SONG FROM THE FOREST

Song from the Forest

My Life among the Ba-Benjellé Pygmies

LOUIS SARNO

HOUGHTON MIFFLIN COMPANY

Boston   New York   1993

For information about permission to reproduce selections
from this book, write to Permissions, Houghton Mifflin Company,
215 Park Avenue South, New York, New York 10003.

Library of Congress Cataloging-in-Publication Data
Sarno, Louis, date.
Song from the forest : my life among the Ba-Benjellé Pygmies /
Louis Sarno.
p.   cm.
Discography: p.
ISBN 0-395-61331-0
1. Benjellé (African people) — Music.   2. Benjellé (African people) —
Social life and customs.   I. Title.
DT546.345.B45S37   1993   92-26839
967.41 — dc20   CIP
Printed in the United States of America
MP 10 9 8 7 6 5 4 3 2 1

CONTENTS

PREFACE

I WAS DRAWN to the heart of Africa by a song. In retrospect it seems wondrously strange that a mere song should have lifted me out of the rut of my life, and sent me off on an adventure that has wrought such deep and permanent change in me, an adventure that continues still.

Music has always had a profound influence on me. As a boy I wanted to be a composer like my heroes Beethoven and Schubert. But as I grew older my life turned in other directions. I never lost my love of music, but circumstances led me ever farther afield, until even my precious record collection lay five thousand miles away. Gradually my favorite symphonies and sonatas faded into cherished memories of a life I had left behind.

And then, alone in a northern European capital one winter night, I turned on the radio — and rediscovered music. The song on the air was unlike anything I had ever heard: voices blending into a subtle polyphony, weaving a melody that rose and fell in endless repetition, as hypnotic as waves breaking on a shore. At the end the announcer spoke in Flemish, and all I learned was that the song had come from somewhere in central Africa.

I was surprised that a music so alien to what I had grown up with should captivate me. It was as if during the years of quiescence the faculty in me that responded to music had pupated and metamorphosed into something unfamiliar and improbable. I became obsessed with that song and set about trying to track it down. By the time I did, I had come across several recordings of similar music, and I knew that it was a song of the Pygmies.

The Pygmies of central Africa are the largest population of hunter-gatherers remaining on earth. The name "Pygmy" itself dates back to ancient Greece, although Pygmies appear in the historical record long before that time, and we know from those early accounts that their music was a source of fascination for the ancient Egyptians. After Aristotle, however, the Pygmies were considered to be a myth, and only in the second half of the nineteenth century were they "rediscovered" by modern Europe. These denizens of the rain forest have survived to the present day with their culture largely intact, carrying with them a music that may well antedate the emergence of agriculture.

I ferreted out every available recording of this music, eventually raiding museum collections to satisfy my hunger for it. But the more I heard, the more restless I became. The music seemed to stir in me a vague memory, something that might have come from a dream. And as that inaccessible part of me was awakened, it was coupled with a powerful longing. Bewildered, I made plans to go to Africa in search of a Pygmy music that was not on any record. What seemed to call me was not the songs I had heard but a music I could only imagine must exist.

Several major groups of Pygmies live in central Africa. In the eastern Congo Basin in Zaire there are the Mbuti and the Twa. In the western Congo Basin, the Aka live between the Ubangi and Sangha rivers, the Baka live west of the Sangha, and the Bongo live in the Ogooué River basin, in Gabon. Within each group there are smaller clan divisions. The Ba-Benjellé are the westernmost clan of the Aka; their territory includes some of the least-known rain forest in the world.

I decided to search for my music among the Ba-Benjellé. I would fly to Bangui, capital of the Central African Republic, then proceed overland for six hundred miles to the remote village of Bomandjombo, in the heart of Ba-Benjellé country. In the surrounding forest, I thought, I would make contact with the Pygmies.

And so, hardly understanding the urgency that drove me on, I bought a one-way ticket to Bangui, since I could not afford the return. Early one cold morning in Paris, full of trepidation, I boarded a plane that would take me into the equatorial heart of a continent where I did not know a soul, on a quest for a music that might have been nothing more than a state of my imagination.

SONG FROM THE FOREST

ONE

Ainsi Donc la Vie

W E HAD SEVEN HOURS before landing in Bangui — not
much time for a journey between two worlds but more than
enough for me to reflect on the implications of my undertaking. I
had quit my job in Amsterdam, given up my apartment, and made
my farewells as if I were never coming back. My friends had been
impressed by what they called my courage in taking such a leap into
the unknown. But I couldn't help wondering: is it really courage
when one acts out of compulsion rather than choice?

Originally I had intended to visit the Mbuti Pygmies in the Ituri
forest of northeastern Zaire. For more than a year I had corre-
sponded with Colin Turnbull, whose book *The Forest People*, an
account of his two years among the Mbuti in the late 1950s, was
one of the main inspirations behind my own venture. Turnbull had
generously offered to provide me with a recorded message to his
Mbuti friend Kengé, introducing me as his "brother." In any case I
need not worry about my reception, he assured me — if I really
liked their music, the Pygmies and I would get along fine. As for
financing my expedition, once I reached the Pygmies I could get
by on two dollars a day — plus, he added mysteriously, tobacco
expenses.

It was all the encouragement I needed. I would go to the Ituri, and Turnbull's voice on tape would guarantee my acceptance.

Yet here I was on my way to a rain forest nearly a thousand miles west of the Ituri to visit a group of Pygmies known as the Ba-Benjellé. Several factors had influenced my choice. The Ba-Benjellé lived near vast tracts of undisturbed forest. They had been one of the first Pygmy groups recorded, during a French expedition into their territory in the mid-1940s, but since that time they had been left alone. The Mbuti, on the other hand, had become the focus in recent years of intensive research by teams of specialists. The Ituri forest was bisected by a road that had become the major artery for traffic between east and west Africa. Admittedly the road was all dirt and in atrocious condition, but it was used by the overland trucks that annually carried large groups of European tourists through the forest on their way to or from Nairobi. The road that snaked into Ba-Benjellé territory, in contrast, simply ended at a wall of forest twenty miles south of Bomandjombo.

Above all, I was drawn to the Ba-Benjellé by their music. The early recordings I had located had a rhythmic complexity that was lacking in the Mbuti music I'd heard, and the melodic phrases were longer and more intricate. In the sixties Simha Arom, an ethno-musicologist, had ventured into the northern fringe of Benjellé country, where the forest gives way to savanna, and several of the pieces he had recorded intrigued me with the possibilities they hinted at.

For a while I was lost in speculation of what I would find. Half-way across the Sahara it occurred to me that my customary reticence with strangers would never do for making friends in a country where I knew no one. I decided to strike up a conversation with the passenger next to me, a bearded man with an unforgettable name: André la Guerre. André had been living and working in Paris for a year and was on his way to visit his family in Bangui for Christmas. I asked him to teach me some phrases in Sango. Originally a trading language along the Ubangi River, Sango had spread in the early part of this century to become the national language of the Central African Republic (as opposed to the official language, French). It was used extensively on the radio. I learned how to say "I am walking from village to village," "How far to the next village," "I want to visit a smaller village," and "I want to go into the forest."

"Why are you going to Centrafrique, anyway?" André finally asked.

"I want to visit Pygmy villages and record their music."

"Ah, the Pygmies!" André exclaimed.

He had never met a Pygmy himself, he admitted, but he had heard plenty of stories about them in Bangui. I was going to have a problem making contact with them, he thought. They weren't used to strangers and would probably flee as soon as they saw me.

It was dark when we landed at M'poko Airport in Bangui. As we filed off the plane I took my first breath of African air: the scent of wood smoke sweetened with a trace of blossoms. Warmth and humidity enveloped me.

The scene in the customs building was chaos, crowds of people surging toward the wooden tables to expose the contents of their luggage for inspection. I was apprehensive that my thirty blank cassettes would pose a problem, but when the inspector uncovered them and I explained their purpose, he scrawled the mark of approval on my bags with a piece of chalk.

By now it was close to midnight. Yellow Peugeot taxis had converged on the airport to wait for the plane, and their drivers were competing for fares, grabbing bags by force and pulling the owners along by the hand. Several tugs of war ensued. I viewed the scene with trepidation. Suddenly hands were lifting my bags.

"Come," a young man said, and before I had a chance to reply or negotiate the fare, we were pushing our way through the crowd. When we reached his taxi I was relieved to see André la Guerre waiting for me with a smile. He was surrounded by family members — men, women, and several children. His taxi-driver friend would take him home, he explained, and then drop me off wherever I wanted to go.

"Are you sure there's room?" I asked doubtfully — we were at least ten.

André and the driver laughed. Of course there was room!

We all squeezed into the taxi and drove off. Soon we left the main road and turned onto a track leading into a jumble of one-story mud-brick houses. The headlights flashed across palm and mango trees and clumps of papaya and banana plants. We were in one of the *quartiers*, where most of Bangui's half-million inhabitants lived. The *quartiers* were like a series of African villages compressed together. Water was drawn from wells, and at night the only light came from kerosene lanterns.

After delivering André and his family to their home, the taxi took me at my request to a "cheap hotel." On one of the main roads into the town center, it was tucked into a grove of palms lit up with a string of Christmas lights. I disembarked and gave the driver a tip.

The receptionist, asleep behind his desk, woke up only long enough to register me and hand me a key. An old man carried my bags to my room. After a cold shower — there was no hot water — I crawled into bed for my first sleep in Africa.

I AWOKE IN THE MORNING to a babble of voices. It was only seven, but by African standards I had slept in. I lingered in bed until seven-thirty, bracing myself to confront an unfamiliar world. I had a full day ahead — obtaining permits, making travel arrangements — and I didn't know where to begin. I dressed and sat on the bed a moment longer. Finally I opened the door and stepped outside.

A dazzling light blinded me for a minute. When my eyes adjusted I saw that the road was thick with traffic — not cars but pedestrians. The women were wrapped from neck to ankle in bolts of bright-patterned cotton cloth, the African version of the sarong. Many carried bunches of fruit on their heads. Some men pushed two-wheeled carts piled high with the skinned and quartered carcasses of cows; others carried radios or nothing at all. Groups of schoolchildren with notebooks chattered loudly. Teenage boys sold cigarettes and candy or strode along with portable displays of belts, shirts, and neckties. The middle of the road was left to the mopeds, which puttered past steered by men in suits, their briefcases lashed to the seats behind them. Now and then a yellow taxi sped by.

The same receptionist was still on duty when I went to inquire about the price of my room.

"Fifteen thousand francs," he said.

"Fifteen thousand francs a *night?*" I asked — that was more than fifty dollars, and I had only five hundred dollars to my name.

My heart sank. I was going to have to move even before I confronted the government bureaucracy about permits. But where to? At the moment my only friend in the world was this bleary-eyed receptionist, Claude. I invited him to join me for a cup of coffee. He replied that he was nearing the end of his twenty-four-hour shift and intended to go home and sleep, so coffee was not what he wanted. But he would gladly drink a beer.

We sat out on the shady terrace. Claude opened his bottle of Mocaf, the local beer, with his teeth. I launched into an explanation of my visit, concluding with a lament about the hotel's rates. I just couldn't afford to stay another night.

My predicament seemed to arouse Claude's sympathy at once. Fifty dollars a night *was* a lot, but what was I going to do? This was the cheapest hotel in town! For a while we ruminated in silence. Claude sighed and shook his head. If only he had electricity, he muttered, he would happily invite me to stay with him.

"Electricity?" I exclaimed. "But I'm going to live in the forest with the Pygmies! I don't need electricity!"

Claude laughed and shook my hand.

CLAUDE LIVED in Galabadja, a *quartier* several miles from Bangui's small commercial center. On our way there in a taxi Claude warned me that his household had not been tranquil recently. He had taken a second wife, Nadine, and his first, Odette, was not happy with the arrangement.

As we made our way along one of the many footpaths that crisscrossed the *quartier,* passing directly through countless family scenes, people stared curiously. The word *moonju* (white man) rose everywhere. Once or twice children screamed at the sight of me and fled. Odette and Nadine greeted my arrival with frank astonishment, but after Claude explained that I would be their guest for several days, their surprise changed to delight at such an unusual prospect.

Before evening my presence had provoked a flurry of social visits from relatives and neighbors, who dropped by to welcome me, find out why I had come, and drink beer. Claude's older brothers De-mien and Roland, who lived in a different *quartier*, came by in the evening to verify the rumors about a *moonju* staying with their little brother. The next afternoon they returned with their wives and children and several friends. Socializing was what life was about in the *quartiers*.

Claude worked alternate twenty-four-hour shifts at the hotel. On the days when he was at home, there was usually friction with his two wives, never directed at each other but at Claude. Odette did most of the household work, but whenever Claude gave her an order, she carried on as if she hadn't heard. The arguments that resulted were a source of amusement to Nadine, who laughed loudly at every insult. One night Odette threw a beer bottle at Claude. It whirled past his head, missing him by inches. In a fury Claude ran and tackled her. They rolled around in the dust for a minute. Suddenly Claude screamed and leaped up. Odette had bitten him in the thigh.

Yet on those evenings when he was at the hotel, life at Claude's was tranquility itself. Odette and Nadine seemed as fond of each other as two sisters, and cooperated in all the chores. Sometimes they sat together and talked in low, melodious voices, giggling frequently. At such times I found Sango a most evocative language, its rhythms and sounds conjuring up images of centuries of village life along the Ubangi.

Meanwhile I had permits to obtain, and after a couple of days of relaxation, during which I slipped into the easygoing pace of life around me, I established a new daily routine. On the mornings that Claude descended into the city, I accompanied him to the hotel, then continued on to the various government offices I had to visit. On Claude's advice I went first to the official tourist agency and explained my plans. They pointed out that there were Pygmies living within sixty miles of Bangui. Like the Mbuti, these Pygmies — the Aka — had seen many anthropologists over the years. Genetic studies had been carried out among them, and their music was perhaps the best documented of any Pygmy music in Africa. Why not avoid all the inconvenience of a visit to Bomandjombo, the agency suggested, and simply visit the Pygmies around Mbaiki, a two-hour drive to the south? They could issue me a permit in one day. When I insisted on my original intention, however, they told me I would have to obtain an "authorization to circulate" from the department of mines. The province contained diamonds and had been declared a mineral zone.

The department of mines was in another part of town. When I told them I wanted to make recordings, they sent me on to the department of arts and culture. There my plans were greeted with suspicion. Why was I so adamant about visiting Bomandjombo? Who was I to assume there was such a difference between the Pygmies at Bomandjombo and those near Mbaiki? Besides, what could I have in mind but exploitation of the Pygmies? I would return with my recordings to America and make lots of money, leaving the Pygmies as poor as ever.

Their final accusation stung me, and I retorted vehemently that any profit I made, if profit were even possible, I would deliver to the Pygmies personally. We argued until closing time at one P.M. As I was leaving, they told me to return the next day with two photos of myself — they would process my application after all. On my way back to the *quartier* I stopped by the hotel for a beer with Claude to celebrate my first glimmer of success.

My permit was ready in a week. The director himself pulled it out of a special folder with a triumphant flourish. With this piece of paper, he proudly explained, I would have no trouble obtaining authorization from the department of mines. The minister of communication himself had signed it.

Back at the department of mines I was told I needed two more photographs. Another week passed, and then one day a clerk holding my application took me by the hand and led me across town and up a wooded hill to a small building. There the details of my application were entered in a ledger, and the permit was signed and stamped. All I needed now, the clerk cheerfully explained, was the signature of the director of mines.

The next morning I returned. The secretary told me to sit down and went into an adjoining office. A moment later the director emerged and looked at me.

"So you're the one who wants to record the Pygmies," he said sternly.

I braced myself for bad news.

"I have signed your paper," he continued, holding it out. "I hope you have an interesting journey."

BOMANDJOMBO LIES four hundred miles southwest of Bangui as the crow flies, but to get there I had to travel three hundred miles to the northwest, skirting the forest, then, at a town called Baoro, turn south for nearly three hundred more. I would be traveling by bush taxi. Claude expressed a desire to accompany me, but the owner of his hotel had recently fired most of the staff, and Claude was scheduled to begin forty-eight-hour shifts at the reception desk until replacements were found.

Dawn had not yet arrived when Claude shook me awake. He would help me carry my bags to the road where the bush taxi going in my direction cruised in search of clients. We had more than a mile to walk. All was silence as I packed my last things, but when we stepped outside and prepared to set off, Odette and Nadine, as well as a dozen neighbors, emerged from the darkness to bid me farewell.

By the time we reached the pickup point it was light. We sipped coffees from a nearby stall. Ahead a blue station wagon swerved into view and raced in our direction. Two dusty men sat on the roof rack. A third dangled precariously out the back door, holding on with one hand and shouting destinations. The wagon was painted with floral designs and bore the motto *Ainsi donc la vie* (thus is life).

"That's it!" Claude cried and started to wave his arm.

Ainsi donc la vie screeched to a halt next to us.

"Nola?" the man at the back asked.

Nola was more than five hundred miles away, an ambitious goal for this jalopy. The two men on top lashed my bags to the roof rack with long strips of inner-tube rubber. Claude and I embraced a final time.

The crew of Ainsi donc la vie consisted of the driver and three assistants, whose job was to improvise repairs on the road. The job of the driver, a tall thin man with a wispy mustache, was to drive like a son of a bitch. For a couple of hours we sped around the outskirts of town looking for clients. We picked up far more than I thought could possibly fit in the back, and I realized I had lucked out with my seat in the front between the driver and a two-hundred-pound woman.

Soon the outlying houses of Bangui were behind us, and heavily wooded hills rolled briskly by. The driver was a Moslem and devoutly religious. At one point he stopped to get out and pray. I quickly understood his reasoning: the way he drove he had to be prepared to enter paradise.

A hundred miles from Bangui, at a town called Bossembelé, the tarmac ended and the dirt road began. Soon we began a long descent. Each bump in the road sent Ainsi donc la vie cruising through the air for several yards. Still the driver pressed his foot on the accelerator. At the bottom of the hill the road veered to the right, but we continued straight ahead, plunging off the road and into a field of tall grass and finally crashing into a ten-foot-high termite mound.

The mechanics were the first to leap into action. The rest of us were too stunned to move. The driver got out and dusted himself off, casually inspecting the front of the taxi. Miraculously no one had been hurt. We sat along the fringe of the road while the mechanics effected repairs. I fell into conversation with a neatly dressed Cameroonian named Blaise who carried a satchel bursting with papers. He was returning to Yaoundé from an important but secret diplomatic mission, he claimed. There had already been several attempts to steal his papers. Now he was anxious to be on our way, lest we have to spend the night in Yaloké, known for its thieves.

We resumed our journey a few hours later. It was just after dark when we rolled into Yaloké. Without a trace of concern, the driver informed us that Yaloké was the end of the road for Ainsi donc la vie. They would spend tomorrow making repairs. Our bags were unloaded in the middle of a crowd of onlookers, and we were left to fend for ourselves.

The other passengers quickly dispersed into the night, scarcely inconvenienced by the turn of events. No doubt they had family or friends to stay with in Yaloké. Only Blaise and I lingered near the taxi. At last a boy volunteered to lead us to an *auberge*. He made to take Blaise's satchel and carry it for him. Blaise clutched it to his chest with a violent motion, looking at me as if to say "You see?"

IN THE MORNING we boarded a bush taxi called Rapide Car heading for the Cameroon border. We reached Baoro without incident, and I disembarked to wait for a vehicle going south to Nola. A group of old men resting under a mango tree told me a bush taxi was due in thirty minutes.

Half an hour later, to my pleasant surprise, I heard the roar of an approaching engine. A long, torpedo-shaped vehicle came careening around the bend, shooting out a wake of pebbles. Something about it inspired confidence: here was a bush taxi that intended to get to where it was going. Its name was proudly blazoned in pink letters: *Tranquille Car.*

The vegetation had thinned out to scrub at Baoro, but soon we were racing through a landscape of dry woodland. Termite towers of bright red laterite flashed by, some fifteen feet tall, looking like the eroded castles of a bygone civilization. I was wedged firmly but by no means uncomfortably between two passengers. The afternoon heat would have been unbearable but for the stiff wind that blew in through the paneless windows, a welcome side effect of our relentless velocity.

For some time we hurtled on. Conversation was rendered futile by the roar of the engine. Then, unexpectedly, we began to slow down. Ahead, on the side of the road, in the middle of nowhere, stood another torpedo-shaped bush taxi named Tranquille Car. Countless passengers lounging in the grass propped themselves up to watch our approach. Their driver ran toward us.

They had broken down yesterday, he explained. It was a bad place to be stuck. Bandits had been known to ambush bush taxis along this stretch of road. He paused to ask for water. People handed over water bottles, and the stranded passengers, who had converged around our vehicle, drank thirstily. An emotional discussion ensued, a decision was made, and a collective groan rose from my fellow passengers.

"What is it?" I asked the man next to me.

"We are taking all those people with us," he replied with disgust.

Our Tranquille Car was designed to carry thirty passengers, and we were full to capacity. Tranquille Car number two, of identical design, had likewise been carrying a full load. Now they forced their way in, the mechanics shoving them from behind. Tempers were frayed and hostile words exchanged. Some passengers ended up in positions that had no point of contact with either floor or seats. Two hours elapsed before we resumed our journey.

We were still on the road at sunset. An attempt was made to activate a tiny light, but it failed. Two students, sprawled on the heads and shoulders of the passengers beneath them, got into an argument about electricity. One of them calmly removed his glasses and handed them to a friend. Then he lunged across and grabbed the other student by the throat. Fists and feet thrashed wildly. With cries of rage we pulled the assailants apart. For a moment they continued the battle with insults: "You're a barbarian! You tried to choke me!" "You savage! You were going to rip my ears off!"

Soon a weary calm descended on us, and Tranquille Car trundled on in tortured silence.

AFTER SPENDING THE NIGHT in Nola, I found a bush taxi bound for Bomandjombo. We broke down only once, in a hot village surrounded by manioc fields and tall forest. Our driver borrowed a resident's moped to return to Nola for a part, delaying us for seven hours.

Late in the afternoon we turned off the main road onto a sandy track — once a mere foothpath — that cut across a savanna of scrub and stunted, wavy-trunked trees. Sometimes we slowed down for a small herd of long-horned cattle attended by a few men wearing robes and armed with bows and quivers of long arrows. They were Mbororo, nomadic cattle herders from the north, part of the great Fulani nation. At sunset we entered the forest and were immediately consumed by darkness.

With the headlights on, we seemed to be driving through a tunnel. Tendrils of vegetation reached out, slapping the windshield as we sped past. I was so exhilarated that I could not resist sticking my head out the window to breathe in this lush world. After I was smacked in the face several times by branches, the other passengers told me to stop being so stupid and roll up the window. Now and then a passenger would disembark where a few kerosene lights indicated a tiny village. We finally reached Bomandjombo at nine.

My bags and I were deposited at a small wooden police post, where the man on duty invited me to stay the night. During the short interview that preceded sleep I explained my purpose in coming to Bomandjombo. He assured me I'd come to the right place: there were Pygmies everywhere.

TWO

Ba-Benjellé or Bust

BY DAYLIGHT BOMANDJOMBO was a big letdown, especially after the dramatic ride the night before. A large village — 1,500 people — it had lost most of its traditional charm with the opening of a sawmill in the early seventies, when former president Jean-Bedel Bokassa had declared the region open for commercial exploitation. The original villagers — the Sangha-sangha tribe — were swamped by newcomers from all over the Central African Republic who came to work in the lumber industry. Once, so the story goes, Bokassa visited Nola and was so well entertained that he vowed to make it the seat of a prefecture. Bomandjombo became, by association, a kind of subprefecture. It was given gendarmes, police, and a mayor with his own guards. Visually, the town was a scar on the bank of the Sangha River. The ugliest part was the neighborhood thrown up for the sawmill workers — straight rows of identical wood houses with hardly a tree. The ground was fine sand, and the equatorial sun beat down mercilessly. Across the river was dense, misty forest from which elephants sometimes emerge to bathe.

I stepped out into the bright early morning. The Sangha, a few yards away, sparkled like a jewel. A long cream-colored sandbar ran down the middle of it. I could just make out a lone fisherman in a pirogue, moving downriver in the jungle's shadow.

A villager was waiting for me. He had gotten wind of my arrival and had come to be my guide to the nearby Pygmy camps. His name was Christian and he was already drunk. I later learned that he worked the night shift at the sawmill, so six in the morning was the end of his day. But in fact Christian was a lush. At any time of the day or night, he was sure to be loaded.

Christian was a diminutive man — I would meet Pygmies who towered over him — with the most gravelly voice I have ever heard. A bachelor, he had come from Bangui a year earlier to work at the sawmill. He was a good-hearted man, impossible to dislike even though often a pain in the neck.

Christian and I checked out three Pygmy camps that morning. Few residents were at home; presumably most were off hunting. I was surprised to find that the beehive-shaped huts were made of strips of plywood scrap scavenged from the lumberyard instead of the large oval leaves I had seen in photographs. A few had palm leaves thrown over the plywood, which was anchored to the frame-work with haphazardly placed stones, lengths of bamboo, and blocks of wood. I had never seen such shoddy dwellings.

The first two camps were just north of Bomandjombo. As we made our way to the third camp, Amopolo, half a mile south of the village, near the sawmill, I began to have doubts that I had come to the right place.

Amopolo, named after a stream that fed into the Sangha, was really three or four camps separated by patches of jungle that had overgrown abandoned manioc plantations. A maze of pathways connected the camps, which were all within shouting distance of one another. The paths were so arranged that you could go into town or into the forest without passing through any of the other camps. Christian led me from one to the next. Only a few small children and women were around. Finally a sleepy man emerged from his hut to greet us. He said little but smiled a lot. His front teeth had been chipped to points. I gave him a cigarette.

As we stood there, smiling silently at each other, the sounds of a harp reached me. From another direction came the flutelike yodel of a woman singing a lullaby. There was a strange and powerful tranquility in the air. I felt, *this is the place.*

"I'll stay at this camp," I blurted to Christian.

"Ah, *voilà!*" he cried triumphantly.

In Sango, he explained to the man why I had come. The *moonju,*
he said, would sleep two weeks at Amopolo (I hoped to stay three
months, but I didn't want to overwhelm the Pygmies with my am-
bition so early on). The *moonju* wanted to record the Pygmy dances
with his radio. In exchange he would give them coffee, sugar, salt,
and cigarettes.

The Pygmy listened politely and seemed to agree to the arrangement, but his assent was unsettlingly passive. It carried no sense of
conviction. When we turned to leave he reached out his hand as
though to shake mine — but no, it wasn't that. He wanted another
cigarette.

On our way back to the village we almost bumped into a Pygmy
woman on the path. She smiled shyly in surprise at the encounter.
She wore a porcupine quill through the pierced septum of her nose,
but when I looked away for a second, then back again, I noticed that
she had surreptitiously removed it.

IN THE AFTERNOON, accompanied by Christian, I carried my bags
over to Amopolo. Since he had served his purpose by introducing
me to the Pygmies, I kept hoping he would leave. I even bought
him a few drinks in the village in an attempt to incapacitate him,
but he was still going at full steam.

A group of men had already assembled at Amopolo to wait for
their guest. They'd heard the good news. I did not realize then that
they regarded *moonjus* as good pickings, but I did notice something
predatory in the way they so eagerly welcomed me. They led me
to my new home in the largest of the Amopolo camps. The remains
of what looked like a tiny garden shed, it was, literally, a dump.
Inside was a heap of unidentifiable garbage.

An old woman hastily swept out the shed, scooping up the trash
with a stiff piece of antelope hide, but it was too late. I already knew
I was getting the worst room in the house. After some shouted
instructions a boy appeared with an old cracked door, which he
placed on the sandy floor. My bed presumably.

Christian was not on intimate terms with the Pygmies, but he knew some of the more famous and infamous characters, and he began the introductions. A short elderly man named Simbu was pointed out as "chief" of all Amopolo. I would be sleeping in Simbu's camp. Dimba, a sharp-faced man whose toes had been eaten away by leprosy, was the patriarch of one of the other Amopolo camps. His son Etubu had married Simbu's daughter Kukpa. Kukpa's maternal grandmother, Esoosi, with piercing eyes, wielded considerable influence. Her oldest son, Singali, was a tough-looking guy, notorious for his wild drinking binges in the village. One of Singali's best friends was Balonyona, husband of Matangu, the woman with the porcupine quill.

When I opened a pack of cigarettes, the men immediately gathered around me. In five seconds the pack was empty. Old Esoosi stood up and gave a speech, whose essence Christian translated as: the *moonju* has come in search of tranquility. He doesn't like noise. So, everybody — don't make noise!

I was reassured by the sentiments until Simbu got down to business. At the end of my two-week stay I was to pay the residents of Amopolo 20,000 Central African francs, nearly $70. I was momentarily staggered by the amount — I had only 35,000 francs left. Even Christian balked at the high stakes. Without a word from me he tried to argue the sum down to 10,000. Simbu, however, was adamant, and since I did not want to make a bad impression on my first night, I finally agreed to his demand. Simbu looked astonished. Moreover, I added, one day I would return with clothes for everyone. Simbu had recovered his equilibrium and his reply was unambiguous: if I returned with clothes for them, that would be very nice. Just make sure I paid the 20,000 francs.

I began wondering if these people really were Pygmies. For one thing, they were too tall. A few of the men must have been five and a half feet. Then there was their dress. Dimba had on some kind of stately white toga. A couple of the men wore hats. One tallish fellow even wore a vest. Trousers were common. And I had been secretly hoping for bark cloth! As for the women, only Esoosi stood out as an individual for me. The rest of them formed a sort of anonymous collective presence in the background. The men were so domineering that I scarcely had an opportunity to take in anything else. They called me, following the custom of most Central Africans addressing whites, *patron*. I hated the word. I knew from my weeks in Bangui that it would vanish only when I won their friendship.

"*Patron. Pour vrai danser bien il faut vous achète la boisson.*"

It was Singali. He gazed up at me with an expression that seemed to say, "Hey, you want us to dance, so how about it?" Behind him stood Balonyona, looking angry.

They wanted the local moonshine, *mbaku*, and they wanted it in large amounts. Christian, whose motive for sticking around now became clear, joined them in trying to persuade me to buy five liters. I talked them down to 3,000 francs' worth — a few sips for each of the women, a few gulps for each of the men. The crowd that had surrounded me during the negotiations split up as soon as I handed the money to Singali. Simbu, who had been lingering on the perimeter, now zeroed in again. He spoke to Christian in Sango. Christian turned to me:

"The chief says he doesn't drink *mbaku*, so instead he wants five hundred francs for his own amusement."

I forked it over. At this rate, I thought bitterly, I'll be broke before tomorrow.

The mood began to grow animated. Some boys beat on the drums. A couple of girls were already singing. Christian went off with Singali to supervise the purchase of the *mbaku*. The man wearing a vest, who introduced himself as Fidel, taught me my first phrase in the Pygmy language: *béké ndaku* — give me a cigarette. Then, with a broad smile, he looked at me and said, "*Béké ndaku.*" People arriving from the neighboring camps lit their way with glowing sticks of wood, which they waved and twirled to keep bright. The requests for cigarettes intensified as the camp filled up. I started to feel besieged. Simbu, the so-called chief, sat on a log and did nothing to bring the anarchy under control. I became impatient for Christian to return.

When the *mbaku* expedition finally got back, it was obvious that the vendor had rewarded them for bringing him business. Christian staggered, defying gravity with each step. Balonyona carried the large bulbous bottle of cloudy moonshine on his head.

"Monsieur Louis!" Christian announced. "We have brought the drink!"

They set the bottle at my feet. Balonyona swayed a little.

"*C'est trop fort,*" he said without a trace of a smile.

A tin cup was fetched, and the distribution of the alcohol began. Christian took charge of the operation. Frequently he stole a swallow or two before handing over each refilled cup. A short young man named Maurice who was built like Hercules drew me aside:

"*Mais il a boire beaucoup! C'est trop voleurs les villageois! Il faut la couper toute suite même!*"

I assumed he was protesting about Christian pinching drinks. I had a word with Christian, and for a while he showed commendable restraint. The women had gathered in large groups in the central clearing, probably according to the camp they belonged to. They laughed and chatted and sometimes sang snatches of melody, like a vocal orchestra tuning up before a concert. I decided it was time to begin recording. I called Christian over and explained my needs. The Pygmies would sing, I would record. Then they would tell me the name of the song, and I would write it down. Then they would sing the next song. It was simple.

"*D'accord!*" Christian croaked.

He tottered over to the drums and made the announcement. Since he spoke in Sango I had no idea if he got it right. It hardly mattered since no one was listening. I was grateful when Fidel stepped out and shouted *Tiens!* at everyone, even though that had no effect either.

Finally teenagers replaced the kids on drums and began to pound driving cross-rhythms. Fidel stood in front of the largest group of women and encouraged them to sing with wavy motions of his outstretched arms, looking, in his vest, like a parody of an orchestra conductor. The men began to dance in a circle around the bonfire. The chorus swelled powerfully — I could feel my eardrums rattle as the women's voices peaked in volume. I switched on the recorder and held out the microphones.

At the end of the song I produced my pocket notebook and pen. For a moment there was complete silence. I could just make out the faces of the women at the edge of the firelight. They were all looking at me. Maurice told Christian the name of the song and what it meant. Christian translated:

"They call the song 'Sombolo,'" he rasped. "It means Sombolo dances well and all the women love to sing his name."

"Sombolo is the name of a man?" I asked with disappointment — I had expected elephant hunting songs, songs for gathering wild honey, odes to the forest spirits.

"*Oui, oui,* Sombolo!" several Pygmies cried. They pointed to a muscular man standing near the fire. He had a face like *Mad Magazine*'s Alfred E. Neuman. I jotted down: #1. Sombolo.

The second song was "Mamadu," the name of one of the teenage drummers. The third song was about a baby born in a hospital. At the fourth song I canceled the whole naming procedure. I could see it was beginning to irritate the Pygmies, who just wanted to dance and were growing impatient. It was all nonsense anyway. I packed away my recording equipment and decided to get drunk myself.

At midnight Christian left for his shift at the sawmill. In his state, I thought, he'll be lucky not to saw a leg off. Nevertheless, I was not sorry to see him go. The dance went on for another few hours. Then the air turned chilly and the women began to wander off in groups, grabbing brands from the fire. In a while all that remained of the bonfire was some embers. I stared at them in a stupor. The chorus of crickets was soothing. My headache subsided to a gentle throb. When I finally looked up, I was alone.

MOST OF THE PYGMIES were back on their feet by sunrise. My own attempt at sleep was disturbed by an incredible itching fit. The beam of my flashlight revealed the cause: bedbugs living in the crack in my "bed."

"I can't sleep here," I complained in the morning to Maurice in French — I'd gotten the impression that he understood French fairly well. "There are little animals that eat me."

I pointed to the crack.

"Aha!" Maurice smiled. "*Mendili.*"

And the matter was dropped. Evidently my sleeping problem was not high on their agenda. Besides, they needed me awake to cadge more cigarettes. From one of the neighboring camps someone shouted, "Is there a dance tonight?"

Maurice looked at me expectantly.

"The money for *mbaku* is finished," I told him, cynically assuming the question was really about alcohol.

Maurice shouted back the news.

"*Merde!*" came the reply.

Fidel stopped by for a cigarette. He was still wearing his vest, but what darkness had concealed, sunshine now revealed. Those fancy frills along the shoulders were actually torn and shredded fabric. Dark stains gave the vest a blotchy look. The original owner had probably thrown it in the garbage ten years ago. So it turned out with all the clothes the Pygmies wore — only a scarecrow would have been caught dead in them.

I was glad to see Fidel. His attempts to impose order on the chaos of the night had impressed me as the gestures of a responsible character. Most important, he had struck me as being almost fluent in French. So now I tried to explain that I was interested in recording the dances the Pygmies did for themselves, not ones they performed especially for me. Fidel listened with a poker face.

"That's it," he readily agreed with a smile, once it became clear that I'd finished.

I gave him his cigarette and he walked away.

My next-door neighbors on the right were Balonyona and Matangu, with their four-year-old son, Mbutu. Farther along was Esoosi's hut, and beyond hers was Singali's. A mean-looking old lady lived on my left. When our eyes met I smiled, but she held her scowl. Her hut was especially dilapidated. The chief, Simbu, lived opposite me in the biggest hut — a single, roomy beehive hump. Other huts had tunnel entrances that reminded me of igloos.

During the morning many men visited me for cigarettes. They never stayed long, except for Maurice, who hogged the only patch of shade near my hut and appeared to have no intention of moving for the rest of the day. Every time I took out a cigarette to smoke, I felt obliged to give him one. He stashed most of them in his shirt pocket without a word. At one point he dropped off to sleep.

Toward noon the heat grew fierce. I was cross-eyed with exhaustion and dizzy with hunger. The camp had emptied out. I assumed everyone had gone hunting, and despite my disappointment with their music I could not help but admire the sheer vitality of these people who could dance all night and then hunt all day. But I was wrong — most of them were in their huts, sleeping it off. Eventually Simbu emerged and headed across camp toward me.

"*Patron*," he mumbled as soon as he arrived, "there's nothing to eat."

Balonyona evidently overheard, for he shot out of his hut.

"Everyone danced well for you," he stuttered in his rapid-fire French, "and now we are hungry!"

My idea had been to eat *their* food. Now it seemed they expected *me* to provide the food, not only for myself, but for them as well! Full of hidden rage, I shelled out another 1,000 francs — 500 to each of them. When Singali dropped by later in the day with the same lament, I explained that I had already given Balonyona 500 francs for food.

"You gave Balonyona five hundred francs?" he spluttered in surprise.

"*Oui*," I replied.

He rushed off to find Balonyona.

THE REALITY OF LIFE among the Pygmies, as opposed to what I had imagined while planning my trip in Europe, proved to be very trying. I had naively believed that my enthusiasm for their music would compel the Pygmies to accept me into their hearts almost immediately. Instead they seemed intent only on milking me for all I was worth. It was as though they had visitors all the time and had mastered the art of exploiting the tourists. Yet except for the Yugoslavians who ran the sawmill (and they kept to themselves), few whites ever passed this way. But what dismayed me most about the Pygmies — in particular the men, since my interaction with the women was still minimal — was how contemporary, even hip, they seemed. I found it hard to reconcile the people before me with the image I had held of hunter-gatherers, whose every gesture, I had imagined, would be full of ritual significance, every utterance full of wisdom. I noticed no ritual at Amopolo, and its absence prejudiced me against the Pygmies, as if it were their fault for losing it. It had not yet occurred to me that their rituals might be so well integrated into the daily routine that they would escape my notice.

The camp came to life each morning around five. Two hours later, as the women gathered and sat in groups, repairing baskets and gossiping, the men would set out with their spears and machetes. After a while the women followed, slipping their empty baskets over their heads, whooping, yodeling, and singing snatches of song as they rushed off. The hunt was obviously a lot of fun. As I listened to their voices echo through the forest, growing fainter until they became indistinguishable from the fluting of birds, I felt a powerful longing to accompany them. But I felt that the Pygmies would not welcome the idea, and I could not bring myself to ask. All they gave me to eat was manioc and boiled tadpoles, which tasted like mud. I never saw a scrap of meat around camp, but I thought it unlikely that they were returning empty-handed from the hunt every day. I decided they were hiding food from me, and the hunt was the last place they would want me to be.

For several days I was ignored. Simbu, Mandubu, and her mother, Esoosi, made a minimal effort to see to my care, providing me with at least one meal of tadpoles a day. During the middle of the day, when the sun crept slowly into the center of the cloudless sky and lingered for several hours, I was often completely alone. The only thing I could look forward to was my daily bath in the Amopolo, in the large pool by the rickety plank bridge. Usually one or two teenage boys accompanied me, sometimes Mamadu, the drummer, or Biléma, whom I learned to recognize by the fake glasses he invariably wore, made from stalks of bright yellow straw. Often it was a morose youth whose name I didn't know. Except to ask for the soap, they never said a word.

By five in the afternoon, as the sun changed from a white-hot glare to a softer pinky orange glow, my spirits would begin to revive. As the first of the Pygmies returned from the forest, villagers from Bomandjombo started to arrive. Groups of village women brought dried manioc, salt, peanut butter, soap, little balls of fried sweet dough called *makala*, and bottles of home-brewed *mbaku*, all of which they hoped to barter for forest products such as mush-

rooms and *koko,* an edible leaf. At first these women eyed me sus-
piciously. The few men who came from the village were friendlier
and never failed to greet me. Trade between the villagers and Pygmies was lively and brisk. Village women poked through the contents of baskets with a zeal that both outraged the Pygmies and
became the object of their derision. The villagers snatched bunches
of leaves from the Pygmies, and gave in exchange small bowls of
manioc. Sometimes the Pygmy women refused the manioc and
snatched the leaves back, which led to arguments. All the while the
Pygmy women were emptying their baskets, whisking the contents
into the darkness of their huts before the villagers could see what
they had.

By dusk the trade had ended and the villagers had left. The camp
gained an air of tranquility that was far different from the stifling
deadness of the lonely afternoons. Women pounded manioc into
flour in large wooden mortars, filling the camp with a rhythmic
thumping. Cooking fires were started. People called out to each
other. From every direction came peals of laughter. At this hour I
sensed that there was more going on than they were revealing to
me, that these people were indeed the keepers of the secret music I
was looking for.

I had my share of visitors in the evenings, and though I could
not delude myself as to their real purpose — a greeting was invariably followed by a request for a cigarette — I found comfort in the
fact that several of the younger men habitually spent an hour or
two with me in front of my hut. I was not included in their conversation (they showed remarkably little curiosity about me) but I enjoyed their presence. I was content to listen and watch and supply
the cigarettes that fueled the talk. I took it as a positive sign that
they had begun to relax in my presence, even though the elders
were conspicuously absent. No doubt they were avoiding me. And
as for the women, whose singing voices sent shivers down my
spine, they remained as elusive and anonymous as ever.

Days passed without music other than the occasional lullaby or
the lines of melody the women sang as they walked off into the
forest. One morning as I washed my face outside my hut, I noticed
a harplike instrument lying, along with a lot of garbage, in the

bushes behind Balonyona's hut. It was made of wood and had nylon strings. I remembered the harp music I had heard on my first day at Amopolo; why hadn't I heard any since? When I showed the harp to Balonyona and asked him if he could play, he plucked a melody for half a minute, fiddled with the seven strings until they were hopelessly out of tune, then left the instrument in the sand and went off to hunt. Did Balonyona really not know how to play the harp? Or had I been rebuffed? The uncertainty only increased my reticence.

One evening I tried a different tack. As the villagers departed, I produced my recorder and inserted one of the tapes I had recorded on the first night. Even before I switched on the tape player, my corner of camp began to fill with Pygmies eager to watch. The sound of their music sent them into gales of laughter at once proud and shy. I realized they had never listened to themselves before. The men took turns crying, "That's me!" The women began to sway to the music. Pretty soon everyone was singing so loudly that their voices drowned out the sound of the tape. When I switched it off, no one seemed to notice. I rushed into my hut to fetch the microphones, congratulating myself on having gotten things going. A dance was definitely under way. I peeled the cellophane off a new cassette.

"Patron," a voice behind me softly pleaded.

I turned around. Singali looked me directly in the eye. His expression said, "C'mon, man! Do I have to spell it out?"

"Tonight we don't need mbaku," I said in French, confronting the issue head on. "The dance has already started!"

"No, it's not true!" Balonyona retorted with conviction. "The women demand mbaku immediately!"

I said I did not believe him. Singali said something to Balonyona, who left. He returned a few seconds later with an old lady.

"Oka," he told her.

She stood in the doorway and gabbled vigorously, jabbing her right hand in the air toward me to stress her point. When she finished, Balonyona led her away.

"What did she say?" I asked Singali.

"She says the women want you to buy mbaku," he replied.

Balonyona had stopped the drums outside and was making an announcement. I heard the word mbaku several times.

"Yay!" everybody cheered.

I was crestfallen as I counted out 3,000 francs. Singali pocketed the money and gushed with unexpected enthusiasm. Tonight, he promised, I would see *real* Pygmy dancing.

Simbu, standing silently in the corner as I prepared to leave my hut, struck next. No telling how long he had been there — probably long enough to have witnessed the transaction between Singali and me. It was unnerving.

"*Patron*," he muttered urgently. "I don't drink *mbaku*."

So this is how it works, I thought with despair as I dug out 500 francs, ambushed from every direction for money! By now my desire to record was completely destroyed. I would have to get used to these sudden mood shifts. In the coming months there were many occasions when the Pygmies raised my spirits euphorically high, only to demolish them that much more effectively a moment later. I even suspected that they were intentionally manipulating my emotions.

The music and dancing progressed predictably. I had heard enough Pygmy music to realize that what I was recording was only party music. Around three in the morning the revelry petered out, and Singali, Balonyona, and I sat by the remains of the fire. We talked.

"If you think the dancing was good tonight," Singali said, "you should hear us in the forest."

I perked up a little and said, "I'd like to."

"Everything is better in the forest," Balonyona added with a rare smile.

It was the kind of remark I had been wanting to hear ever since my arrival. Perhaps there was still hope for my quest!

We went on to discuss many things, though I understood only a fraction of what the two men told me. Pygmy French, I discovered, was nothing more than an adept handling of several phrases mastered through contact with the sawmill. Balonyona showed me his left foot. The skin around the pinky toe looked as if someone had been digging at it with a needle. He tried to explain the source of the ailment.

"Flesh-eating worms!" I cried in alarm. "Here, in the sand?"

I looked down at the flipflops on my feet.

"No, no!" they hastened to assure me. "Only in the forest."

I relaxed again. Toward dawn Singali picked up one of the drums and began to play. He and Balonyona sang a duet until the sun rose. It was nothing special, but I recorded it anyway to commemorate the occasion. I couldn't be sure, but it seemed that I had made two new friends.

AT LEAST A hundred people lived at Amopolo, and I had enough difficulty keeping track of who was who among the men. Among the women, with whom I had little contact, it was next to impossible. I knew old Esoosi by sight, for her intense eyes made it hard to mistake her for anyone else. For some time Matangu, who lived next door, was the only woman I felt I knew, if only slightly. The old lady on my left who seemed to resent my presence turned out to be Matangu's mother, Nyasu. Singali's wife, Eloba, I recognized from her frequent visits next door to chat with Matangu. Like their husbands, the two women were best friends. I often confused Simbu's wife, Mandubu, with her sister, Elika. Elika, whose husband I had not yet met, had three lovely daughters, the oldest a teenager named Bosso. I knew the moment I saw her that I could never forget her.

Returning from the forest, Bosso appeared at the far end of camp and walked across the clearing. The sway of her concave back, a characteristic Pygmy posture, gave her stride a sensuous grace. From her left ear dangled a sprig of white berries. She wore a headband made from a strip of palm, a loincloth, and bunches of leaves around her waist. In the early evening light she seemed to glow. When she caught me watching her, she held my gaze for several seconds before vanishing into her hut.

There developed a kind of secret rapport between us. Although she was married to Biléma, the man with fake glasses, Bosso enjoyed attracting my attention and showing off, and I was delighted to watch. Through her I began to get my first impressions of the women. I noticed that the men had one set of typical gestures, the women another, and that the two sets were entirely distinct. Bosso's every move seemed to spring from an undiluted femininity. Eventually I began to discern the same playful nature in all the women, even my forbidding-looking neighbor, Nyasu.

But at first I saw this only in Bosso. She was the first to arouse my curiosity about the women, to make me notice them in more than a casual way. She was mysterious: what did she mean by her flirtation? When I heard her sing, her voice seemed to come from another world that had a powerful allure. I thought more and more about Bosso — I had definitely fallen under her spell.

ONE AFTERNOON when the coast was clear I counted my money. I had not been keeping track of my finances. After setting aside the 20,000 francs I'd promised Simbu, I had eked out my cash mainly on cigarettes. Every time I lit up in front of a Pygmy, I gave in to his passive look of hunger and handed him a cigarette too. Consequently I tried to smoke mostly in the middle of the day, when few people were around. So far I had been coasting along fine — there was always a 1,000-franc note when I reached for one. But I knew the good times could not last; I had only 8,000 francs left.

I had to face the fact that my coming to Africa in search of the secret music of the Pygmies had been a wild gamble. I didn't even know whether such a tradition existed, but I had thrown every cent of my meager savings into the endeavor. With my one-way ticket to Bangui I was betting that I would discover this music. If it existed, I naively reasoned, it would be a cinch to raise enough money for a more serious and professional expedition to record the Pygmies' music. Now, with my money running out, I was desperate to uncover this music.

Up to this point I had been more or less coerced into buying *mbaku*, and perhaps therein lay the problem: my reluctance might have dampened the Pygmies' enthusiasm. This time I would make the offer openly, emphasizing that I hoped they would reciprocate in like manner. I would buy whatever they claimed they needed for a good dance, and I would make it clear that I was blowing the last of my money on them. Surely they would be touched by my gesture and let me hear their *real* music. Of course I knew it was bribery, but I had come too far to give up now.

In the evening I broke the good news to Balonyona. After listening to my speech about how noble I was being, and how I hoped to hear "true" music, Balonyona replied, "Monsieur Louis, you're a *real* white man!" Then he ran off to spread the tidings.

Arrangements were made rapidly. Singali, as usual, showed up to assume command of the *mbaku* brigade. I had learned that although Simbu did not drink *mbaku*, he did smoke massive amounts of marijuana, as did several other elders. I arranged for a generous supply to be brought in from Bomandjombo. Word of the dance spread, and soon two teenagers were beating the drums in a powerful, speedy rhythm. A third boy banged on a sheet of corrugated iron. Women began to gather in small groups. They talked incessantly, now and then throwing out a yodel or two.

When Singali returned, the noise level intensified. Disputes broke out over the distribution of the *mbaku*. Then Balonyona squabbled with the drummers. In his inebriated zeal he had changed into a grass skirt and insisted on taking over one of the drums. The drummers resisted. The problem was compounded by the refusal of Mamadu, the most popular drummer, to participate, despite the women's pleas. When Singali tried to drag him over, he broke free of his grip and fled.

I had noticed during previous dances that each song had two distinct sections. First came the actual song, with easily identifiable melodies, which after ten minutes or so gave way to a rhythm section in which musical themes were abandoned completely. These rhythm sections, called *esimé*, all tended to sound alike. During them the dancing grew wilder. The women cried out high-pitched phrases and sounds, sometimes an octave higher than I would have imagined humanly possible. Their shrieks were precisely timed, and strictly holding the rhythm or breaking it suddenly with a new one seemed to be a show of virtuosity.

On this night, scarcely did each song begin than it broke into a noisy *esimé*, which in turn quickly degenerated into babble. There were many false starts. The drummers continued without regard to the singers; the singers sang when the drums stopped. Singali got into an argument with Balonyona, which was, remarkably, conducted completely in atrocious French. Balonyona called Singali an imbecile. Singali pushed Balonyona. Balonyona fell backward like a plank of timber. "*Wo!*" the women cried. Balonyona leaped to his feet and skipped around like a boxer, waving his fists and swearing revenge. My last chance to discover the secret music of the Pygmies was turning into a fiasco.

Shaken by my failure, I retreated discreetly into my hut, packed away the recording equipment, and went to bed. I had been so sure that there was more to these people than I had seen, and it was devastating to be proved wrong. I needed time to recover and to reassess my situation. The financial ramifications of my blunder were dauntingly grim.

My absence was not noticed for at least an hour. Eventually Singali staggered into my hut.

"*Patron*," he called into the dark, "you're sleeping?"

"*Oui*," I replied from the depths of misery. "The music at Amopolo is *terrible*."

Singali swayed over me for a moment — perhaps my mood of despair had reached him despite his intoxication. Then he gave up and returned to the chaos in the clearing. The party gained momentum for several more hours, finally peaking in a fight between Matangu and Eloba. Everyone crowded around to watch as the two women tore and scratched at each other; at each blow, the spectators exclaimed in chorus. They parted to make way for the contenders, who plunged first in one direction, then another. Ultimately they tumbled into Balonyona's hut, and within minutes the hut was shredded.

Finally, the crowd intervened, pulling Eloba off Matangu and dragging her away. Silence, as if from a profound sense of shame, quickly smothered the drunken cacophony. In a few seconds the clearing was empty. From the forest rose the gobbled call of a touraco. The bird had probably found sleep impossible during the pandemonium. Another voice rose in the darkness, too — a bleating wail, heart-rending in its sadness. It was Matangu, crying out a lonely lament.

CAMP WAS UNUSUALLY quiet in the morning. People avoided my eye. I determined never again to buy the Pygmies *mbaku* — a purely academic resolution, since I was now almost broke. The few men bold or audacious enough to approach me for a cigarette had to endure my angry harangue: the Pygmies at Amopolo were a bunch of degenerates. I vowed to find *real* pygmies.

I wondered how, with my remaining francs, I would support my own nicotine habit, let alone move to another Pygmy camp. I was stuck with Amopolo, and I knew it. I couldn't even go home until I found a way to pay my fare. Whether the Pygmies liked me or not, I had to hang around for a while. I recorded my desperation in my diary. As I wrote, Simbu, who had been absent from the night's revelry, marched grimly toward me with my breakfast.

"Truly," he apologized with more fervor than usual, "there's no food in our village."

He handed me the bowl of tadpoles.

"But I eat well here," I protested sarcastically.

To my astonishment, Simbu burst out laughing. I had never even seen him smile before. Shaking his head in disbelief, muttering to himself, he left me to my meal.

Toward afternoon I decided to sneak off to the village and buy some peanuts. It was not hunger that drove me — my helpings of tadpole were always generous — but a craving for a different taste sensation. It occurred to me that I could have been supplementing my diet all along. Now that I had thought of it I was nearly penniless.

I felt like a cheat as I followed the road into the village. I had intended to survive on Pygmy foods alone, anticipating all sorts of meat, wild forest nuts, tasty roots and tubers, strange delicious fruits. Instead I was getting tadpoles and manioc. Nearly everything about the Pygmies was proving different from my expectations, and not only different but *worse*. In his letters to me Colin Turnbull had assured me there were few mosquitoes in the rain forest, so I had blithely decided not to buy a mosquito net since the Pygmies lived in the rain forest. But Amopolo was outside of the forest and next to a large swamp. Trillions of mosquitoes fed on us each night.

The stories I had heard in Bangui had filled me with excitement. A woman from Nola had explained, "The Pygmies around Mbaiki are used to strangers. Scientists visit them all the time. But at Nola they are very shy. They look at you sideways, and when you look back they turn away. If you give them just one cigarette, they become so happy! They pass it from hand to hand, and each Pygmy smokes one puff. Then they dance and dance all night." Others had told me that the Pygmies would flee in terror when they saw me, or that they had the power to turn invisible. Bokassa, it was said, had tried to harness Pygmy power in his climb to supremacy. Nothing had prepared me for the reality of Amopolo. Luck had dealt me a bum hand; Amopolo was the pits.

I had worked up quite an anger by the time I entered the village. In a spirit of revenge I gorged myself on *makala* — at ten francs apiece they were a tasty bargain. Then I bought a bag of roasted peanuts to stash away at camp, and a loaf of bread to eat on my way back. I also bought a pack of cigarettes; it would be my secret personal supply once I became destitute.

When I reached Amopolo I was surprised to find a large group of women, thirty or more, in front of my hut, sitting around the base of an abandoned termite mound. They watched me as I approached. I noticed Bosso among them. At first I wondered nervously if they knew about the peanuts, but that cynical thought quickly evaporated under their gaze. They just looked at me. I tried smiling. Only Nyasu, previously such a sourpuss, smiled back. I sat down in front of my hut, facing them. A moment ago I had been in a silent rage against the Pygmies. Now my anger dissolved. I felt strangely comforted and reassured by the women's presence. But what could have prompted it?

After twenty minutes they got up one by one without a word and left. I went inside my hut and discovered a large yellow papaya on top of my pack. Balonyona came over and explained that Christian had dropped by and left the fruit as a gift. Though glad I had missed him, I was touched by his gesture. On the spur of the moment I sliced the papaya in two and gave Balonyona half. It was juicy and ripe. Balonyona returned to his hut with his share. In a moment I heard slurps and hums of pleasure as he, Matangu, and Mbutu consumed the fruit. It sounded as if they had never tasted papaya before.

THE NEXT MORNING at the crack of dawn Balonyona appeared in the entrance of my hut and urgently suggested that we go fishing. Fishing? Except for some of the boys, none of the Pygmies had shown the least interest in fishing. The older hunters practically scorned it. I was not particularly keen on fishing, but Balonyona insisted. Realizing it would be my first walk in the rain forest with a

Pygmy, I agreed. I dug out some hooks and line, and surreptitiously stuffed my mouth with peanuts. I reckoned our early-morning departure would preempt breakfast.

Balonyona evidently meant business, for we set off at once. Several boys tagged along. We headed south, then turned onto a trail that led toward the Sangha. This was hardly the primary forest I had read so much about, with its immense trees, little undergrowth, and perpetual darkness. We were forcing our way through one endless bramble that defended itself with a menacing variety of thorns. Detachable needles embedded themselves in my skin at the slightest touch. Barbed wiry vines crossed the path at ankle and throat height. Tree trunks bristled with steel-hard skewers. Spiked lianas were common. And every now and then we came across the classic rose-type thorn. The jungle grew thicker and the trail vanished. Balonyona hacked at the growth with his small machete and made such good time that soon I could no longer see him. At one point I cried out in momentary panic.

At last we reached a clearing. We had come here, Balonyona explained, to make fishing rods. The boys cut some poles, I measured out line and distributed hooks, and we assembled our tackle. Then we set off once more.

The dense bush gave way to marshy forest. We negotiated carefully along roots and fallen branches to avoid the mud. Eventually the ground dropped away, and for a few precarious moments we clambered across a matting of lianas fifteen feet in the air. Below, elephant tracks cratered the swampy earth, each footprint inundated with black water. After an hour we entered lighter, drier forest. We marched on and on, crossing several likely streams. Each time I suggested that we stop and get down to business, but Balonyona wanted to forge ahead. He knew the perfect place, he explained, to find worms.

At noon we reached a little stream no different from the ones we had already crossed. Balonyona stooped down and began to dig into the muddy bank with his machete. Worms were hard to come by in the rain forest, for their role as the primary aerators of the soil had been usurped by ants. Balonyona found seven worms. He wrapped them carefully in a leaf, handed the bundle to a boy, and led us back the way we had come until we reached one of the earlier streams. We baited our hooks and cast into the water.

Balonyona's line twitched several times. After a little delay he would yank it out. Invariably the bait was gone. In less than twenty minutes only one worm remained. Balonyona was about to bait his hook again when the oldest boy demanded the worm with a vehement authority as startling as it was unexpected. Balonyona gave it to him without an argument.

The boy fished for five minutes and jerked out a minnow.

"Let's go," Balonyona said.

We headed back to Amopolo.

WHEN WE REACHED camp it was nearly sunset, that hour when the light imbues everything with a delicate glow. The usual evening activities filled the air with the welcome sounds of human presence. In the clearing some children were earnestly starting a dance of their own. Three small boys manned the drums. A group of girls sat behind them, talking, laughing, and singing bits of melody. Directing the effort was Bosso's twelve-year-old sister, Mbina, who wore a plume of leaves like a bushy tail. She was intently preoccupied with observing the effect of the plume as she danced forward in tiny rapid steps, shaking her behind. Her lovely bright voice encouraged the others to join in. For a moment it seemed that the song was under way, then they interrupted themselves with laughter, briefly argued over how to proceed, and began again. There were problems in the drum department: the four-year-olds just could not sustain the rhythm. Under Mbina's direction a crew of eight-year-olds took over. Immediately the music grew more powerful.

As I sat in front of my hut, where several men had joined me to wait for cigarettes while I ate my supper (tadpoles again), the children's melodic fragments struck me as altogether different from any of the songs I had yet recorded. They had a delightful quality, as though expressing the essence of childhood. Suddenly I thought, I ought to be recording. Here at last was a genuine example of the spontaneous dances for which the Pygmies were so famous. Never mind that it involved only the children — it might very well be the most interesting music I would ever hear at Amopolo.

By the time I had plugged in my microphones and hung the recorder by its strap around my neck, the music had gathered considerable momentum. I ran from my hut holding the microphones aloft. The chorus of children had tripled in size. They sang with an endearing concentration. Mbina, the center of attention, danced in short sequences one after the other without a pause. Her extraordinary voice pulled the music forward into a kind of joyous excitement. Men and women rushed over to watch and shout encouragement. They pressed together in a circle around the girl. At first everyone watched her, but at some point I became aware that their shouts and laughter were no longer directed at Mbina. A second figure now danced with her. Wrapped from head to toe in dark cloth, and consequently unable to see, it performed a hilarious parody of Mbina's dance, displaying remarkable agility. A minute later it was gone. The children called it back by beginning another song. Mbina yodeled and danced on.

At dusk the mood changed abruptly. There was a lull while the women arranged themselves in three seated groups according to their camp. Mamadu took command of the big drum. The men moved to the sidelines, some of them occupying a low bench made from three long bamboo poles. Now a new kind of music rose in the darkness, a densely polyphonic sound that seemed to embrace the camp in deep longing. A few of the men sang in low voices, but this was clearly the women's music. They sang with subtlety, embellishing the melody at every turn with soft yodels. They emphasized first one part of the melody, then another, giving the song a sense of musical development that belied its essentially cyclic nature. As for the melody, with two short phrases and a final descending yodel, I felt I had never heard anything so beautiful. For me it would become the theme song of those months at Amopolo. Later I heard it as a lullaby sung to crying babies. It cropped up in numerous variations during dances, and its countermelodies gave birth to new songs. Eventually, like all things in the forest, it would fade and vanish. But on that first night it was a glimpse of a timeless, magical world.

No one danced. The three groups of women, each around a small pile of embers, answered one another in a kind of antiphonal fugue.

When the song died away into a few stray yodels, the *esimé* began. The women's cries were whispered into the night, their voices soft and high: *Ya tay!* (Come here!) or *Béké!* (Give!). At a hiss from Mamadu the drums and singers stopped on a single beat.

The women sang for hours. That special melody appeared many times, surged in power, drew me into its promise and inspired a painful yearning. Bosso and her close friend Owoosa, another teenage girl, sat back to back in the middle group near the microphones. Sometimes the two improvised elaborate yodel sequences, leaning their heads to the side and pressing them together during the most inspired moments of their duet. Nyasu, sitting just below my left microphone, yodeled in a low quiet voice, as did other old women, adding a sublime profundity to the brilliant sound of the younger women.

At the time I was puzzled and even disappointed by the uncharacteristic reticence of the men, who sat without singing, except to themselves. Previously they had been such attention-grabbers, running up to the microphones and bellowing at the tops of their lungs, that I had considered them a nuisance. Now they were a collective lump on a log. I pointed a microphone at them to encourage a little participation. Only Dimba's voice rose for ten seconds from a hum to a scarcely audible croon. I supposed they were refusing to sing out of stubbornness because I had not bought *mbaku* tonight.

Occasionally Mamadu took a break from drumming and disappeared. He was, I learned, a temperamental drummer and often behaved as if he felt his talent was not being accorded due appreciation. During his absences the women would sing in a rehearsal for the next song, establishing its tone. There would be cries of "Mamadu!" and "Come to the drums!" Eventually he would return, either on his own or dragged back from his hut, sulking, by one of the women.

Around midnight, after a particularly moving rendition of my favorite song, I loaded yet another cassette into my machine. The women launched into the next song immediately. Gentle and warbly at first, their voices slowly blossomed into yodels of joy. Out of the corner of my eye I noticed a small bush where I did not remember a bush before. It stood a few feet into the clearing and cast a short shadow in the moonlight. As I looked around, I saw other bushes I had not noticed. At the edge of a patch of jungle an immense leaf, low to the ground, bobbed up and down like foliage caught in a breeze — only there was no breeze.

One of the bushes raised itself slightly, advanced farther into the clearing, and became motionless again. Despite the volume of the women's voices, I thought I could hear a soft cry, a high nasal voice that sounded at once nearby and far away. A few minutes later I heard it again, louder and definitely nearer. The music grew intensely excited and slipped into a wild, complex *esimé*.

"Ay-aaaaaaa!" came the cry directly behind me, rising clear above the voices of the women.

A giant leaf, twirling slowly, glided across the clearing and came to rest before the largest group of women. It tilted toward them and beat the ground, heaving up and down in rhythm. Sometimes it screeched with a strangely unhuman voice. The women were practically in a frenzy. Many stood up and danced in place. The leaf brought the music to an abrupt halt with a stabbing hiss. For a moment there was only the sound of the night insects. Then the leaf shivered. The tangled undergrowth that bristled beneath it shook with a windy rush. Falling still again, the leaf spoke.

The women listened in silence. Then a faint far echo answered, jibbering madly in the forest night. "Ooh!" several women exclaimed. Something popped in the nearby jungle, and long sharp hoots rose in the distance. One of the bushes raised itself, ran a few yards, and froze. The leaf shivered and spoke again. At the threshold of my hearing I could make out other voices, echoing one another, screaming out simultaneously or in tandem. The entire forest suddenly seemed mysteriously animated. The leaf declaimed in short rapid bursts of speech. Sometimes it elicited a collective *Ee-ho!* or *Yay!* from the women. Sometimes it inspired that lovely group laugh so typical of the women: *Eh-hay-hay! Whoooh!* Occasionally its remarks provoked an intentionally dissonant cry — two or three notes a half-tone apart, held for several seconds. Meanwhile the bushes continued to maneuver into new positions according to their own obscure designs.

Finally the leaf trembled violently and moved off, screeching a grotesque tune, which the women took up and transformed into a melody of supernatural beauty. Mamadu pounded several times on the big drum, warming to the rhythm. All manner of strange cries and cackles came from the forest. Two or three voices, at the limit of audibility, seemed engaged in a vituperative argument. A nearer voice, hopelessly out of tune, sang with the women.

The music continued throughout the night. The forest spirits returned again and again. Bushes detached themselves from the surrounding gloom and crisscrossed through the camp, spinning like tops. The leaf fluttered and swayed before the women. A third kind of spirit appeared. Pale in the moonlight, like albino creatures that lived in perpetual darkness, they had elongated, blank faces and boundless energy. They scampered and hopped about on all fours like frenetic monkeys. They beat the earth rapidly, emitting reedy grunts, twitching their funny heads from side to side. They ran through fires, scattering the embers in a shower of sparks. One of them ran into Singali's hut and ripped its way out through the wall. When they charged the singers, the women cried "Wo!" and fled in alarm.

The dance started to wind down in the early hours of the morning. Soon the forest spirits withdrew for good, although their voices could be heard through a few more songs. Then came a song from which they were absent. It comforted me, that song, an expression of both fulfillment and regret, with its texture of deep yodels to which there came no reply from the forest. The quiet *esimé* that followed petered out after only a minute. Without a word everyone got up and left.

As I crawled under my sheet in a mood of lingering euphoria, it occurred to me that during the entire ceremony I had not been asked for a single cigarette.

THREE

Heart in the Forest

I N THE MORNING everything looked different. For the first time in my two-week stay I was really seeing Amopolo. The hot, treeless clearing that was always too bright, the dirty white dusty sand, the shabby huts — these scarcely reflected the true reality.

Simbu, serious-faced, emerged from his hut and started across the clearing toward me. He looked as if he were on an important mission. He put down the bowls in front of me. I did a double-take — instead of tadpoles, large chunks of meat! I looked at Simbu.

"That is the porcupine," he said, and erupted in laughter. When he got himself under control he added, "The Pygmies, we eat lots of porcupine." He laughed again.

Meat! I thought.

"Eat *well*," Simbu stressed.

I ate like a carnivore, growling softly.

T HE PYGMIES' DECISION to let me witness the forest spirits was to have far-reaching consequences in my life. What had prompted their decision I could not guess, but I felt immensely relieved in one respect; if they had disliked me, as I had begun to imagine, they would never have allowed it to happen. I could not take the privilege of my acceptance lightly. I had found my music, all right. Its intricacy, subtlety, and profound emotional content convinced me that I had stumbled on one of the most significant cultural traditions of the human race. Here was a music, probably older than the pyramids, that was still alive, and its true artistic value was scarcely understood.

The extraordinary communal intimacy I had felt during the ceremony lingered for many days. Ordinary transactions between the Pygmies and me took on a kind of double meaning, as though each time our eyes met, they were winking, saying "Now you know our secret. Now you know who we are." The ceremony had affected me far more than I could have anticipated.

On the morning after the ceremony I apologized to the Pygmies for all the things I had said to them in my anger. They smiled tolerantly. How could I leave, I asked with sincerity, after what I had seen and heard during the night? They told me little about the forest spirits, other than their generic name, *mokoondi.* I did not harass them with questions. For the moment I was content with the mystery and willing to accept the *mokoondi* on whatever level the Pygmies wished to reveal them.

I BEGAN TO HEAR all sorts of music at Amopolo, especially that of the harp, or *geedal.* Although the harp is played by most groups of Pygmies throughout Central Africa, few scholars believe the instrument originated with them. In more elaborate forms the harp is one of the most widespread instruments in Africa. The Pygmy version usually has only five or six strings. The *geedal* was popular with the boys, who taught themselves how to play it. The women showed no interest. For exuberant virtuosity the finest player was a young man named Akété, who lived in Dimba's camp and was probably the best-dressed man at Amopolo. He even owned a radio! In his performances Akété always teamed up with his close friend Zalogwé, who provided satirical raplike accompaniments to the songs. The result was a remarkably innovative sound, the closest thing I ever heard to Pygmy pop.

Mamadu, the drummer, turned out to be an aspiring harpist. Though only slightly younger than Akété, he was far behind in technique, but he practiced diligently, almost obsessively, into the early hours of the morning. There was only one *geedal* at Amopolo, and every evening, if none of the more skillful players requisitioned it for the night, Mamadu claimed it. Often I heard him repeat a passage over and over until he could execute it smoothly. No one, however, could play like Balonyona. The very sound of the *geedal* seemed to be transformed in his hands. His effortless virtuosity filled each song with infinite variation. Listening to him play was like watching a forest stream. Occasionally, while everyone slept, he sat in his hut and played half the night away. I would drift off to sleep, only to hear the music in my dreams, until the sheer beauty of one of his melodies pulled me awake again. Though I would hear many *geedal* players, I never heard Balonyona's equal, and I appreciated my good fortune in having him as a neighbor.

The teenagers had their own dance, which they called *elanda*. After forming a circle, the girls yodeled a short melody over and over while the boys made deep grunting noises from their chests. Each person took a turn stepping into the circle and dancing solo for a few seconds, then selected the person who was to follow. It was an energetic, high-spirited dance that went on for hours after the older generations had gone to bed. Much of its energy undoubtedly derived from the fact that *elanda* was the most popular occasion for flirting. Rendezvous were arranged, affairs started (many young married couples took part), couples sneaked off unobtrusively one at a time and reappeared twenty minutes later. The atmosphere was charged with amorous intrigue.

The musical games of the children never failed to charm me. Toddlers learned the songs and games directly from the older children. In Europe and America many children's jump-rope rhymes have been found to be centuries old, and I would conjecture that most of the songs that accompanied the Pygmy children's games were equally old. Although *elanda* and *eboka* (drum dance) songs changed over the years, each one rising in popularity and then after a few months falling into disuse and finally vanishing from the repertoire, the musical games remained constant, nothing new was ever added, nothing old forgotten.

For weeks I recorded what must have been one of the most sustained outpourings of music on the planet. I went from *geedal* sessions in the afternoon to *gano* (sung fables) in the evening to the late-night *elanda*. When one group of Pygmies had exhausted themselves with music making and retired for a rest, I was instantly claimed by another. I hardly slept. It astonished me that prior to the dance with the forest spirits, the Pygmies had been able to keep such a wealth of music secret from me.

The music was not confined to such recordable events. Life at Amopolo was accompanied by a musical soundtrack. The strains of the *geedal* in the background rarely ceased, providing the day with a subliminal continuity. In the evenings, when men gathered around my fire to smoke and talk, the *geedal* would be passed from hand to hand. Only when it fell silent did one take notice. Men whistled too. During an idle moment with a child on his lap, a man would suddenly whistle a long lyrical improvisation that seemed to spring from some inner serenity. Mere breaths of air, these forest melodies imbued the few moments during which they endured with stunning poignancy.

In the afternoons, when Amopolo was virtually empty, small groups of children, some so young they had only begun to talk, would start to hum, their voices mingling in a ripple of harmony that spread its gentle influence over the camp. Children farther off, hearing the music, would join in, until in every direction a delicate sound filled the air, as soft as a murmur. Time itself seemed to stand still.

Much as I prized the music of the men with their harp and sung fables and admired the musical invention of the children, there was no doubt that the sound I had come in search of was to be found in the women's province. They filled me with a kind of awe. They were so in tune with one another, so intimate, that collectively they formed a kind of super-presence. They used the same gestures, their voices had the same extraordinary modulations, and they frequently cried out the same words at the same time. When they left for the forest they yodeled out of sheer joy. Often I paused in what I was doing to listen until they were out of hearing, finally realizing, with regret, that what I heard was no longer a woman's voice but a warbling bird.

/ / /

ONE NIGHT I was prodded awake by a painful throb in my toes. They had been bothering me for several days, but when a cursory inspection failed to reveal any obvious cause, I had shrugged off the dull pain as a minor inconvenience. It was only when the pain got decidedly worse that I switched on my flashlight for a closer inspection. Each toe was so badly swollen that the nails had begun to dig into the flesh. Several toes had a thin crust of blood, and tiny brown specks were swarming over my feet. Alerted by the beam of light, they hopped away before I could see what they were. I inspected my toes more closely. To my horror I could make out faint circles of discoloration beneath the skin, each with a black dot in the center. I discovered more in the soles of my feet. There were dozens, maybe hundreds, of them! I was panic-stricken. I switched off my flashlight and lay back, sweating.

In the morning I cornered the first man awake, Singali, and showed him my feet. He sat down and took hold of the right one. Suddenly he whistled in amazement.

"Maganja!" he exclaimed. "Ooh!" Several women came over to look. Singali obligingly held out my foot. "Wo!" they cried in a dissonant chord. Their cry of alarm drew others. Soon I was encircled by spectators eager for a glimpse of my tragic feet. Children crawled to the front between the adults' legs. When they saw the damage they went wide-eyed with wonder.

"What," I asked Singali, "is maganja?"

Singali explained that they were little animals that ate people's feet.

"But you told me they were only in the forest!" I protested.

I was blithely informed that there were no *maganja* in the forest but plenty in the sand at Amopolo. With a sharp sliver of bamboo Singali proceeded to dig them out, one by one. It was an excruciating introduction to one of the major health problems that accompanied the Pygmies' newly sedentary existence: chigoe fleas. The impregnated female burrows into the skin, then dies, but her insidious legacy lives on. The fertilized eggs in her abdomen grow larger and larger until they hatch as larvae, feast their way out of the flesh, drop into the sand, and transform into the next generation of fleas, each waiting for a human foot. Now I understood the source of the many foot deformities I saw, especially among the children. I had assumed they were testimony to a barefoot life in the forest. Much of the damage, I later learned, is reversible, but some children with severely infested feet had taken to walking on the inside of their arches, and gradually their feet had deformed to accommodate this style of gait. There was no reversing *that*.

When Singali removed the fiftieth chigoe I stopped counting. He was still operating on my right foot.

ALTHOUGH MY MONEY had run very low, my visa was good for another two months, and I was determined to spend that time in Amopolo. I wanted the Pygmies to think of me as one of them by the time I left, for I was already planning to return.

Every evening, upon returning from the forest, Balonyona built a fire in front of my hut. Despite the precarious state of my finances, I sometimes provided sugar and coffee, which Balonyona prepared. Normally my hut was the meeting place of adolescents and young men, the group that was most curious about me and most eager to establish friendship. When word spread that coffee was brewing, however, my fire became the most animated corner of camp. Men would emerge one by one from the shadows and gather around my fire. They came to drink coffee and, presumably, to size me up. Many faces were new to me. I met Doko and Wadimo, both smokers of the "big pipe" (Simbu's bamboo pipe for smoking *jama*, a mixture of marijuana, tobacco, and scrapings from a special tree). Doko had a sad, grumpy face and spoke rarely, mumbling in a deep sonorous voice. I never understood a word he said, and even the other Pygmies had difficulty with his speech. Wadimo had an untended Abe Lincoln beard that lent a kind of wisdom to his general appearance. His eyes always had a faraway look. Over the coming months I would learn of his remarkable ability to sit for hours in the same position, knees drawn up to his chest, folded arms bridged across them, as he surveyed the scene before him. Many of the elders shared this pastime, but Wadimo was its champion. Only Dimba could give him a run for his money.

Another visitor, Mabuti, was one of the tallest of the Pygmies, two or three inches over five feet. The sorrowful expression of his droopy eyes was contradicted by a curled upper lip, which gave him the look of a street-corner hoodlum. He made no bones about the motive behind his visits, establishing as soon as he arrived whether coffee and *jama* were on offer. If not, he claimed his nightly cigarette and promptly departed. Otherwise he stuck around until the last drop was drunk and the final pipe-bowl smoked. Many Pygmies had begun to call me Monsieur Louis, a welcome change from *patron*, but Mabuti pointedly called me *patron* at every turn, emphasizing my status as an outsider. For Mabuti my only value was in what I could give him. I realized that my acceptance by the Pygmies was not yet unanimous.

One evening Simbu, the "chief," arrived with a friend whom he introduced as his brother-in-law, formerly a renowned elephant hunter. "My name is Emile," he told me, "but you can call me Mobo." He was Bosso's father. Mobo, even smaller than Simbu, reminded me of an elf. There was an irrepressible twinkle in his eyes, and his dimples made him look so friendly that it was nearly impossible to deny his requests. The first thing he asked for, as soon as he sat down, was marijuana.

"I am the grand smoker," he explained. I gave him two hundred francs and he set off at once for the village. When he returned he had a smoke-up with Simbu. Then, unlike any of the other Pygmies, he proceeded to tell me about himself. He had had two wives, but the first had recently died. He had just arrived from her camp with his young son, Johnny. Mobo had spent years hunting elephants with both spear and gun. One day he was arrested by the authorities, locked up, and warned that if he ever killed another elephant he would be sent to prison in Bangui. He wisely gave up his elephant-hunting career.

Though my role was still that of passive observer, I enjoyed these coffee nights immensely. When the coffee boiled, Balonyona would remove it from the fire, and the gathering of dignified elders would spring to life. The men always brought their own drinking vessels, a variety of ancient soup cans, plastic bowls, jars, empty perfume bottles, aluminum pans, even a dented tea kettle. As Balonyona ladled out the coffee and plopped lumps of sugar into each container, a heated argument was certain to follow. Everyone wanted more sugar, even before tasting his coffee. Eight lumps seemed to be the acceptable minimum. Balonyona would resist at first, but after a five-minute argument would acquiesce to each demand. As soon as one man got as much sugar as he wanted, he would switch to Balonyona's side in the disputes with those not yet satisfied, telling them to restrain themselves, that there was not enough sugar. I was always served my portion in the only real glass at Amopolo, with the additional honor, unrequested, of twelve lumps, which turned the coffee to syrup.

As my relations with the Pygmies grew warmer, my initial perceptions began to change. My first impression had been that the Pygmies of Amopolo had strayed far from their roots and had degenerated into a decultured people. Now I realized that the behavior I had seen was the facade they used to deal with the outside world and conceal their real world. I was still struck, however, by how unexotic, how contemporary, they seemed. Many of their preoccupations seemed mundane, even laughably trivial. Often they discussed the day's hunt, but just as often they bragged about their plans to score a handful of cigarettes the next day, or fifty cents, or a pipe-bowl of marijuana.

Their lives were filled with physical hardships, yet my overall impression was one of self-indulgence. They were capable of great feats of endurance and physical labor — but only when strictly necessary. Otherwise their favorite pastimes were napping, talking, and making music. They loved to laugh. Everyone who has met Pygmies has noticed their sense of humor. There was a definite element of anarchy in their society; when they cooperated it was by choice. Anyone who didn't feel like hunting, for example, stayed home. Their tolerance for individual behavior went against everything I understood as the basis of an organized community. There was no need for pretense; in fact pretense was used only as a way to provoke laughter. Their only form of social coercion, if it could be called that, was derision, which was highly successful. Men and women had distinct roles, but the society was essentially egalitarian. If anything, power tilted slightly in favor of the women. As I would learn, the women could be extremely obstinate. On a collective level, their stubbornness was a powerful social force.

Simbu, though originally pointed out to me as chief, exercised little direct authority over the day-to-day affairs of the camp. None of the elders did. On the rare occasions when one of them tried to order the adolescents around, he was usually ignored. There was, however, a hierarchy of authority based on age groups: children, adolescents, adults, and elders. Among the men this took a remarkable form in their ritual of sitting down, or taking their places.

The rule seemed to be: never sit on the sand. The higher above the sand your seat was, the better. And in the choice of seat, privilege went according to generation. If someone of an older generation came along and claimed your seat, you had to surrender it. If someone from the same generation claimed it, you shared. The women, on the other hand, had no hierarchy for sitting down. They gathered in close groups, sitting directly on the sand, legs extended in front of them.

Around my fire at night there was always a selection of possible seats: a log, a broken lounge chair, one or two pieces of firewood, a large wooden mortar. The lounge chair, of a kind made in Bomandjombo, was shaped like a V, so that when you sat in it your knees stuck up as high as your head. It was extremely uncomfortable. Nevertheless, because it was usually the highest seat available, it was the most desirable. One of my favorite pleasures of an evening was observing the comical interactions as the men sat and resat according to their rules. One night an enterprising boy dragged over the big drum, turned it on its side, and sat on it. Within minutes he was sharing his seat with four others. Simbu came over with the big pipe, pulled up a large leaf, and sat down. He scarcely ever pulled rank for a seat, and sometimes even sat directly on the sand, which few men did. Soon Dimba arrived and claimed the lounge chair. Mobo and Doko took the log, and Mindumi balanced himself on the largest piece of firewood. I was sitting on the mortar. Mabuti strolled up, surveyed the situation, and opted for the drum. The boys adjusted their behinds to provide him with a perch. But Mabuti was not the sort to accept this compromise. For a moment he stared at them as though he could not believe his eyes. Then he grabbed the drum, tipped it until the boys fell off, set it upright so that it was now the highest seat, and sat on the drum skin.

Much as I prided myself in having made an important breakthrough with the Pygmies, I remained peripheral to their existence. My natural reticence prevented me from forcing myself on them, and they made little effort to include me in any activities other than music making. Except for my fishing expedition with Balonyona, I had not been included in their hunts in the forest. But even in less important matters they were still not forthcoming. For example, there was the question of my bathing place. For weeks I had been bathing in the large pool by the bridge. It was on the main road — the only road — and though traffic was sparse, no more than two or three vehicles a day, the pool was frequented by villagers from Bomandjombo. Early on I had begun to suspect that the Pygmies had their own secret bathing spot in the forest, where I often saw them head. And the women, when they went to fetch water, followed the same trail into the forest.

One afternoon I was lounging in front of Balonyona's hut while he plucked idly on the *geedal*. Eventually he put aside the instrument and fetched a wafer-thin piece of soap, carefully wrapped in a leaf.

"I'm going to bathe," he announced and set off toward the forest.

"Don't you bathe by the road?" I could no longer resist asking.

"I bathe in the forest," he answered without explanation.

"You mean there's a place in the forest?" I persisted.

"*Oui,*" he replied simply, as if it had never occurred to him before to tell me.

"Can I come too?" I asked.

His face went blank as he said I could. I did not think he really welcomed the suggestion, but from that day on I bathed in the forest, and no one objected. It was a lovely spot, shaded by a colossal tree, with walls of luxuriant foliage tumbling down into the water. More important, no villagers bathed there, and often we lingered in the pleasant shade long after bathing.

Another sore point was food. For days the women returned every evening with foliage infested with small, hairy caterpillars. The women roasted them, and everyone ate them with a side dish of *gozo* (manioc dough). Yet they always gave me meat. Why didn't they ever give me caterpillars? One day I remarked to Simbu, still my primary supplier of food, that he didn't have to give me meat every meal. I wanted to eat everything that the Pygmies ate.

"Meat is *good,*" he replied. "We want you to eat *well.*"

Later that day I tried another approach.

"What are those called?" I asked Balonyona as he munched on a bowl of caterpillars.

"*Bokongo*," he replied.

"Are they good to eat?"

Balonyona looked concerned. "No, Monsieur Louis, they are not good to eat."

I was so surprised by his answer I didn't know what to say. A few days later Simbu brought over a dish that I had eaten a lot of lately and that I had privately dubbed "hard-core food": it was antelope offal, stewed in a mixture of palm oil and blood. I could make out noodlelike strands in the ruddy gravy, only I knew they weren't noodles, they were boiled arteries.

"Always meat, meat, meat!" I whined in a mild fit of temper. "I already told you I don't need meat every meal. Why don't you give me *bokongo* to eat?"

"No," Simbu replied emphatically, wagging a finger at me, "*bokongo* is not good for the whites."

What did he think he was doing, I wondered, protecting me from caterpillars?

"I want to eat *bokongo*!" I insisted.

Simbu stoically carried away the meal and returned with a bowl of *bokongo*.

"From now on," I said as I ate, "if it's good for the Pygmies, it's good for me."

They took me at my word. The next morning I was no sooner out of bed than Simbu brought me over a meal of ten giant white grubs cooked in their own fat. They were, I knew, considered a delicacy. Under Simbu's gaze I picked one up and started to eat. It had the flavor of sweet butter. "*Maboongi*," Simbu said with a grin as I started on the second grub. I ate all ten.

These were small victories, but they marked my first attempts to convince the Pygmies to stop treating me like an outsider. Once they had accepted my presence, it was up to me to initiate each new step. When I finally pushed, they gave way, but they definitely left the pushing to me. Each time I made a move toward integration, I worried that I might be imposing myself; their very passivity made me reluctant to force my wishes on them.

One of the barriers I knew I had to confront was language. Usu-

ally we talked in Pygmy French. I had picked up a few phrases of
their own language, mostly what was useful to the Pygmies for me
to know, but I realized that to make further progress I needed a
teacher. I wondered who among them would be willing, since we
did not really have a common language. I also had the feeling it was
not a task any Pygmy would relish, and I had little to offer in
return.

One night around the fire I announced that I wanted to learn
their language. I wanted a teacher for one hour a day, whom I
would pay with cigarettes (I was no longer handing them out). For
several minutes the men praised my decision. Yes, they said, they
would teach me. That way we could stop using French. The conversation eventually died down. Who, I asked, wanted to be my
teacher?

Everyone stared into the fire. Suddenly Balonyona leaped up.

"Monsieur Louis!" he cried in agitation. "You want to learn the
language of the Pygmies? I, Balonyona, will teach you immediately! *This* is the language of the Pygmies!"

He stooped over and plucked something off his calf with great urgency. "*Jaku!*" he cried. He plucked off another one. "*Jaku!*" He began to stamp his feet furiously, scrabbling at his thighs, his crotch,
his torso. "*Jaku jaku jaku!*"

The others jumped to their feet in alarm. I stood up too, and then
I noticed a black stream like an oil slick snaking out of the bush, up
behind Balonyona, and scattering under the steps of his frenzied
dance. Driver ants! Balonyona was crawling with them.

THE NEXT DAY Mowooma came to my hut. I knew I had never
seen him before, for I'd definitely have remembered him. He was
five feet tall, skinny and dark-skinned, with a smallish head and a
mean-looking scarred face. He spoke in a speedy slur, in a voice so
emphatic it sounded angry. Mowooma had heard that I wanted to
learn the Pygmy language and that I was paying in cigarettes. Today he would teach me for one pack. His fee was out of the question; we eventually settled on two cigarettes. I opened my notebook
and the lesson began.

"*Bhembpungungwa,*" Mowooma said.

"*Bhembpungungwa?*" I repeated.

"Eh-heh," he replied. "Write it down." He watched carefully as I wrote, a contemplative smile transforming his face, miraculously, into an expression of innocent friendliness. When I finished he asked me to read it aloud.

"*Bhembpungungwa*," I read. Mowooma smiled with satisfaction. "But what does it mean," I asked, "in French?"

"Never mind what it means in French!" he replied impatiently. "You already know French!"

I knew there was no point in arguing against his logic. He resumed the lesson. "*Inderti inemwotiti*," he said, and instructed me to write it down. When I had amassed half a page of incomprehensible scribblings, which threw me into a kind of despair, Mowooma had me read it all aloud.

"*Voilà!*" he cried triumphantly when I finished. "*That* is the language of the Pygmies!" I paid him his two cigarettes, and he departed a happy man.

The Pygmies called writing "marking paper." They had encountered it enough times in their dealings with outsiders that they appreciated its importance, but exactly how it worked eluded them. The young men could draw some numbers and letters, and whenever they got hold of paper or cardboard, they used a piece of charcoal to fill it with their strange alphabets, later mounting these cryptic signs on trees around camp. A couple of the boys could write their names, but only as a series of memorized marks. As far as I could tell, what most impressed them about my writing (I had begun to keep a diary) was the neatness of the script.

Often, as they watched me write, they praised my mastery to one another, contrasting it with the way the villagers from Bomandjombo wrote. Those villagers thought they could write, they'd say, but what a joke! Now they, the Pygmies, had someone who really knew how to write! Once my dotting of a few *i*'s caused Zalogwé, who had been observing me closely, to gasp in wonder. Another time Biléma, after silently watching me write for an hour, suddenly spoke his name with a smile and told me to "mark" it on my paper. Sometimes they mimicked me, bending over and making minuscule writing motions on their knees with a stick. Once Akété accompanied his performance with a speech, speaking in a nasal whine that I assumed was an imitation of my voice. It certainly sounded like someone from New Jersey.

Reading also fascinated them. I had brought only one book with me, Lévi-Strauss's *Tristes Tropiques*. Each afternoon as I read, my hut "regulars" — Biléma, Akété, Zalogwé, Mamadu, and a few others — congregated around me. They could watch me read for hours, discussing it the whole time. If I paused for a moment, they asked to borrow the book. Then each one would take a turn, flipping the pages with immense care and "reading" by staring at the text with every semblance of concentration. When I finished reading *Tristes Tropiques* I decided it was good that I didn't have any more books. Reading always takes one away from one's surroundings. I was exactly where I wanted to be, so why read? A young man named Mokoko, seeing me leave the book in the sand, asked if he could have it. I gave it to him, and he bore it away into his hut like a treasure.

Gradually, despite initial difficulties, I built up a Pygmy vocabulary. Nouns were the easiest to learn, although I was confused at first by the differences between singular and plural. These lessons always began spontaneously. We would be sitting around when suddenly a couple of men would start pointing at things and naming them. I would get out my notebook and write down the words. Just as abruptly the lesson would stop.

For some time I had been trying to learn their name for themselves. When talking to me, they always referred to themselves as "the Pygmies." They acknowledged the name Ba-Benjellé, but used it only to distinguish themselves from the Pygmies across the Sangha River, whom they called BaNgombé. The BaNgombé belonged to a different linguistic group and called themselves Baka. In Sango the Pygmies were called BaBinga, but they didn't like that name. Bomandjombo villagers called them Béka, which in the Benjellé language was an interjection meaning "friend." Pygmy men often cried out when they heard some important news, "Ooh! *Béka!*" But in Lingala, the principal language of neighboring Congo, and a major ingredient in both Sango and Benjellé, *béka* meant "monkey." It was hard to tell in which sense the villagers used it.

For all the times that I asked them their name, however, the

Pygmies always avoided telling me. Eventually I dropped the subject. Then one day, in the course of an anatomy lesson, Balonyona told me without prompting: they were all Bayaka. He was a Moaka (singular for Bayaka). I was a *mondélé*. The villagers (non-Pygmy Africans) were *bilo*.

In records kept by the Egyptians, who contacted Pygmies around 2000 B.C. and left the earliest accounts of them, the Pygmies are referred to as Akka. Today one group in the Ituri forest is called Aka by their non-Pygmy neighbors. Eight hundred miles to the west, not far from Bangui, the Pygmies call themselves Biaka. I was with the Bayaka. In southern Cameroon there are the Baka, and the Ba-Bongo in central Gabon have another name: Akoa.

SCARCELY A MONTH after my arrival at Amopolo I had to face the unpleasant fact that my money had run out. All that remained was the twenty thousand francs I had promised Simbu. I decided to give it to him immediately, before I spent it. It would be interesting to find out what it was like to be totally broke among the Bayaka. I pocketed the cash and went to speak to the chief.

"Today I have no more money," I began. Simbu maintained a blank expression — he'd heard those words from me before. "All I have is the money I promised to give when I left." I produced the bundle. "Is it all right if I give it to you now and continue to sleep at Amopolo?"

"*Oui*," Simbu said quickly.

I gave him the money. Almost immediately Simbu began to peel off thousand-franc notes and hand them out. He reserved one for himself and gave two to old Esoosi to hold for the women. The atmosphere in camp soon grew festive. People were dressing up in their finest rags. Everyone babbled with excitement. Then I realized that they were leaving the camp in droves.

"Where is everybody going?" I asked Balonyona as he put on the single plastic sandal that he owned. "To Mosapola," he replied. "The Pygmies there are holding a dance."

Gee, guys, thanks for telling me! I thought. "Is it far?" I asked.

"Five kilometers," Balonyona said noncommittally. He stood up to go.

"Can I come?" I finally asked.

"Let's go," Balonyona said.

We had to pass through Bomandjombo on our way to Mosapola, and our journey was not without incident. The Bayaka went crazy with purchase power. They bought cigarettes, coffee, sugar, biscuits, and beer bottles of *mbaku*. They shouted to each other from one shop to the next. They gathered in groups in the middle of the road, doling out cigarettes, swigging from their bottles. They argued and laughed at the top of their lungs. Balonyona bought me a pack of cigarettes. Singali gave me two hundred francs. Biléma gave me a package of biscuits. As soon as we passed the gendarme post at the north end of town they stopped to roll a joint.

The road climbed out of the valley, passed a series of manioc fields, and entered the forest a mile later. On either side a wall of spectacular trees loomed up. Bosso, Owoosa, and Mbina looked tiny as they clambered onto felled trees along the way. We heard the drums of Mosapola before we reached it. When we did, I had a momentary pang of regret. The camp was beautifully situated. Although it was right on the road — unlike Amopolo, which was set a hundred yards back — this stretch of road was isolated and in full forest! Except for a few hours around noon, when the sun hovered directly above the gap of the road, Mosapola must have been shady all the time. When I had first come to Bomandjombo, I had passed Mosapola in the dark without seeing it. Had I passed by in the daytime, I probably would have told the driver to let me off there.

My regret was short-lived, however. As soon as they saw a *mondélé* in their midst, the Mosapola Bayaka began to crowd around me with demands for cigarettes and *mbaku*. Before I could disillusion them concerning my financial state — clearly, a white man without money was a contradiction in terms — the Amopolo Bayaka jumped to my defense with a loyalty I scarcely expected. Singali and others quickly explained that I was destitute and that it did not matter — today they would supply the tobacco and drink.

Gangba, the chief of Mosapola, a patriarch with a full white beard, invited me to sit with him in front of his hut as the dance resumed. The women gathered at one end of the camp and started to sing. Men and boys, many of the latter with hats made out of strips of palm leaf, gave high-pitched cries. At the back of the camp men constantly walked up a path into the forest, curtained off with palm leaves. Soon a chorus of two-note cries approached. The curtain parted and out came a group of men and boys wielding sticks and leafy branches. They surrounded a central figure, tapping it with their sticks, and as the entourage made its way into the clearing I got a closer look. The figure, draped in a mass of raffia fibers, was shaped roughly like a haystack. It neared the women and began to whirl, its raffia dress fanning out. As it whirled it grew in height and moved across the clearing. The women set off in pursuit, dancing after it. Suddenly it collapsed flat on the ground. "Yo!" everyone cried. It leaped up again. The women retreated, laughing and shouting. The figure began to dance again. It was Ejengi.

Ejengi is the most famous and possibly most widespread of all the *mokoondi*. I had once come across a recording of an Ejengi ceremony from northern Gabon. And I had seen in the American Museum of Natural History in New York a set of Ejengi's raffia clothes that Colin Turnbull had brought back from the Ituri forest. What surprised me now as I watched was that unlike the *mokoondi* I had seen at Amopolo, which emerged only at night and vanished by dawn, Ejengi came out and danced in the daytime. I was also surprised to see several villagers — *bilo* — taking part in the ceremony alongside the Bayaka. Other *bilo* who stood around watching were obviously terrified of Ejengi. Whenever he made a move in their direction they fled, bumping into Bayaka and tripping over objects in their panic.

The song gave way to an intense *esimé*. The women shrieked as though possessed, their cries weaving into a rhythm of bewildering complexity. Ejengi's movements grew bolder, he shot up in height, tilted to one side and whirled, the raffia fibers fanning out and flowing in a circle like an endless cascade. He ran, ranging farther and farther afield, the women pursuing, their cries growing ever more frenzied. "Yo!" came the collective shout as Ejengi collapsed. It was an overpowering sound, all the diverse rhythmic elements suddenly converging on that one note.

As evening approached and the forest darkness began to spread over the camp, Akété danced over to me and pointed to a cheap, colorful watch he wore: six o'clock. I took the hint and at the end of the song packed away my recording equipment. After bidding farewell to Gangba, Singali and I set off at high speed toward Amopolo. There was no moon, and soon we were walking blindly in absolute darkness, faster and faster. I made it a point of pride not to fall behind. We entered Bomandjombo like two front-runners in the final leg of a walking marathon. As we passed a shop I detoured to make a purchase. Through the generosity of the Bayaka I had amassed eight hundred francs that day. Now I bought a box of sugar and a bag of coffee. When we reached camp only Simbu was there, keeping lonely vigil by a fire in front of his hut. He rose and came over to greet us at once, obviously happy to see somebody. Singali got a fire going in front of my hut, and we brewed up the coffee. It was just boiling as the others returned, filling the camp with excited chatter, making a welcome end to an extraordinary day.

By LIVING WITH no money among the Bayaka and sharing their economic perspective, I came to appreciate their predicament. They stood literally on the border between two worlds. The forest was directly behind them. Half a mile down the road was Bomandjombo. The authorities there, in keeping with government policy, pressured the Bayaka to integrate with the national population, to abandon the forest and form large villages. Amopolo was one such village in formation. And village life was alluring — with its tobacco and alcohol, of course, but also luxuries such as soap, flashlights, cooking pots, and above all, clothes. The Bayaka loved clothes. And in Bomandjombo the men were required by law to wear shirts. (Curiously, no such law applied to the women.)

On the other hand the Bayaka could get along without money by exploiting the forest, obtaining products form the village world like manioc and salt through barter. They earned more expensive items like clothes and iron for their spears by hunting for the villagers. The *bilo* who owned shotguns often hired Bayaka men to hunt for them. Others hired them to lay wire snares in the forest. In exchange for the meat they brought back, the Bayaka would get a pair of trousers or worn shoes. They rarely considered these transactions fair, but this was their only means of acquiring the products of civilization. The danger was that as pressures to conform increased, the Bayaka were spending more and more time in these new pursuits at the expense of their traditional activities.

A major problem for the Bayaka was how to share the spoils of civilization. A well-honed system of rules governed the division of products of the hunt. In the absence of wealth, all of the Bayaka had maintained the same material level of existence. But with the appearance of Western clothes and other markers of status, some began to look distinctly "poorer" than others. A man who pursued traditional activities and avoided employment by the *bilo* became "poor," even though he might be eating better than someone who spent this time working for clothes. So far the strong social cohesion of the group had withstood this strain, but the problem remained: how to redistribute the new forms of wealth to maintain the egalitarian nature of their society?

A few of their solutions seemed to be partially successful. In the case of clothes, friends of the same generation "borrowed" items from each other, sometimes for an indefinite period. Even Akété's radio went from hand to hand, though whoever borrowed it had to provide batteries. Once Biléma carried it around for a whole day. The lack of batteries didn't prevent him from enjoying temporary ownership. When it came to cigarettes, which only the men smoked, sharing was the rule, but usually not without an argument.

One evening as I sat at my fire with several of the elders, a young man named Yongo came striding triumphantly over. Yongo was one of the "wealthy" Bayaka. He was so well dressed (though always in the same clothes) that the first time I met him I thought he was a *bilo*. To reinforce that impression, he was speaking in Sango to two Bayaka. Then I had noticed his eyebrows: they were shaved into two arching rows of vertical lines, a style practiced only by the Bayaka. Yongo sat down and spread eight packs of cigarettes out on the ground. He had obviously just been paid in cigarettes for some work and was inordinately pleased with his sudden fortune in tobacco. He kept rearranging the packs, picking them up, counting them (in both Sango and French), and blowing sand off their shiny red surfaces as the elders silently watched.

"Brother," Mobo finally said quietly, rousing Yongo from his pleasant reverie, "give me one. Give me a pack."

Yongo handed one over without protest. Then he arranged the

remaining seven in a row, removed the open, half-finished pack and set it apart, and stacked the unopened packs in piles of two.

"Give me," Simbu said, reaching out a hand. Yongo hesitated, picked up a pack, and gave it to Simbu.

"Where's mine?" Dimba called out in his sharp voice.

With an impatient click of the tongue Yongo thrust a pack toward him. He spread the remaining packs on the sand and began to count them in earnest. By now he no doubt regretted coming over to my fire, but it was too late. To the elders he was a sitting duck, and the requests continued relentlessly. Soon he was down to one and a half packs.

An old man named Bombé made his move. "Give me a pack," he gently harangued in a scarcely audible voice. "I'm an old man. I sleep alone. I smoke cigarettes. Give me my pack."

Yongo stared at the ground, sulking. For one thing, he knew that Bombé didn't smoke. On the other hand, he had this surplus, and here was Bombé, easily the oldest man at Amopolo, asking for a share. Yongo did his best to look deaf. Bombé continued in the best "old man's" voice he could manage — it seemed to quiver with frailty. Finally Yongo exploded in anger. He threw the last unopened pack at Bombé's feet, swiped his half-pack off the ground and marched off in a tantrum. The elders didn't bat an eyelash.

As time went on, the Bayaka began to include me in their network of sharing. I usually received enough cigarettes to blunt the edge of my nicotine craving. Sometimes these transactions were a little complicated. One day Simbu came over and told me that Singali, who had been away for a couple of days on a hunt for a *bilo*, had just returned. Then he gave me two cigarettes and a small bag of marijuana. Singali showed up a minute later and sat down with us. Simbu told me to give the cigarettes and marijuana to Singali. Singali broke up one cigarette and mixed the tobacco in with the marijuana, kept half of the blend for himself, and gave me the other half with the remaining cigarette. Simbu then asked me for the marijuana back, leaving me with one cigarette.

Another day Bakpima, the patriarch of a small family group that had set up camp across the road from Amopolo a few weeks earlier, visited me with a plastic jug of palm wine he had tapped himself.

Bakpima was dark for a Moaka, with short legs and a large head. He was incredibly strong. By birth he was a BaNgombé from across the river, but his parents had joined the Ba-Benjellé when he was a child. He was on his way to Bomandjombo, he now explained, to sell his palm wine. As soon as he sat down, we were joined by several other men. Everyone's eyes were fixed on the gallon of palm wine. No one wanted that palm wine to reach Bomandjombo. Bakpima wanted to drink it as much as everyone else, but he also wanted to sell it for five hundred francs. The men lamented that the *mondélé* had no money. Surely he would buy it if he had money. To make sure, they asked: would I buy the palm wine if I had the money? Yes, I said. You see? they said to Bakpima. He would buy it if he had the money. After a significant pause Mobo suggested that since I was willing to buy it in principle, why didn't I buy it on credit? Bakpima was immediately agreeable to the idea — never mind that I wouldn't have any money until I came back for a second visit — and the palm wine was promptly poured and enjoyed.

ABOUT TWO MONTHS into my stay Balonyona introduced a new man, Mokoko. "From now on," he said, "it will be Mokoko who makes your fire, who makes the coffee and guards your things. My job will be to hunt so that you always have food." I didn't have the heart to tell him there would be no more coffee, that I was broke. Mokoko was Singali's oldest son from an early marriage. He had arrived at Amopolo with his wife, Sao, and they had put up a small hut next to Singali's. Sao's cousin Ngongo, a bright lad of ten, lived with them. They had come from Mombembé, a tiny fishing village on the Sangha, far removed from any road. Apparently the Bayaka shared the village with a local fishing tribe, and there was some intermarriage. Sao's father was a *bilo*. In Mokoko's description the patriarch who presided over Mombembé was a *bilo* who was seven feet tall. Mokoko took his responsibilities toward me very seriously. He was also a wonderful singer, and his deep voice enriched many music sessions. Sao, a giggly woman, was more outgoing than most. By the time I left Amopolo, I considered them two of my closest friends.

Bombé was another recent arrival, and he quickly became one of my favorites. Despite his great age — among the men he belonged to a generation by himself, the eldest of the elders — he was vigorous and sharp-minded. He led a nomadic existence, wandering from one Bayaka settlement to another, rarely settling in one place for more than a few weeks at a time. His wife, Balé, also wandered, but they rarely stayed in the same place at the same time. This couple was involved in a perpetual dispute and was always divorcing and remarrying. They left messages for each other ("If you see Bombé, tell him . . ." "If you see Balé . . .") concerning the latest point in their ongoing argument. On the infrequent occasions that they did run into each other, they would stand face to face and make derisive remarks for several minutes.

One afternoon Adamo, Singali's older "brother," appeared at Amopolo. He was actually Singali's first cousin, but a first cousin was always called brother or sister. Adamo had moved to his wife's village, fifty miles to the north, several years earlier. The village, Monasao, was on the southern edge of a savanna whose stunted trees I had passed through months before. More than a thousand Bayaka lived in Monasao, which had been established more than a decade earlier by a Catholic priest named René. It had a school where the children learned to read and write French, a small hospital, and a church. Every family was required to cultivate its own plantation of manioc.

Adamo was drunk. A broad-shouldered man, he lurched over to my hut and plopped himself down on a broken wooden crate. He looked at me with an inebriated sneer, his eyelids drooping halfway down his eyes.

"It's me, Adamo Bertrand!" he finally announced, thumping his chest several times.

"My name is Louis."

"Yes! I know!" he cried with force. He pointed to his head and emphasized in a softer voice, "I know." He leaned toward me, reeking of *mbaku*. "The big brother of Singali," he confided, "me!" He pointed at Nyasu's hut. "My wife," he said in a soft voice, and then shouted, "My wife! Nyasu. Matangu is my daughter." He looked me in the eye. "Watch out!" he warned. "I'm a big man at Amopolo! Monsieur Adamo Bertrand!"

"Uh-huh," I agreed.

Adamo hiccuped, looked like he was about to puke, got it under control with a hefty swallow, and ranted on. "Singali? Pah!" He waved his hand contemptuously. "A child. A little boy. But Adamo!" He jabbed his chest with a thumb. "*Oui! D'accord!*"

I sat patiently through more than an hour of Adamo's self-aggrandizing ravings, all the while thinking: what a pain in the ass! Gradually he ran out of steam. He stretched out directly on the sand and started to snore. He roused himself slightly once to roll on his side and throw up. Then with a groan he turned his head away and was promptly snoring again.

Esoosi came by a little later to clear away the vomit, muttering in her disapproving way, "You see? *Mbaku* is bad."

"It *is* bad," I agreed.

From within Balonyona's hut came a series of tongue clicks. "Adamo!" Matangu called out softly, and gave a sorrowful little laugh.

My first conversations in pure Yaka (the Bayaka's name for their language) were with Bosso's little sister, Mbina. She occupied a special place in my affections; after all, she had started the dance that led to my first sight of the *mokoondi.* Even for a Moaka she was exceptionally musical and eagerly participated in most musical events. When I recorded the boys playing the *geedal,* she alone of the females sat and watched us. For some reason Mbina had begun to take an interest in my comings and goings. If I was leaving camp when she was around, she would ask as I passed, "*Looyay, ové dwa gangwé?*" There was magic even in the way she spoke, singing the final syllable on a sharply rising note.

I would reply in Yaka, "I am going to the village" or "I am going to the forest."

"*Oka!*" she always approved.

ONE DAY I was returning from bathing when I heard a very strange kind of singing. I stopped and listened.

"What is that singing?" I asked Balonyona as he passed by. "Is that the Bayaka?"

"*Oui,*" he replied. "An old woman died this morning."

"Oh," I said stupidly.

"I'm going over there now," he continued. "Let's go."

We reached the camp and joined a group of men sitting in the *mbanjo*, the men's meeting place. The old woman, I gathered, had just been buried a little way off in the jungle. A number of women were gathered in a close bunch inside and around what I presumed had been the old woman's hut. They were singing the strange music I had heard; it was *élélo*, the death lament. *Élélo* begins upon the discovery of a death and continues, with little interruption, until the corpse is buried. Afterward the lament is sung intermittently by close family members for another week or two, but it no longer draws in all the women of the camp. It is not so much sung as sighed, though at its most intense the sighing becomes a heart-rending wail of despair.

The *élélo* now was subdued, fading away, significant pauses breaking up its continuity. Now and then a few women would arrive from another camp, sit down, and join in for a while. Others would get up and leave. Several women looked at me, seemed even to stare. Did they regard my presence as an intrusion? After an hour Balonyona and I left. On our way back to our camp, I couldn't help asking Balonyona if there would be more music that night. Having heard the *élélo*, so different from any of the Bayaka's other music, I felt an agitation that would go away only when I had captured the music on tape. In a way it was a burden, this compulsion to record.

That evening Balonyona sat in front of his hut strumming the *geedal*. He was a temperamental player in a very Western artistic sense. I eagerly took the opportunity to record him. Zalogwé strolled over. For a few minutes he listened respectfully. At the end of the song he interrupted to tell us the dance would begin soon at Mindumi's camp.

"*Eboka?*" Balonyona asked.

"*Elanda*," Zalogwé replied. I was disappointed. I had accepted the fact that I would not be recording *élélo* that night, but I had found consolation in the hope that at least I might record the *mokoondi* once more. Now I learned that the dance would just be the teenagers' flirtatious dance. As far as I knew, no forest spirits ever came for *elanda*.

The dance was already under way when we arrived, but it was scarcely worth recording. I had been expected, however, and the small group of boys active in the dance wanted me to start recording immediately. I explained that I wanted to wait until more dancers showed up. "No, no!" Yongo insisted. "Begin immediately! People will come!"

I turned the recorder on. The *elanda* was completely uninspired. It had an unbalanced quality, the singing never straying from the lower registers. Then I realized that no women or girls were present. In fact, there were no women anywhere in the camp. The men noticed me looking around. They redoubled their effort, but my inclination was to stop recording. Then, beyond the low voices of the men and the falsetto yodels of the boys singing in imitation of the women, I heard the unmistakable sound of the women's voices — many voices. They were approaching from my left and singing.

For a moment the men's *elanda* faltered. Yongo, Zalogwé, and others shouted at the boys, whose rendition of the women's singing had temporarily lapsed while they listened to the real women. They tried again. Just then the women emerged into the clearing, at least thirty of them, their powerful voices drowning out the men's insipid *elanda*. They crossed the clearing and gathered in one great mass in front of the dead woman's hut. Bilema's mother tapped an irregular rhythm on an old, beat-up aluminum lid. They formed a tight circle, all facing inward. From the tiny hidden space at the center rose a deep hooting cry. Biléma's mother, the only woman still standing, waved the lid over the source of the hooting. The other women, arms stretched out in front of them, swayed to the overwhelming current of their own music. They were totally oblivious to the men.

It took me only five seconds to decide to abandon the men and record the women instead. As I moved toward the women I heard Yongo call out, "Monsieur Louis! The *elanda* is getting better! We're really going now!"

The women's singing possessed the drive of a force of nature. Ululations of irrepressible energy erupted everywhere — the only other times I had heard the Bayaka women ululate before were at the first sighting of the new moon each month. The hooting cry, which seemed to rise out of the earth, filled the music with urgency. I could feel its vibrations in my chest. Where was it coming from?

I watched Biléma's mother carefully, but she was singing even as she swooped the lid like some kind of conjurer's wand over the center of the group. Sometimes a second or third voice, from the right or left, would hoot in accompaniment, imitating the cry coming from the center. The arms of the women nearest the center concealed whatever was there. Suddenly the voice died away in a deep gobble.

"Wo!" the women cried in a long descending note, followed by ululations.

I was shocked — had I really just recorded that?

A fracas broke out behind me. Yongo and some of the men began to argue with the women: they should join in the *elanda* so that everyone could take part, instead of trying to hog the evening for themselves. The women, however, ignored their pleadings and began their next song. As the music rose in volume, the men and boys left the clearing in one mass movement. Only two little boys stayed behind and joined the circle of women at its outer fringe.

The music continued for a minute before the two boys were discovered. The women shouted wild threats and made violent motions. Two girls got up and chased the boys away, one of them so frightened he was crying as he ran. Then, like an ocean tide, the music surged once more. Now as I watched I caught glimpses of the figure in the center — a woman on her knees, crouched so far forward her face was almost pressed against the earth, her shoulders and back rising and falling as she danced. The women's arms would part slightly as she rose briefly into view, then close over her again as she sank back out of sight.

Sometime after midnight the women paused to tell me the music was over. I knew it wasn't (it went on until dawn), but respectful of their wishes, I packed my bags and left. Besides, I was terribly shaken: I had just fallen in love with the women of Amopolo.

Soon after that magical evening, Mokoko came by and watched me for a moment. "Well," he said, "are you coming?"

"Where?" I asked.

"Hunting!"

Finally I began to accompany the Bayaka on many of their hunts.

In the beginning it was exhausting. I didn't make things any easier for myself by lugging my recorder — my self-imposed albatross — wherever I went.

The day's hunt always started out pleasantly enough. The men set off first, along wide trails that were easy to follow, but at a daunting speed. On the road they usually ambled along at an excruciatingly slow pace, but as soon as their feet hit a forest trail they really moved. Inevitably we would veer off the main path onto a side trail that wound between jungly hummocks, across patches of mud and the occasional stream, over tree trunks and roots, under lianas, along scarcely visible detours to avoid obstacles such as a recently fallen tree whose branches had torn down lesser timber during its fall. Finally we would strike off onto a trail cut only the previous day. Just as I was beginning to feel miserable — eight o'clock in the morning and I was already worn out — we would stop. Suddenly, all around us, the hunting nets appeared. The scene caught me by surprise every time. Each net, draped in a mass over a sapling that had been cut off at about five feet, had a flower-shaped umbrella of big oval leaves pinned on top. They were almost invisible in their jungle surroundings.

We usually waited for the women, who would be at least half an hour in coming. (Once in a great while they never showed up at all.) The men would get a small fire going, take down their nets, then sprawl out in exaggerated postures of relaxation. Although back at Amopolo there was so much fuss to avoid sitting in the sand, the Bayaka showed no aversion to sitting on the forest floor. So what if a big black ant scurried across your belly? You just ignored it — it would reach the other side soon enough. Many men snoozed. If there were any cigarettes, they were lit up and passed around. Chatter was good-natured and pleasant. Now and then someone would whoop a hunting cry.

Gradually, first one man and then another would get around to the business of the hunt. Someone would go to a nearby tree and hack off a piece of bark with a resiny, brick-red inner surface. Scraping off the resin into a leaf, he would spit into it. The rest of us were invited to spit into it too. The leaf was curled into a funnel and the contents squeezed out, a few drops onto each net. Someone else would pluck several leaves off a special plant, place them on the embers for a moment until they wilted and turned hot, then press one of them onto his forehead. Others would reach for the remaining leaves. Some of the men and boys chopped down saplings for new spear shafts. One or two others strung out their nets, taking out tangles and repairing holes.

At last the women would begin to arrive in small parties, their much slower approach heralded by yodels and hunting cries. They would find their own spot not far from the men and sit down, joined by more and more arrivals. As their own chatter, more lively and musical than the men's, gained momentum, the men would urge each other, "Let's go!" A few would stand up, gather their nets over their shoulders, rest their spears on top like rifles — blade pointing down — and set off into the bush.

Now we moved silently, following trails that were indiscernible to my eyes. The animal we were hunting was the blue duiker (*mboloko*), a shy, solitary browser, frail, trembly, and no larger than a lamb. Its smooth coat shimmered with a blue hue. The Bayaka would pause at a haphazard arrangement of leaves on the ground or a slight disturbance in the soil and discuss it in urgent whispers. One of them would pop a leaf over his clenched fist — a sharp report that carried far — and the men would fan out left and right, stringing their nets in a large circle. Each hunter had a designated place in the circle, according to family groups, and set his net up between the same two men throughout the day. The hunters moved swiftly and without a word, first hooking one end of the net to a sapling or liana, then dropping the net along the ground. Wives and daughters followed, securing the net above and below to saplings, roots, branches, and vines. For some reason the circle of nets was never closed. One end would curve in, the other out, leaving an open corridor that seemed to have some mystical significance. The women stationed themselves strategically out of sight in the vicinity of the nets. The men disappeared into the cordoned-off jungle. For a moment there was a tense silence. A leaf popped, and the hunting cries began.

Yelps, rising falsetto howls, and simple yodels shattered the still forest air. As the startled duikers began to run, the hunters shouted to each other, warning of approaching animals. The cries grew more coordinated, moving as an ensemble in one direction, then another. Suddenly a woman would yowl with excitement. A duiker had hit the net. Sometimes a nasal bleat of despair signaled that the duiker had been caught. Or the laughter of the women would assure us of an evening meal of meat. If an argument erupted, it meant the duiker had gotten away.

The nets were only three feet high and never held a duiker for more than a couple of seconds. To make sure of the catch some-one — usually one of the women — had to rush and tackle it. The animals were dispatched with either spears or several blows to the head, using the nearest piece of wood. Sometimes the men managed to spear one of the much larger red duikers (*misoomi* and *mbom*). And every now and then a porcupine would panic and run into a net.

When it was decided that every animal inside the circle had either been caught or fled, the hunters rapidly walked along gathering up their nets, piling them in folds over their shoulders. I was always amazed that so few tangles resulted from their haste. The women, never idle for a moment, immediately began skinning and quarter-ing the catch. They divided up the meat on the trail. Complex rules regulated the sharing. The animal belonged to the hunter in whose net it had been caught. The woman who tackled it, the owner of the spear that killed it, the hunters who helped drive it into that particular net — all claimed a piece.

While on the move from one hunting site to the next, the women were always finding things to eat: *koko, payu, kana, bo-kombu* — leaves, seeds, nuts, and mushrooms — as well as other delights, such as *yoko, ékuli,* and *isuma,* edible tubers; *mola,* a sweet juicy root; and *mayingoyo,* a small orange fruit with a re-freshingly tart pulp. Like other little fruits, it was always eaten on the spot. At every moment, both the men and the women kept an ear to the trees, listening for the sound of a beehive. At every break in the canopy they paused to scan the sky for bees in flight. When they located a hive, they memorized the tree and moved on. The men would return for it the next day or next week. But the honey was already theirs.

Around midday Bombé, who carried his net but never deployed it, would give a two-note cry at regular intervals, the signal for lunchtime. Everyone assembled. The women unpacked the food wrapped in leaf bundles, and we had a picnic. Some women worked on the *payu*, extracting the edible center which would be used for the evening sauce. We ate more snacks found on the trail and smoked cigarettes. And then we were off again, hunting until late afternoon.

In the beginning I found these hunting expeditions grueling. I had trouble just keeping my feet on the trail. Camouflaged roots were constantly tripping me up. Branches poked at my eyes. Sandpapery vines rasped my shins and throat. Everything clutched at my microphones. Once we left the trails behind, each inch of the way deepened my misery. Spiderwebs formed a maddening gauze over my face. Ants fell down my back and bit me. Debris got into my eyes. To top things off, whoever had the last net always led me swiftly all the way around the circle, through thick vegetation, until I ended up back where we started, and was instructed to sit down.

One day I decided to leave my tape recorder behind. I'd already recorded every phase of hunting several times, including the killing of the prey, the arguments, even the sounds of lunch. I was obsessed with the sound world of the Bayaka. But enough was enough. I would go into the forest with arms as free as a monkey's. Bwanga, one of Singali's brothers, was my companion for the day. As we bounced along the trail I noticed a difference immediately. I could actually gaze around and *see* the forest for the first time. What struck me at first was how unexotic it looked. Most of the leaves had a waxy texture and uniform shape — oblong, tipped with a downward-pointing drip spout. There were no fancy crenelations, no serpentine tendrils, no carnivorous bug traps. Along the streams or where a tree had fallen, however, the sunlight released vegetable life at its most fantastic. Gradually the sheer immensity of the forest — the height of the canopy, the girth of the trees, the lianas contorting through the vaulted understory — impressed itself on my senses. We were like scurrying ants, creatures of the leaf litter. Sometimes the thickness and closeness of the tropical undergrowth bewildered me with its organic detail. Then we emerged

into spacious, echoey *bimba* forest, the canopy held aloft by towering *bimba* trees, the earth covered in a brown carpet of leaves,
bimba seedlings and saplings filling the air with green. These trees
formed their own groves apart from other species. Because of the
poor quality of their wood, they had been spared the depredations
of the lumber company.

Bwanga and I raced along ahead of the others. Bwanga, who had
a beautiful voice, sang in a smooth falsetto a long wordless improvisation that went on and on. If only I had my tape recorder! I
thought. His voice resonated, rich with instant echoes that bounded
back from the trees. Soon we entered denser forest. Now, as I
started to pay attention to the forest floor, I noticed that much of
the litter *was* truly exotic. Big green fruits like bowling balls spread
over one area. Older specimens had rotted away into round shells.
All of them were broken open and hollow.

"Are those edible?" I asked Bwanga.

"Only to the elephants," he replied.

We passed areas strewn with blossoms, some as big, colorful, and
fragrant as roses. There were familiar-shaped seedpods, only ten
times the normal size. A whole selection of fruits speckled the
ground, almost all inedible. Some, however, looked delicious, and
one variety, like a pink apricot, even smelled delicious. Was it
poisonous?

I stayed with Bwanga during most of the day's hunt. It was extraordinary how much easier and more fun it was to move through
the forest unimpeded by a thousand dollars' worth of recording
equipment. I hadn't realized how handicapped I'd been. Once, when
the nets were being set up, Bwanga decided to sit the hunt out. He
flopped his net in a coiled bundle on the ground and we lounged on
its ample folds. Hunting nets make comfortable cushions. While we
sprawled, the hunting cries drew dramatically near. Bwanga, in response to a cry, sat upright with taut attention. He leaned forward.
There was a sudden rustle of leaves. Something blurred through
the foliage. Bwanga was already speeding toward the net when a
blue duiker hit it. He tackled the animal in a flash.

Late in the day, on the penultimate hunt, I left Bwanga and sat
alone near Beedyaba's net. (Beedyaba was Wadimo's oldest son.) I

sat a few yards outside the circle, the net practically invisible even at that close range. The hunt commenced and I drifted off in a daydream. All at once I realized that the cries were approaching fast. I strained my eyes in the direction of the net, on the alert for any action. I now knew what a duiker in flight looked like: the only visible motion was the flick of the leaves it hit in its passage. The rest was just a blur.

An animal shot out of the bush and hurled itself into the net. I banged swiftly through the undergrowth. Startled for an instant, the blue duiker regained its balance and turned to flee. I threw myself on top of it just as it began its getaway.

The Bayaka were mildly amused. Beedyaba, to whose net the animal was credited, came over and killed it. "Monsieur Louis," he called to someone in the nearby bush, "just caught an antelope."

"Monsieur Louis?" came the reply.

"Oui, Monsieur Louis."

The unseen hunter chuckled.

AS I DEVELOPED the stamina for hunting, I began to enjoy our expeditions more and more. Hunting was fun! I thought of the contrasts between hunting and agriculture. Who in his right mind would want to trade such an invigorating day's work for the drudgery of life in the fields? And for what? Manioc? Bananas? Hunting gave you meat. And as for gathering — it was sheer delight. The women strolled through the forest as though they were in a vast grocery store — only here everything was free. And each day's hunt was full of little adventures, excitement, moments of idyllic contemplation or laughter. No two days were the same.

On one of the rare mornings when the men and women left for the hunt together, Motadi (Matangu's younger brother) led the way. As usual, I was second in line. Motadi raced along at a speed that was a new challenge to me. My walking reveries, normally pleasant as I contemplated the remarkable world around me, soon became tinged with irritability. Why was Motadi walking so fast? Once we left the main trail behind, he seemed always to choose the path of greatest resistance, plunging into thickets, ducking under lianas, hopping from branch to branch along fallen trees with a mind-boggling ease and dexterity. I would reach a tangle of growth he had just passed through at an unbroken pace only to discover that it was impossible to advance without untying a complicated mesh of vines. How had Motadi done it?

On and on he forged. I began to grow annoyed. I considered Motadi for the first time. Although he lived next door in Nyasu's hut, we had never had much to say to each other. I even had the feeling that Motadi didn't like me, this *mondélé* who had moved in with them, pretended to be a Moaka, who thought he was such a hotshot in the forest. Pretty soon I convinced myself that he was testing me, trying to put me in my place. I felt a flash of anger, and I determined not to flag. As I tromped grimly along, ignoring the continuous bumps, scrapes, and scratches the forest was inflicting on me, I slowed down just long enough to take a quick peek behind. Mbina was right at my heels, a small carrying basket hanging from her head, her littlest sister, Mowa, in a sling on her side, a sprig of leaves in her left hand. I felt instantly humbled.

Another time some boys came across a giant millipede (*ngongolo*). They are harmless creatures but impressively large, and everyone avoids touching them. Women find them especially repellent. Ngongo found a stick and nudged the millipede gently until it assumed its defensive posture, curled up. He maneuvered it onto the stick and raised it, the usual procedure for removing a *ngongolo*. One then catapults the creature into the surrounding bush. Ngongo, however, hid behind a tree and waited for the women, who soon appeared. Bosso, I noticed with a certain amount of guilt, was in front. Ngongo leaped out and thrust the dangling millipede toward them. Bosso shrieked and fell down. During her fall, in a kind of reflex action, she slapped the *ngongolo*. It broke in two and vectored through the air. Bosso screamed again, now in genuine revulsion. She had just *touched* a *ngongolo!* Eeyuck! Everyone burst out laughing. Bosso laughed so hard that when she stood up she immediately fell down again, bumping her head against a tree. That made her laugh even harder.

One day in the forest during a lull in the hunt I found myself standing near Mbina and another girl. It was my first extended close-up view of Mbina, and I looked at her carefully, scrutinizing her facial tattoos for the first time. Many men and women had these blue-green tattoos. On the men they were usually just a few bars, lines, or zigzags above the bridge of the nose, between the eyebrows, and up the middle of the forehead. Some of the women had more elaborate patterns. Akété's mother, Belloo, was a walking constellation of swirls, circles, loops, and squiggles. These designs are called *matelé* by the Bayaka. I had seen photographs of the bark cloth still made by the Pygmies of the Ituri forest, which the women decorated with abstract painted designs. The Bayaka no longer made bark cloth, but the *matelé* they tattooed on their faces and, less extensively, their arms and bodies looked like fragments from these bark cloth designs.

Mbina's tattoos were minimal: a row of little vertical lines on either side of her forehead. Who, I wondered, did the tattooing? Her parents? (I didn't yet know that the women did the *matelé*.) What impulse inspired that particular design? Was it a creative whim? Did the artist interpret a child's nature symbolically, or was the design an attempt to impose a nature?

I looked from Mbina to the other girl, whom I had seen once or twice recently, always in the forest, always with Mbina. She looked a little older, and had lighter, honey-colored skin. She was very pretty. What struck me immediately were her fascinating tattoos. A wild jumble of dashes crisscrossed and intersected each other from her forehead halfway down her temples. Although the marks were paint, visible only close up, they possessed the energy of pure chaos, no attempt having been made at any kind of symmetry. What on earth, I wondered, was the artist thinking when she did *that?*

The girl turned suddenly and looked at me. I realized that I'd been staring and turned away.

THREE MONTHS into my visit one of my microphones began to malfunction. I noticed the problem during an afternoon *geedal* session. One of the VU meter needles kept going dead. If I fiddled with the microphone jack, the needle would suddenly leap back to life. I switched the recorder off and took the microphone jack apart on the spot. The Bayaka stopped the music and crowded around to watch. After a short examination I discovered the problem. A tiny red wire's contact with the conducting plate had broken. I should have had a spare microphone cord, but I didn't.

Over the next several days I attempted to tie the minute bundle of exposed copper threads to the conducting plate. Like Edison in search of the perfect filament, I patiently tested many different materials. A strand of polyester carried me through half a night of songs to celebrate the appearance of the new moon. A thread of canvas from my threadbare sneakers kept me going for an hour of musical games. Sewing thread was the least effective — it hardly lasted through a single *geedal* song.

Another problem was my rapidly dwindling supply of batteries. I had brought along more than enough batteries to cover all my cassettes. In fact I had used up all my blank cassettes weeks earlier and was now recording over the least remarkable material whenever something special came up. What I had not calculated for, however, was the number of hours the batteries would be used for playback. It should have been obvious: the Bayaka were great enthusiasts of their own music and wanted to listen to themselves all the time. It was impossible to deny their requests — after all, it was their music. The only batteries available in Bomandjombo were made in Cameroon; they were powered by gasoline, and after ten minutes their power would ebb and surge erratically. They might have sufficed for flashlights, but to me they were useless. Besides, I had no money to buy them.

And so for the first time I began to think about leaving, a painful thought, dictated by circumstances beyond my control. I would leave, I told myself, only to return better prepared. At the same time I was immensely relieved that I didn't have the means to leave; I was stuck.

ONE MORNING, just as I finished repairing my microphone with my latest inspiration — a piece of tough, wiry grass — Bwanga and Zalogwé carried the two drums over to Mindumi's camp. The women were all wandering in that direction too, and when I heard drumbeats and saw the men begin to leave, I asked what was up.

"*Eboka* for the women," Balonyona explained.

"Now, in the morning?" I asked, surprised. It was the perfect opportunity to test out my repairs.

The first dance had already begun when I arrived. All the women of Amopolo seemed to be there, sitting in two large groups and singing. Except for the percussionists, Bwanga and Zalogwé, the men, though a great many were present, hung around in the background unobtrusively. A single woman danced in the clearing, but she was not a Moaka. A *bilo*, she belonged to the indigenous river tribe, the Sangha-sangha. Wearing a grass skirt, she danced gracefully and modestly. Now and then one of the Bayaka women ran into the clearing, grabbed her by the wrist, and raised her arm in the air as though she had just won a boxing match. The song ended with a short *esimé*. After a break the second song began. A different *bilo* woman, wearing the same grass skirt, danced. Both village women left before the third and final song, during which no one danced. I was slightly mystified by the proceedings, but my puzzlement was overshadowed by my elation: the microphone repair was a success!

Two or three mornings later — I had not made any recordings in the meantime — Bwanga and Zalogwé again took the drums away, and the women all migrated toward Mindumi's camp.

"What's going on?" I asked Balonyona.

"*Eboka* for the women," he replied. What, again? I fetched my recorder and went to check it out.

The scene was much the same as for the earlier dance. The same Sangha-sangha woman was dancing in the clearing. The previous time she had danced topless, but now she wore a shirt. She was young, although from her pendulous breasts she was obviously already a mother, and attractive despite a slight crossing of one eye. Instinctively I liked her. The women's singing was more powerful on this occasion. They were giving it their best. At the start of the *esimé* the Sangha-sangha woman left the clearing. The next song was beautiful. Its melody had only three notes, and the effect was hypnotic. I recognized it from the last time, but now the song was laced with subtle and intricate harmonies that added a thousand little currents to its overall flow. The song ended, not with an *esimé*, but with a new melody, which lasted only a minute, that did not sound like the Bayaka at all. I thought it might be a song of the Sangha-sangha.

During the lengthy pause that followed, the camp was filled with the chatter of the women. The men were also talkative. Now and then someone pounded on the drums. I waited. The microphone, which I handled delicately, had recorded without a hitch. Ten minutes passed, then twenty. Soon it be a half-hour. I told Zalogwé that I had recorded enough and would go back to my hut, but he insisted that I wait, there was one more song.

The mood appeared to be heating up again. Esoosi, Biléma's mother, and a third old woman kept going up and down one of the paths that led into the jungle. The erratic drumming began to pick up and then stabilized into a powerful, deep-toned throb. Soon afterward the women started to sing. The melody was radiant, gliding away in dense polyphony and reemerging, only to soar off once more. At first no one danced, but after a couple of minutes a girl in a grass skirt, urged by the three old women, stepped out into the clearing. She was crying, covering her face with one hand.

"Dance!" the women encouraged her. She took a step or two. "Yay!" the women cheered her on. Her face still covered, the girl began to dance forward in tiny spurts. She took her steps with increasing confidence, and as she approached the center of the clearing, her hand dropped away from her face. It was the girl with the crazy tattoos.

Her dancing grew more assured. Soon she seemed to lose herself in it, dancing out of the pure joy of movement. Her initial shyness dissolved, as if she were leaving the world behind, the crowd forgotten. Her womanhood seemed to blossom as she danced. The women finally called her back amid more cheers. She left the clearing and disappeared up the jungle path. The drums pounded on for a while, but the dance was over. The women were dispersing.

I didn't know it yet, but I had just made my final recording.

SOON AFTER that wondrous dance, I became seriously ill with malaria. First a wave of cold swept over me. All my strength seemed to ebb away and I was overcome by violent shivers. I felt that I was surrendering my body to the shivers, released from all responsibility for fighting the fever. The malaria had won. I spent a delirious night, shifting constantly in bed to try to relieve the terrible aching of my body. No position was comfortable. As my fever raged, my mind seemed to split into several voices, all speaking at once in a kind of mental fugue. During the night I was dimly aware of a succession of Bayaka at my bedside. They were, they later told me, deeply alarmed by my condition — not because they liked me but because they were afraid that if I died at Amopolo, they would be blamed.

In the morning the fever abated, and I felt well enough to bathe in the stream. But by nightfall it returned with even more force. The next morning, though again I felt better, I knew I had to find a way to leave Amopolo. The Bayaka encouraged me to go. Go to America, they told me; when you get better you can come back. And don't forget to bring us those clothes you promised.

I ARRANGED TO FLY free of charge to Bangui with the Yugoslavians from the sawmill. Their supply plane, an eight-seater, flew in twice a month. On the day I was to leave, most of the Bayaka made their farewells in the morning before going hunting. They had been very casual about my departure, and I had felt a little hurt. For me, leaving was so emotional that I couldn't understand their composure. They might never see me again, and it hardly seemed to matter. They accepted at face value my promise to return, while privately I was tormented with the thought that I might not be able to afford to come back. It was important to me that they really believed I would return, as if their belief would somehow ensure it.

Balonyona alone stayed behind to wait with me. I was deeply grateful, for of all the Bayaka I felt closest to him, and I was glad that my impending departure did not leave him unmoved. Just to be in his presence was a comfort. What I would miss most, I realized, was simply the company of the Bayaka. During my months at Amopolo I had come to regard them as the most well-adjusted people in the world. Their undaunted preoccupation with enjoying each moment as it came, with no concern for the consequences, made them free from neuroses. They were an example to me of how the full potential of the individual could be realized in the absence of the complex constraints imposed by modern civilization. Originally I had thought many of their concerns petty and trivial. Now, on the contrary, it was the machinations of the world I was returning to that struck me as superficial, even idiotic.

Balonyona was playing the *geedal*. He began to pluck a familiar tune, only now he improvised new words: "*Merci Looyay . . .*"

Merci for what? I was the one who was indebted.

At one point he paused and stared blankly ahead. "Monsieur Louis," he finally said, speaking in slow, careful French, "if you want to return, you must leave your heart at Amopolo."

I was surprised that he was expressing such a sentiment in this familiar way. "How do I leave my heart?" I asked.

Balonyona smiled suddenly, as if the joke were on me. "You already have," he said, and plunged back into his *geedal* playing.

FOUR

Dzanga-Sangha Days

F ROM AN ALTITUDE of 30,000 feet, sunset over the flat expanse
of central Chad was a spectacular display of fiery light. More
than two years had passed since I had left the Bayaka, but I was
finally on my way back. I had had difficult times in Europe and
America, but in the end my recordings of Bayaka music had aroused
enough interest to finance my return. Walter Slosse, who hosted a
weekly series about ethnic music on Dutch radio, scheduled two
programs of my recordings. Later he found a company that designed and built a solar battery recharger that I could take with me.
The Pitt Rivers Museum, part of the Department of Ethnology and
Prehistory at Oxford University, awarded me a grant to carry on
my research and agreed to house all the material I collected. In New
York I met the musician Brian Eno, whose albums I had once collected, and he commissioned me to bring back recordings of forest
sounds and ambient music of the Bayaka. He had been asked to
participate in New York's next Winter Festival and had decided to
create a rain forest environment, for which he needed recordings.
The festival was to be held in eight months. I expected to be gone
for six months, so I looked forward to taking part in it.

In Europe I had come across a book by Simha Arom about making field recordings. Arom had been recording in Central Africa since the mid-1960s, and his work had immeasurably enriched the repertoire available to the West. His recordings, including an album of the Ba-Benjellé Pygmies, a deluxe three-record set of the music of the Aka (Biaka), and an album of the Baka in southern Cameroon, were part of the inspiration that had led me to Amopolo. Arom was a professional musicologist, and his method was to organize special recording sessions of select pieces. In effect he recorded concert performances of the music.

The more I thought about Arom's method, the more convinced I became that my search was different. It was not just the music that I was after: I wanted to record how life really sounded among the Bayaka when no outsiders were present. Arom recommended against making recordings of ceremonies; most took place at night, and recording conditions were far from ideal — there was talk and laughter, pauses, moments of total chaos. But what I loved about these ceremonies was their spontaneity. However beautifully the Pygmies might sing during organized sessions, they simply never reached the ecstatic inspiration that characterized their music when the *mokoondi* were present. I wanted to record the Bayaka when they sang to the forest spirits, not when they sang for me. I wanted the laughter and shouts and arguments of the children as they sang and played musical games for themselves, not the tame sessions they might perform for my microphones.

Though my first visit with the Bayaka had lasted only three months, the intervening time had in no way diminished the impact of that stay. They had been the most vivid three months of my life, and I had kept the vision alive by listening to my recordings. Sometimes my longing to return left me quite agitated, especially when it seemed that I could never afford to go back. I really had, as Balonyona said, left my heart at Amopolo.

In Bangui I set about getting a new permit to live among the Bayaka. On my first visit the process of negotiating for permits from two government departments had been slow and frustrating. And in Bomandjombo, I had produced only one of the permits and discovered that it was sufficient. So now I decided not to bother with the second permit. To my delighted surprise it took only three days to obtain the necessary authorization. Almost before I knew it I was ready to leave for Bomandjombo.

On the eve of my departure I went to one of the markets to eat some *mishwi* — grilled chunks of beef garnished with chili pepper and salt. *Mishwi* vendors always wrapped the purchase in a sheet of paper. Pages from textbooks, school exercises, computer printouts, magazines, ancient government documents — all ended up as wrapping paper in the markets. I bought a triple portion of *mishwi*, which warranted a full sheet of paper. When I unwrapped the meat, I noticed that the paper was a letter with a familiar signature. I realized where I'd seen it before: on the money. It was the signature of the man who was now president of the country.

My journey to nola was a bumpy race through the Central African countryside. That night I had a vivid and disturbing dream: I had arrived at Amopolo. Balonyona came up to greet me. He embraced me and began to cry. At first mistaking his tears for an expression of joy, I soon realized that he was crying over some deep sorrow. I woke up wondering what made him so sad.

The second day of the journey I shared the cabin of the bush taxi with the driver and a policeman traveling to his new posting in Bomandjombo. The driver was describing an accident on this stretch of road in which more than twenty passengers had died. He said the wreck was still there; we would pass it in a minute. But as we rounded a bend, a bush taxi came hurtling directly at us. Our driver steered our car off the road and into the jungle, narrowly avoiding a head-on collision. Farther on a large monitor lizard scampered briskly across the road and disappeared into the bush.

The policeman began to look worried. "Isn't there anything on this road?" he finally asked.

"Nothing but the forest," the driver replied. The policeman shook his head in despair.

At the Bomandjombo police station most of the familiar faces were gone. Only Gabriel, whom I had befriended on my first visit, remained, and he would be leaving in a matter of weeks. Still, I was so elated at having arrived that I ordered a round of palm wine for everyone. Gabriel filled me in on events since my departure. The major development was that the sawmill had shut down. Everyone was out of work, and Bomandjombo was really suffering. There wasn't even any medicine. Many people wanted to return to their native villages, but few could afford to. The sawmill had been in operation for seventeen years; people had built homes and started families. Where could they find the money to transport all those children and possessions?

Gabriel told me that Singali was the new chief of Amopolo. He asked if I remembered Balonyona and went on to relate that he had been attacked by a gorilla and bitten in the head. I remembered my dream and for one horrible instant was afraid that Balonyona had died. But Gabriel assured me that Balonyona had survived the attack, though he had spent a month in the hospital in Nola. Finally I gathered up my bags. They were heavy, and I had nearly a mile to go. But I politely declined offers of help from the police. I wanted to arrive at Amopolo alone.

I reached the turn in the road, where it veered south for its final twenty miles. Amopolo was just a hundred yards along on the left. Some children were playing in the road. A man with baggy shorts was walking slowly toward Amopolo. As soon as I stepped into view he turned around. Even from a distance I recognized the disdainful cast of countenance — it was Mabuti. His eyes widened with delight. I could almost read his thought: a *mondélé* is coming! Then his expression turned into one of genuine surprise. He had recognized me.

"It's the *patron!*" he cried. "Monsieur Louis!"

I wagged my head in acknowledgment. The children dashed off into the camp, and soon a roar of many voices rose up. "*Merci, patron, merci!*" Mabuti gushed obsequiously as he shook my hand. He took my two largest bags. Up ahead people began pouring out into the road, and soon I had a crowd around me. Bosso was the first to greet me, shaking my hand with a big smile on her face. She held a toddler at her side, a boy, the spitting image of Biléma. It reminded me of how much time had passed. Mbina, now a strikingly beautiful teenager, came up to greet me. Others flocked up in quick succession. Old Esoosi kissed me on my chest.

Mabuti remained by my side, holding a raised arm out to me

and grinning as though he personally had arranged my appearance. As we made our way into the camp, the teenagers congregated in the clearing and began an energetic *elanda*. It was such an overwhelming reception that I grew apprehensive about their reaction to the bundle of Salvation Army clothes I intended to distribute. It was not, I now realized, much of an offering after my long absence.

The men led me to a large new *mbanjo*, the men's meeting place. Amopolo hadn't had a proper one during my last visit. Much about Amopolo had changed. Gone were the little beehive huts. In their place stood rectangular houses made from bamboo and palm thatching. Many were still under construction. The few beehive huts that remained looked sadly doomed. In addition, the several camps that had made up Amopolo had been merged into one large chaotic settlement. Amopolo was now a village. The layout of the houses was bewildering. Some were back to back, some were clustered in miniature neighborhoods, a few were attached like townhouses. Others stood off alone like islands. There had been a general migration closer to the road, and the bush had been cut back considerably. The whole scene was, I felt, bitterly disappointing.

In no time at all I distributed three packs of cigarettes. Everyone kept thanking me for coming back. Many called me *patron*, as if in their enthusiasm they couldn't help themselves. I could hear their speculations regarding the contents of my bags. When I asked where Balonyona was, they told me he was drinking in the village with the new chief, Singali. Simbu soon returned from the nearby raffia swamp, where he had been gathering palm leaves. He had rushed back as soon as he heard the news. He smiled happily, though I privately wondered what circumstances had led to the usurpation of his authority. Was this venerable elder now compelled to obey commands from the relatively young Singali? The thought made Simbu look slightly pathetic. I presented him with the machete I'd bought for him in Bangui, when I believed he was still chief.

My bags were carried off to one of the smallest new-fangled huts. I never learned whose home it had been before I occupied it, but it was obviously one of the first bamboo huts ever built, before they had learned to do the work properly. Still, it was a mansion compared to my previous Amopolo house. To the left was Mamadu's hut, which he shared with his mother, Bessé, and his brothers. To the right was the back of Motadi's hut, where his mother, Nyasu, my old neighbor, also lived. Several yards directly ahead was the framework of Mokoko's hut. The biggest advantage was that my view of the large central clearing was blocked by Motadi's hut. Instead I had a view of a kind of small back courtyard.

These changes threw me into a crisis of self-doubt. Had I been right to come back? I saw around me nothing but decay. As the snotty-faced children crowded around, their parasite-infested feet emitted a ghastly stench. And I saw how many deformities the adults had — missing fingers and toes, gaps where teeth had been chipped down or knocked out, split earlobes. On my first visit I had been surprised at how tall the Bayaka were; now I was taken aback by their small size. Their distinctive physiognomy was more exaggerated than I remembered. I wondered if I had romanticized these people while I was away. As I looked at the eager faces all around me, it struck me as wildly unlikely that I might have any close friends among them.

The teenagers' dance was still going strong when Singali and Balonyona returned. Balonyona, wearing an enormous black cowboy hat, embraced me for a long time, gasping *merci* over and over as though I had just saved his life. I thought about my dream again, but when Balonyona finally backed away he was smiling. I mentioned that I had heard about the gorilla attack. Balonyona removed his hat and pointed to a large bare patch on the crown of his head, traversed by a scar.

"I suffered much," he explained in French, the Bayaka's language of choice when inebriated. "I slept five months in the hospital in Nola. My head is not good like this! With the sun — *ooh!* But this hat, Monsieur Louis, it just won't do!" He leaned toward me and lowered his voice. "You don't have another one for me, do you?"

On the spur of the moment I handed him the other machete I'd bought in Bangui, the one I'd intended for myself. He took it and walked quickly off to his hut.

"Monsieur Louis, it's me — Singali Jerome."

Singali, rocking gently, stood before me. His shirt, several sizes too small, was pulled tightly across his chest and held together by a single button, giving him an exaggeratedly muscular appearance. His eyes were bloodshot and watery. We shook hands, and I gave him a durable pocket knife I'd purchased in America. He pocketed it without a glance.

"It's me, chief of Amopolo," he resumed. "Look." He pointed at a tiny metal button pinned to the upper left-hand corner of his shirt. It bore a miniature portrait of the president. "*Voilà*. Chief. Me." He smiled for the first time. I wondered if I should congratulate him. "You come to my village. It's good. Dancing tonight. It's me the chief who says so." He paused. "Monsieur Louis, give me a cigarette."

Amopolo seemed to have grown considerably. There were many people in the crowd I had never seen before. One crusty older fellow with an untamed beard reached out his hand as soon as our eyes met. "Monsieur Joboko Jerome," he croaked with a friendly smile. Another grand patriarch with light skin had an almost Oriental look, more like a !Kung than a Moaka. He sat motionless, scrutinizing me with squinted eyes, his lips slightly parted in an expression of disbelief.

As I sat and talked with everyone, trying to describe what had happened since they last saw me, I began to feel that it was good to be back after all. One of their first questions concerned my recorder: had I brought it? I produced it now and put in a cassette of music I had recorded at Amopolo. It contained a little bit of everything: *geedal* music, drum dances, sung fables, *elanda*. They were thrilled by the sound of their own music and laughed as they recalled the occasion for each piece. When a lullaby began — Matangu singing to her crying daughter — there came a sudden hush. Balonyona pushed forward and grabbed my arm.

"Listen," I said, "it's your baby, Mbota!"

"Monsieur Louis," Balonyona cried in anguish, "she died!"

I switched off the recorder. Mbota had been born during my first visit, and I had become very fond of her after helping cure her conjunctivitis. Balonyona urged me into his hut, calling Matangu and his son Mbutu over too. The bamboo hut, still unfinished, lay a fair distance from mine. As small as mine, it seemed even more cockeyed in its angles. That it managed to stay together was something of an engineering marvel. The four of us gathered close together on the littered sand floor. Balonyona told me to play the tape. During the lullaby the family sobbed quietly. Sometimes Balonyona cried out, "Mbota!" Then, sitting next to me, he hugged me and wept.

AND SO, after a gap of more than two years, I resumed my life at Amopolo. For several days there was so much music that I began to take it for granted. On my first night the Bayaka had appealed to my sense of celebration and persuaded me to contribute some money for *mbaku*. The dance they held rivaled the worst I'd seen during my previous visit. They didn't even need my money for *mbaku*. A party of men, including Singali and Balonyona, returned from the village smashed during the dance. One man was especially obnoxious, howling into the microphones in a drunken, hoarse voice. He looked vaguely familiar, and I realized I'd seen him several times before, always at night, always when *mbaku* was on offer. The teenagers' *elanda* songs, I noticed, had all changed. The men and boys were ready to make *geedal* music at the drop of a hat. All I had to do was sit next to someone idly strumming on the instrument, and before I knew it a full-fledged *geedal* session was in progress. Everybody wanted to be recorded playing the *geedal*, and I discovered several budding talents as well as some accomplished musicians like Mosio and Badjama. But the most startling discovery was that Mamadu was now a master of the *geedal*.

I first heard Mamadu play in the middle of the night when I woke up from a dream to the sounds of the harp coming from his hut. The playing lacked the virtuosity of Balonyona or Akété's style. Mamadu, in mastering the *geedal*, had taken a different route entirely. His playing sounded simple and static until you heard the complexity underneath, each hand playing in a different time signature. The songs were meditative in nature. Many of the melodies, I learned later, were his own creation. He was the most prolific composer for the *geedal*. For a long time I had to content myself with his nocturnal performances, listening from my bed as he played into the dawn. I had been sorry to lose Balonyona as a neighbor, but now I realized how lucky I was to be near Mamadu.

At first he was too shy to perform before the microphones. Then one evening his younger brother, Ezanga, began to play the *geedal*. He tried his hand at one of Mamadu's songs, a new composition I'd heard him working out over the past few nights. Ezanga faltered along for several minutes while the audience grew increasingly impatient. Suddenly Mamadu appeared and demanded the harp. He sat down and without another word played the melody that had stumped his brother. It flowed along, inspiring an accompaniment of soft percussion and yodels that gave me goose bumps.

One day I passed a boy sitting with an instrument on his lap that I'd never seen before. It was a long stick with an off-center bridge. Three nylon strings crossed the bridge, forming six segments of different lengths. A six-note harp-zither! I thought with excitement. How could I have missed it during my first visit? "Wait here," I told the boy and rushed off to get my recorder. When I got back I found, not the boy, but Mabuti sitting with the instrument. Though it was only morning, he was truly drunk.

"Today," he slurred in French, "the *patron* records Monsieur Mabuti François for the *mondumé*."

"*Mondumé*," I repeated. "Is that what this instrument is called?"

"*Oui, oui!*" Mabuti nodded. "He is the *mondumé*. I know?" I wrote down the word. "To write," Mabuti continued, "me he knows? Monsieur François. Today he plays the *mondumé* for the *patron* for me. *Oui. Patron*, give me a cigarette." I gave him one. "Because me," Mabuti said, "he knows the *mondumé*. Good, okay. Open the radio."

I turned on the recorder. Mabuti, the unlit cigarette dangling from his lips, started to pluck the strings with his two forefingers. After a few seconds he stopped.

"*Patron*," he said, "give me fire." I switched the recorder off and lit his cigarette. "*Merci*," he thanked me. He puffed several times on the cigarette. "Me he says *merci* to the *patron* for me because . . . because . . ." He hucked and spat. "It is the *patron* for me, no?" He adjusted the instrument on his lap. It was resting on a pot to amplify its soft sound. "Okay, open the radio."

I turned on the recorder again. Mabuti played for ten seconds.

"Monsieur *patron*," he said suddenly, interrupting his playing. "Where is the gift for me?"

"Gift?" I asked.

"*Oui*, the gift! Because me he knows the *mondumé*. A watch, a radio with four batteries, okay."

I told him that I wanted to hear him play first. He began playing once more, this time long enough to start singing, in a high falsetto voice that wavered uncertainly. It sounded ridiculous. A whole minute passed before he paused to ask for another cigarette. I made several more attempts to record a full song, but Mabuti was incorrigible. He asked for money, he asked for cigarettes even as he smoked them. Finally he got completely absorbed in tuning the strings. I got up and left.

THE BAYAKA KEPT TRYING to persuade me to reveal the contents of the two duffel bags in my hut. I kept stalling because I was afraid they would feel disappointed when they saw the meager offerings, mostly second-hand T-shirts and shorts. My delay, however, only served to heighten their expectations. Finally I decided to get it over with. I would hand out the clothes and suffer the consequences.

I lugged the duffel bags out to the *mbanjo*. My passage across camp provoked a rising murmur of excitement. Almost instantly I was surrounded. I emptied the contents of the first bag in a pile and picked up the first item to give away. It was a T-shirt with a colorful illustration of a big cooking pot over a log fire, with two human legs sticking out the top. The caption read: SOUTH PACIFIC ISLAND COOKING.

Hands shot out. Everyone squeezed closer. "Give me! Give me!" came the shouts. I held the shirt toward Mamadu. He snatched it. There was a brief tug-of-war with a young man named Engulé, then with a mighty yank Mamadu triumphed. He headed for his hut with the prize.

The second item was a T-shirt with what looked like Chinese characters, only if you looked carefully you could see that the characters spelled FUCK OFF. It went to Simbu.

When I reached the end of the pile I was consternated to see that the number of people pressing in around me had not diminished. I began to distribute the second bag of clothes. Arms waved frantically in the air, hands grasping. "Where's mine?" both men and women cried. The children, growing desperate as they realized that they would get precious little, swiped items totally inappropriate for them. Halfway through the bag it was obvious that I didn't have enough for everybody. The mood was becoming slightly hostile. I surrendered the clothes, and the responsibility to distribute them, to Singali. He was the chief, so *he* could decide who would be left out. The furor went on a few minutes more, then reluctantly the crowd dispersed, complaining. Singali came to my hut to report that he had given everything away. The only problem was that he hadn't kept anything for himself. Could he at least have the duffel bag? I was so grateful that he asked that I gave it to him without hesitation.

Over the next several days everyone wore their new clothes. Many items were loaned back and forth before settling down with their original owners. Others were traded. There were certainly some odd choices. Dour Doko tramped around every day in a girl's pink blouse with butterfly designs and puffed sleeves. A T-shirt with prison stripes became Balonyona's uniform, his signature. Soon, even in the dark, when all facial details were obscured, I learned to recognize the shadowy figures who approached by their clothes.

Despite the affection I felt for the individuals of the village, I was disturbed by the Bayaka's sedentary existence. They seemed to be entrenching themselves permanently along the road, a process strikingly symbolized by their new bamboo houses. Traditionally, house building was done by the women, who could throw up a beehive hut in a matter of a day or two. Now house building had become men's work, and it required not days but months — partly because the men worked so irregularly.

Many of the men, rather than go hunting, now worked on their houses. Mokoko's was nearly done. Judging from the corner poles, Mowooma's would be large enough to fit six of my huts inside. Mindumi, on the other hand, continued to live in a beehive hut, dwarfed by the bamboo houses springing up all around it. As the jungle was cut back more and more, Amopolo grew. It was a revolution in tradition. The investment of so much labor probably meant that the Bayaka would be less willing to abandon their homes than before. The bamboo huts seemed to herald the end of the Bayaka's nomadic days.

Early one morning the mayor of Bomandjombo visited Amopolo, accompanied by his guards, four young men in khaki fatigues, to survey the progress on the huts. The mayor proudly explained to me that he had ordered the Bayaka to build them as part of his effort to civilize the Pygmies. They had to live in normal houses like other people. The mayor was pleased with the work that had been accomplished but unhappy about the pockets of the village that remained entirely beehive, as well as about a couple of traditional huts near the road, fully visible to passing traffic (not that there was any) and presumably an embarrassment to the local government. He regretted that Amopolo was laid out so haphazardly. The "citizens," as he called the Bayaka, should learn to organize their village in straight lines like civilized people. Also, they had forgotten to make windows.

After the mayor left I talked to the Bayaka about the bamboo huts. I was surprised to hear that they liked them. "The big huts are *good*," Simbu said, though he still lived in a beehive hut, and except for planting four corner poles, had made no attempt to build a bamboo hut. I had to admit that for the sedentary life they seemed to be adopting, the new huts were an improvement. I doubted that I myself would find life in a beehive hut very tolerable, but I was sorry to see them disappear. I found some comfort in talking to Joboko. First he claimed that the beehive huts were bad (although he lived in one himself), but when he realized that I liked them he reversed his position. As usual, it was difficult to tell what he really thought.

"What kind of houses do you make in the forest?" I asked, though I had no idea if the Amopolo Bayaka ever moved into the forest anymore.

"We make the little ones," Joboko replied.

The village was constantly changing shape. Families abandoned one site for another. Mobo moved three times in a month. Sometimes a bamboo house would be evacuated as the family moved to a different neighborhood or staked a pioneering claim in some newly cleared recess. One day Mitumbi and his group arrived, and overnight a whole new neighborhood developed. Within days the first bamboo corner poles were up. It was depressing.

One day I asked a *bilo* if the Bayaka of Amopolo always lived in the same place. "They are always here," he assured me with a cheerful smile. "Even if you come back ten years from now, you will find them here. Do not worry, they are civilized." He had no idea how sad his answer made me. Yet on other occasions I heard remarks that gave me hope. One villager told me, "In July they all disappear. No one sees them again until December." I had been planning to leave at the end of June.

The bamboo huts were not the only change. The appointment of an official chief was also the work of the *bilo*. On those rare occasions when government representatives from Bangui visited Bomandjombo, the Bayaka were routinely asked to dance in the village. It was part of their duties as "citizens" of the nation. The Bayaka regarded these duties as a nuisance, and their compliance was always problematical. In fact, at the first sign that their services were required, they would flee into the forest and remain until the *bilo* authorities left, empty-handed. The mayor then hit upon the idea of appointing an official Bayaka chief who would be responsible for overseeing their compliance with his orders. If the chief should fail in his responsibility, he would be arrested.

Singali's position carried a certain amount of prestige — for example, he now had three wives rather than one (monogamy was the Bayaka norm) — but in the opinion of most Bayaka the position brought more headaches than rewards. It was no easy task to bring anarchy under control; often it was only the threat of imprisonment for Singali that persuaded everybody to cooperate with the demands of the mayor's office.

During my absence Amopolo had also acquired a mayor. Although the Bayaka spoke disparagingly about the *bilo*, there was also a feeling of rivalry, a sense that anything the *bilo* did, the Bayaka could do better. Now that they had a village and an official chief, the Bayaka decided they should have a mayor. They picked Mindumi by unanimous consent. Whereas many of the elders grumbled over Singali's appointment as chief, Mindumi was an obvious choice for a position of authority, however illusory that authority might prove in the day-to-day affairs of camp. Mindumi was not in the league of the grand elders like Simbu, Dimba, Wadimo, or Joboko, but ranked with the generation of Mabuti, Singali,

Doko, and Mobo. One of the most tranquil souls at Amopolo, he was accorded a respect beyond his years, and his presence had a powerful calming influence on the village. In the evenings he liked to sit in front of his hut with his wife, Zabu, and children around him and watch the scene before him with a contented smile.

A story I pieced together over the next few months gives an idea of Mindumi's character. Zabu was one of Bakpima's daughters. They had two sons and a baby daughter. The older son, named Bakpima after his grandfather, was usually called Landi. He was the spitting image of his father. The younger son, however, looked just like a young man named Tété. Zabu had had an affair with Tété, and it was obvious to everyone that he was the younger son's real father. But Mindumi's love for the boy was undiminished; he even named him Tété.

Mindumi's selection as mayor of Amopolo was duly recognized by the authorities in Bomandjombo, including the mayor, who addressed Mindumi as "Monsieur the mayor." Not long after my return Amopolo acquired a third authority figure and I was a witness to the creation. Late one night I was catching up on events in my diary by flashlight when Mabuti, drunk again, shuffled up to my hut. "Gofra!" he called, the Bayaka's way of announcing their arrival, and entered my hut. Reluctantly I got out from under my mosquito net.

"It's me," Mabuti said, "the captain!"

"Captain?" I asked.

"Oui, oui!" he cried. "Because Singali is the chief, Mindumi is the mayor, but me, Monsieur Mabuti, he is the captain!" He gave me a salute. "Because me," he continued, "he commands the military of Amopolo." He executed a few robotlike maneuvers around my hut, marching, swiveling about-face, standing at attention. I started to laugh. "Patron," Mabuti quickly said, taking advantage of my lightening mood, "give me a cigarette." I handed him one. He saluted me again, spun around, and marched off into the dark.

I dismissed the incident as merely a clever way to wangle a cigarette in the middle of the night. Mabuti, however, did not forget his inspiration. Over the next several days he amused everybody with his outlandish caricatures of military bearing. He even made himself a kind of crop out of a metal wire and a piece of wood for the handle, and carried it with him everywhere. Often he led the children, who were only too happy to participate in his game, in military exercises around the camp. Whenever he joined a group of elders to smoke the big pipe, he never failed to snap to attention and salute before sitting down. He was so persistent in perpetuating his fantasy that eventually his claim was recognized, not only by everyone at Amopolo, but by the Bomandjombo villagers as well. From then on the *bilo* mayor would have to consult with Mabuti, as well as Singali and Mindumi, in his dealings with Amopolo.

Bomandjombo had several kinds of uniformed authorities, and it took me a while to sort them out. The national gendarmes wore camouflage, the police favored pale blue uniforms, and the mayor's guards usually tromped around in khaki. One afternoon I was startled by the arrival in Amopolo of two men in what looked like combat gear. A variety of knives and daggers hung from their belts. They looked alarmingly like soldiers, and they had recently been drinking. When they suggested that I take their photograph, I instantly complied. After eliciting my promise to make large prints for them, they wandered off, and I breathed a sigh of relief. A few minutes later, however, I heard a loud commotion in a far corner of camp, where Bakpima lived. We all ran over.

What I found did not reassure me. The two uniformed men were surrounded by scores of angry Bayaka. One of the men was holding a shotgun, which Bwanga told me they had just confiscated. Apparently the owner of the gun (a woman from Bomandjombo) had hired a Bayaka hunter named Mbinjo. The "hunting guards," as Bwanga called the two men, had discovered the gun and were trying to confiscate the basket of smoked meat that Mbinjo had brought back from his week-long hunt. Mbinjo himself had fled into the forest, so the hunting guards had grabbed a man named Omoo and ordered him to take the basket of meat to their headquarters at the old sawmill office. Omoo, his beard unshaven and his hair uncut for months, had a wild look. He heaved the basket up, slipped the bark strap over his forehead, and carried it ten yards before protests from the Bayaka persuaded him to drop it on the ground. He refused to carry it another inch. The guards grabbed Bwanga next. Bwanga ignored them and began to walk away. The taller guard, who was holding the shotgun, was rapidly going berserk. Now he ran up behind Bwanga, raised the gun, and slammed the butt into Bwanga's back. Bwanga stumbled forward.

For five minutes we had a shouting match. I had no idea of the guards' position in the hierarchy of local authority, nor even what their function was, but I threatened them with legal retribution: I was going to the police. The guards momentarily relented, and the shorter one urged his excitable companion to give him the shotgun. Then they rallied: I could go to the president himself — the law was the law, and hunting with a gun in the reserve was forbidden.

I stomped off down the road, my bravado now a complete bluff. The guards' remark about the law had flustered me. On my first visit the entire forest had been a free hunting ground. And what was this "reserve" the guards had mentioned? I turned around and started back.

"And I found that green stuff in the basket!" the tall guard was shouting. "The marijuana! MA-RI-JUA-NA!" He rifled through the basket looking for the evidence. It had vanished.

We passed each other going in opposite directions. The guards carried the basket between them. "What happened with going to the police?" the short guard taunted.

"Who's carrying the meat?" I retorted.

THE NEXT DAY I learned about the Dzanga-Sangha Dense Forest Reserve by talking to its director. The World Wildlife Fund was trying to persuade the government to establish a reserve in the extreme southwestern corner of the Central African Republic. Two areas would be declared national parks, where all forms of hunting would be forbidden. The reserve had not yet been voted into law by the government, but the antipoaching laws were already in effect. One area was called Dzanga after the most spectacular of its many *bai* (naturally occurring meadows in the forest). The abundant wildlife in the surrounding forests visit these *bai*, attracted by salt deposits in the soil. The most impressive gatherings are at Dzanga, where elephants emerge from the forest and congregate in the *bai* every afternoon. Usually they remain throughout the night and leave shortly after dawn. Unlike the more accessible savanna elephant, little is known about the life of the elusive forest elephant. Dzanga is a researcher's paradise, where family relationships among the elephants can be observed at leisure. Enormous flocks of gray parrots also gather there. Their extraordinary whistles and calls, blending with the evening cries of monkeys, and the deep purrs and occasional trumpet blasts of the elephants, create a sonic environment of primeval beauty.

The second park area was to be at the extreme southern tip of the country, an expanse of uninhabited primary forest called Ndoki. Here the waters of the Ndoki River seep across the border into the Congo Republic, finally joining the Sangha River a hundred miles farther south. The Ndoki is surrounded for most of its length by vast, impenetrable marsh forest. According to the Bayaka, these marshes are the home of the legendary *mokilimbimbi*, a creature larger than an elephant that looks like a rhinoceros. Several respectable institutions, including the University of Chicago, have sent expeditions to look for it. One expedition in the 1980s returned with photographs of what were purported to be giant footprints that resembled those of a rhinoceros.

In the areas of the forest reserve outside of the national parks, where there were several *bilo* villages and Bayaka settlements (including Amopolo), hunting would be restricted to the Bayaka's traditional methods. The reserve has one of the world's richest concentrates of primate species, including chimpanzees and a large population of lowland gorillas. The concept of the Dzanga-Sangha Reserve was the brainchild of two American scientists who had carried out research in the area, Richard Carroll and Michael Fay. The idea was not only to protect the wildlife but also to provide the indigenous Bayaka with a context in which to pursue their traditional lifestyle.

When I heard about the reserve, I knew it was potentially of great benefit to the Bayaka, despite the confrontation of the day before. By protecting the wildlife against the depredations of poachers, the reserve would secure an important food source for the Bayaka, and thereby preserve their net hunting into the twenty-first century. It was ironic, however, that just as the reserve was being set up, the Bayaka were giving up many of their traditional ways.

/ / /

MY WRITING CONTINUED to be a source of fascination for the Bayaka. Sometimes around my fire they would say words and ask me to write them down. Then they would peer somberly at each word in the firelight, discussing it, even praising its design, for all I knew. One night Bakpima was suddenly inspired to learn how to write. He took my pen and paper, and for several minutes carefully drew a series of squiggles.

"What does that say?" he asked.

"It doesn't say anything," I replied.

The others, who had been momentarily impressed by Bakpima's handwriting, now cried out in ridicule.

"I can write *Saturday*," Yongo volunteered. I gave him the pen and paper. He labored over the word as though it were a math problem, but when he showed me the result, I was impressed. He had written the word correctly.

"I'll write *Thursday*," I said. They scrutinized the word.

Bakpima suddenly demanded the pen and paper again, claimed he had figured out how writing worked. He scribbled down some wavy loops and pointed at them. "*Sunday*," he said.

On my first visit the Bayaka had been but dimly aware of the days of the week. Only a few of the teenagers knew all seven, and no one could recite them in the proper order. Now even most of the elders knew the sequence of days, and the Bayaka were happy to use Sunday as an excuse to take the day off from hunting. At one point they devised a simple abacus calendar to keep track of the days, a piece of rope strung with seven wooden beads, which they hung up in the *mbanjo*. On Sunday all seven beads were pushed to the top of the string. On Monday the first bead was pulled to the bottom, on Tuesday the second, and so on until Sunday, when all seven beads were pushed back to the top. There were problems. Sometimes nobody remembered if a bead had been pulled down for the day; consequently on some days two or even three beads were pulled down, on other days no beads were pulled down, and now and then a bead was actually pushed up to compensate for a presumed pulling down of too many beads. Whoever decided to adjust the abacus to the correct day would first have to consult the others. These short conversations resembled the best of Abbott and Costello:

"Today's Monday?" Balonyona asks as he contemplates the abacus.

"No, today . . .," a pause while Biléma thinks, "is Wednesday."

"Yesterday was Wednesday," Lalié says. "Today's Tuesday."

"Yesterday was Saturday," Biléma replies. "Today's — Sunday?" Everyone agrees it can't be Sunday.

"Ah!" Balonyona realizes, "yesterday was Monday!"

"Today's Tuesday," surmises Kukpata.

"Tuesday," comes the collective endorsement. There is a pause, invariably followed by everyone saying, "Tomorrow's Wednesday." Balonyona adjusts the abacus.

SINCE MY SECOND arrival I had been administering eye medicine in an effort to get the rampant conjunctivitis under control. My daily medical rounds definitely made a difference, but an unwelcome side effect was the terror my approach now inspired in the children. To counter this I began to buy them *makala* and bananas from the *bilo* women who came every afternoon. It didn't take the children long to catch on. Soon, whenever they saw me negotiating with a villager for *makala* or bananas, they gathered around me and waited expectantly. There were a lot of children, and the purchases became a major daily expense. Gradually my generosity overcame their fear. Individually each child still approached me with caution, snatching his banana and running away again. But collectively they lost all fear. One day as I returned from an outing in the forest a group of children sitting in the *mbanjo* cried out in one musical voice, "*Elobayé!*" When I cried it back they tittered with laughter. The greeting quickly became a ritual at camp. Even the most timid toddler would respond to my "*elobayé*" with his own. Pretty soon, wherever I went children called out the greeting to me, sometimes in a scarcely uttered whisper.

Mbina became a frequent visitor to my hut. Whenever I played one of my recordings, she showed up to listen. If my hut was filled with men and boys, she sat just outside the entrance, but if my audience was women, Mbina sat inside too. She continued to hold a special place in my heart, and her presence filled me with delight, only now my feeling of affection for her was growing confused, for

Mbina, on the verge of womanhood, was turning into a real beauty. Sometimes I found it difficult to take my eyes off her when she was around. On those occasions when she caught me looking at her she would hold my gaze, her ordinarily dreamy eyes suddenly becoming direct and bold. Invariably I was the one to look away first. I wondered if her sister, Bosso, had mentioned our innocent flirtation from my first stay at Amopolo. In the forest, where I was actively recording and photographing every phase of the hunt, Mbina usually remained near me. While others did their best to ignore my camera Mbina seemed to enjoy the attention. (On my first visit I had brought a camera but had been too shy to use it. The Bayaka were never completely comfortable with me in my role as photographer, and neither was I; eventually I sold the camera.) Consequently she became a frequent subject; I worried about what the Pitt Rivers Museum would think when they saw all those photographs of her.

One day the women took me into the forest for a day of music and games. They played at spear-hunting gorillas and elephants. In one of the games Bosso played the elephant. Later they gathered in a tight circle and sang, while from the center rose a deep hooting cry. It was the same music I had recorded during the death lament for the old woman. The women now explained that the hooting voice was their very own *mokoondi*, and they called their special women's music *lingokoo*. As we talked they crowded in around me, leaning on me, draping their arms around me, teasing me with thinly veiled suggestions. Did I have a wife? they wanted to know. She left me years ago, I told them. The women burst out laughing.

ONE MORNING I set off with Biléma and Kukpata — now Amopolo's favorite drummer — for an Ejengi dance. We followed the road south for several miles, then turned off onto an overgrown track, which ended at a wall of immense trees. We plunged on into the forest. The trail descended steeply. Soon we reached a dark, marshy world pockmarked by elephant tracks and crisscrossed by lianas and aerial roots. After several miles we arrived at the tiny, picturesque village of Mombembé on the Sangha. The village, presided over by an old patriarch named Yono, was unusual in that *bilo* and Bayaka lived together in relative harmony. The leaf huts of the Bayaka were interspersed with the larger wooden cabins of the *bilo*. Yono himself was well over six feet tall. He had two wives — one nearly as tall as he was, the other a Baka woman from across the river. The entire village spoke Yaka and lived by hunting and fishing.

I was led to a broken chair near Yono's house, which stood on stilts. Yono handed me a bowl of palm wine. Behind me a curtain of palm leaves hung across a jungle path — Ejengi's doorway. Boys rushed up and down the path, crying out the distinctive two-note motif which I would learn to associate exclusively with Ejengi. Soon others from Amopolo arrived — Mokoko, Ngongo, Singali, Bwanga, Yongo, even old Bombé. They told me the women were on their way. To bide the time I snapped some photographs. The dance had not begun, but Ejengi appeared a few times, running through the village and keeping the Mombembé women on their toes. At first I kept the camera pointed obviously away from the forest spirit, but Yono suggested I photograph him and Ejengi together, and I happily obliged. Ejengi ran over and posed next to Yono, who held an elephant spear in one hand.

The women started to arrive in large groups, and immediately the village livened up. Bosso and Mbina had both dressed up for the occasion with head scarves and what must have been all the clothes they owned. The drums, which had been sounding intermittently the whole time, now picked up in speed and force. Even as more people from Amopolo arrived, the women clustered at one end of the village and started to sing. Ejengi emerged from the forest and came to a standstill beside me, accompanied by numerous boys. Mabuti hurried over and in short rhythmic sentences declaimed Ejengi's thoughts. Then, with Mabuti shouting, *"Oka!"* (listen), Ejengi and his entourage hurried across the village.

The dance began. The chorus of Bayaka women predominated, though some village women sang too. One of the most enthusiastic singers was a woman of mixed blood — possibly, I speculated, a daughter of Yono's by his Baka wife. Yono stood in front of his hut to watch, holding his elephant spear at his side. The familiar moves of the dance unfolded, the women pursuing Ejengi during the *esimé* sections of the music, only to turn and flee when Ejengi reversed direction. I noticed two *bilo* men sitting in front of one of the huts. They had been rubbed with a reddish oil. Their faces, arms, and bodies were decorated with a white sap in a pattern of dots and dashes, and they were adorned with many necklaces. They were being initiated, I guessed. One was a boy, but I was surprised that the other was a grown man. All day they sat motionless, looking down between their knees.

By now I had my recorder in action. One of the *bilo* women, who had brewed up some *mbaku*, saw her opportunity. Between songs she suggested that the *mondélé* who was photographing and recording them should pay a fee in the form of buying her entire supply of moonshine. The Amopolo Bayaka knew that I refused to buy *mbaku* and responded unpleasantly to such requests. Now, however, being a guest in a village that was not acquainted with my quirks, I accepted Singali's strong advice that I had better make an exception. Forking over 4,000 francs, I took consolation in the fact that no would be able to drink enough to get drunk. Nevertheless, for a while my mood was spoiled and I sulked by a large tree, my recorder inactive. The dance continued with no concern for my mood. Bosso, perhaps emboldened by her share of *mbaku*, threw many long glances my way. I felt the old thrill that eye contact between us used to evoke. Pretty soon I was back on my feet recording. I was in luck, for the dance that began as I switched on the recorder heralded an hour of uninterrupted singing, alternating with frenzied *esimé* sequences. Mokoko's wife, Sao, was especially active in the *esimé*, shrieking up a storm.

Late in the afternoon Mokoko told me that I should start back; the others would return later. As it turned out, most of them stayed another two days. I returned to Amopolo with Ekumu, a young man who was the tallest Moaka I ever met. During most of the arduous walk I felt a deep satisfaction with my day's work. The final long dance alone had made the five-hour round trip worth it. I played that dance many times for the Bayaka in the months to come.

/ / /

WHEN THE YUGOSLAVIAN overlords of the sawmill shut down their enterprise and fled the country, they left behind not only heavy debts but a lumberyard full of gigantic logs. For nearly two years the logs lay there, slowly rotting. One day an old *bilo* woman who wanted to plant corn in the overgrown field next to the sawmill set fire to the scrub. Unusual winds during the night blew the fire over into the lumberyard. For seven days and nights the blaze roared. The local authorities could do nothing but watch helplessly as tens of thousands of dollars' worth of tropical hardwood was reduced to ash. Clearly visible from Amopolo, the fire at night was a dramatic sight, silhouetting palm trees like a glorious sunset.

One night during this fire I visited Mindumi's part of camp to watch an *elanda*. However, that night the teenagers were simply too boisterous to concentrate on dancing and had moved on to more direct forms of flirtation, chasing one another, wrestling, scheming, gossiping. One found a giant millipede and pursued the others, who fled with shrieks of revulsion. There was no point in watching, so I went and sat down in the *mbanjo*.

Just then a crouching figure leaned toward me out of the darkness and began to speak in pure Yaka. It was a rough but expressive voice, and as it rambled on I began to comprehend, almost by a kind of osmosis, what the man was saying. He had heard of the *mondélé* and his radio, and of how the Bayaka's singing made his heart turn beautiful, so he had come to see this *mondélé* with his own eyes. He would sing for the *mondélé*'s radio too. His name was Gondo, and he was famous for his storytelling.

With a start I realized that he had reached out his hand to shake mine, but it was so big and spatulate that in the dark I mistook it at first for a foot. When I grasped his hand, the skin felt like tree bark. Others began to wander over. Noticing Gondo's presence, they grew excited. "Gondo is here!" they cried. "Gondo!" A group of us headed back toward my hut. My sense of direction, always faulty in the dark, soon led me astray. Singali called me back to the correct path, and as I rejoined the others I heard Gondo chuckle behind me, "The *mondélé* doesn't know the way." What puzzled me was that his voice seemed to rise up from the ground. We reached my hut, and in the light of the fire, flickering still, I turned to see Gondo emerge from the shadows. His body was arched like a banana — his name means "banana" in Yaka — and he walked on his feet and hands, his neck craned up so that he could look ahead. I never learned whether his walk was the result of an accident or a birth defect, but he could cover several miles in a day.

I had made many recordings of *gano* (sung fables) with various storytellers. Among the best were Balonyona, a man named Ndimo, who was married to Bakpima's sister, and Mabuti. None of Amopolo's storytellers, however, could be called a master of the art. I had heard better storytellers on records.

Mokoko brewed some coffee. Word of Gondo's arrival had spread, and most of the teenagers left their games to assemble around my fire for a glimpse of the legendary storyteller. Gondo sat in the firelight, his face contorting into fantastic expressions, his voice mutating into a dozen others, his head bobbing like a pigeon's as he told his stories. At first only the adults accompanied him with a chorus. The teenagers appeared altogether too astonished by this rare and curious visitor to do anything but stare. Mbina sat through two fables without singing a note, craning her neck the whole time for a better view of Gondo. Eventually, during a story about my journey to Amopolo, which had everyone cracking up, the teenagers redeemed themselves with some lovely singing.

ONE MORNING on my way to the Bomandjombo market to buy some peanut butter, I ran into the man who had made such a nuisance of himself when I first arrived, bellowing into the microphones. Now, seeing him in daylight with his distinctive perpendicular ears, I suddenly remembered who he was.

Sombolo had been present at Amopolo during my first visit, but for the most part he had kept his distance, presumably scoring cigarettes from me through intermediaries. I never saw him in the daytime. Only during the height of nighttime drunken revelries would he appear, a figure, by association, of chaos and confusion. At a little over five feet he was tall for a Moaka. He was also one of the lightest-skinned, with that uncommon but by no means rare Pygmy trait of reddish hair. He had a magnificent build, muscular but not too broad, with longer legs than the Moaka norm. His one physical defect, which I noticed now for the first time, was a knob that protruded from the back of his skull, directly in the center. It was the result, I heard later, of a nasty fall during one of his many *mbaku* binges. Sombolo was infamous as the heaviest drinker at Amopolo.

On this day Sombolo was on his way back from the village, where he had downed a glass or two of *mbaku*. Seeing me, he swerved around and tagged along, talking amiably. No doubt he reckoned that he could cadge at least one drink out of me. I was determined to resist.

At the market three different women tried to persuade me to buy their peanut butter. Sombolo immediately antagonized all three. He insulted their peanut butter, told them they didn't know how to make it properly, accused them of charging inflated prices. When I made my purchase, Sombolo harangued the woman for being stingy with her scoops and then badgered her into giving me two extra spoonfuls. As we left the woman called out, "Monsieur Louis — next time come with Balonyona! Sombolo is nothing but trouble!" Sombolo laughed.

On the outskirts of town Sombolo steered me over to the very last shop to look at a pair of bright red nylon gym shorts. We stood there for a moment. "Genuine shorts," Sombolo muttered with admiration. His own attire was obscenely threadbare. On the spur of the moment I bought him the shorts.

ONE NIGHT A DRUNK and agitated Singali staggered into my hut. He had a bone to pick with me. Why had I given machetes to Simbu and Balonyona but not to him? Didn't I know that he was the chief? I was living in *his* village, and it was *my* village too. So where was his gift? When I reminded him of the knife I'd given him, he was momentarily distracted and thanked me, but soon he returned to the subject of the machetes. He had three wives, and he wanted three machetes. *Three.* No — one, two, three. Four! He wanted *four* machetes. I realized I'd blundered by not presenting Singali with a special gift. That he had waited so long to voice his complaint meant he must have been brooding over it a long time. I promised to order him his machetes. The American director of the

Dzanga-Sangha reserve, who was living in one of the abandoned sawmill houses by the river, was going to Bangui in a few days, and I would give him money to buy the machetes. Singali was appeased.

A week later, when my order of ten machetes arrived, I carried them back to camp. I was hoping I could slip into my hut unnoticed, but word of the machetes had spread throughout camp, and the Bayaka were on the alert. They guessed immediately what was in the box as I scurried across the clearing. "*Boonu*," they all muttered as they watched me pass. "Machetes." I stashed the box inside and joined the group of elders in the *mbanjo*. We sat silently for a moment.

"*Oka*," Bombé said at last, "I don't have a machete. I'm an elder. Where's my machete? I don't have one. Are you going to give machetes to the children first?"

When he put it that way, I hadn't much choice. I fetched him a machete. They were big heavy ones forged in Manchester, England, far superior to the small, thin machetes that most Bayaka owned. Bombé accepted the machete with remarkable self-control, setting it down beside him with scarcely a glance. He would, I knew, check it out carefully later. Dimba, however, could not afford that luxury. His lips puckered in admiration. He turned to me at once: "Where's mine?" He knew I understood that the same argument Bombé had used applied to him, as the oldest man at Amopolo without a new machete. There was no need for him to repeat it. Dimba was always efficient in matters of Bayaka etiquette. Joboko and Wadimo got machetes next, followed by Akunga, a heavily bearded elder with a grouchy face. Both Joboko and Akunga asked for theirs, but Wadimo sat as still as a statue, ostensibly unconcerned but actually watching closely out of the corner of his eye. At some point during the proceedings I became aware of Ewunji, who had arrived unnoticed at the *mbanjo*. Now he fixed on me a gaze of intense concentration. I handed him a machete and he nodded his head sagely, as if approving my grasp of Bayaka etiquette.

Suddenly I realized that I had only two machetes left. The chief had ordered four. What should I do? I resisted Doko's pleas; he would just have to wait until I ordered more. And that, I realized, was what I had to do.

If I learned a lesson from the machete incident, it was how susceptible I was to the Bayaka's forms of persuasion. Once I accepted their basic tenet of sharing surplus, all the subsequent points in their arguments seemed to follow logically, so that if I resisted the conclusion — that I should give them whatever they were asking for — I was the unreasonable party in the debate. Since I was trying to live as much as possible according to Bayaka rules of conduct (and compared to the Bayaka I had a surplus of everything at least in the form of money), I was fair game for the demands. In addition, I had told them that a museum had given me money for their music, and that gave their demands an added moral force of which they were fully aware: they were simply asking for what was rightly theirs.

The nights had become uncharacteristically cold. I had not brought a sleeping bag, and my only defense against the cold was two sheets. The Bayaka maintained fires in their huts all night, but even so I knew they must be suffering. An evening that was balmy for me made the Bayaka shiver. The cold nights must have been truly chilling to them. From my bed I could hear them wake up in the night, crunching embers and blowing on them to reanimate their fires. My two sheets were probably even less effective against the cold than their fires, but at least there was some psychological comfort in wrapping myself up in them. None of the Bayaka had sheets.

Tété, who had one of the most beautiful and versatile voices among the men, found the cold particularly unbearable. Several times he had asked me to buy him a sheet. I refused, knowing that if I bought him one, others would start to hit me up for sheets. Tété suggested I give him the sheet surreptitiously. He would sneak over in the middle of the night when everyone was sleeping, slip the sheet under his T-shirt, and sneak back to his hut. No one would be the wiser.

"What happens when you wash the sheet and hang it out to dry?" I asked. "Everyone will know where it came from." Tété had no reply; I'd stumped him. But it was only a temporary victory.

One day Tété pointedly asked me how many sheets I had. He knew I had two, and he knew that I knew he knew. He had me.

"Two," I replied.

"Give me one." He pressed home his advantage relentlessly. "It's cold at night. I can't sleep." So in the end Tété got his sheet. Unwilling to part with one of mine, I bought him a new one. We actually did make the transfer late at night, when no one saw us. But it would be only a matter of time before the sheet was noticed, and the requests for more would start to multiply.

SOME MONTHS INTO my stay I realized I would have to cash some traveler's checks. The only place I could do this was Bangui, a six-hundred-mile journey. I planned to ride in style with the park director, who drove to Bangui almost every month. My days of riding bush taxi, I hoped, were over. One night in the *mbanjo*, I announced my imminent bankruptcy to the men, then cheerfully added that I would be going to Bangui in a couple of weeks to get more money.

As the days passed, word of my impending trip spread around camp until it achieved a kind of mythical status. Tété's sheet had not gone unremarked, and in Bayaka logic, that meant everyone was entitled to a sheet. One afternooon when I was hanging out in front of Singali's hut, the women made it clear to me that they expected me to bring them all underpants. Esoosi stood up, flapping her loincloth emphatically as she lectured on the need for underpants, practically exposing herself to drive the point home. Okay, I agreed amid laughter, underpants. They watched with deep satisfaction as I wrote it down. What else? I asked. Clothes, Singali's first wife, Eloba, said. She meant the wraparound cloth worn by most African women. Earrings, Mbina told me in no uncertain terms. Necklaces, Sao added. Pots, Simbu's wife, Mandubu, added.

The men approached me individually, usually at night, always with an air of secrecy. "When you go to Bangui . . ." they would begin. Each acted as though he were the only person who had thought of approaching me in this manner. Balonyona made a special trip to my hut late at night to ask for a pair of flipflops, assuring me the transaction would be kept strictly confidential. Little did he know that Singali, Bwanga, Biléma, Joboko, and Mabuti had preceded him. A few minutes after he left, Etubu came in to ask for a knife to sharpen arrows for his crossbow. The entire population of

Amopolo had turned into children, telling Santa Claus what they wanted for Christmas. Even Gondo, the master storyteller, sent word through the grapevine that he wanted a machete and a sheet. What was I getting myself into?

One evening two *bilo* from Mombembé arrived at Amopolo. One was Yono's oldest son, not quite as tall as his father. They had heard of my impending departure for Bangui, and had come expressly to ask me to bring them a guitar. I politely told them I could not afford such a purchase, but that I would bring Yono a machete. They expressed mild disappointment over the guitar and promised to tell Yono about the machete. Then they bade me a safe trip and said they were leaving. It was six miles to their village.

"You're returning to Mombembé tonight?" I asked incredulously. It was already dark, and most of the way was through tangled jungle, along a twisty trail at times invisible even in daylight.

"*Oui*," Yono's son replied.

"But it's already late!" I protested.

"We will run," the second villager said matter of factly. And they promptly got up and left.

On the night of my departure (the park director planned to leave at midnight) I joined the men in the *mbanjo* for a few minutes. A large group of women gathered near the entrance to the camp. Little was said. Though I would be away for only a week, I felt overcome by emotion.

"*Dwa na loli*," the men told me. "Go gently."

The women came up one by one to shake my hand. "Make sure you come back!" they said — as if there was any doubt. As I walked down the path toward the road, Mbina called out, "Come back quickly, Looyay!"

FIVE

Ngbali

T HE WORLD WILDLIFE FUND pickup sped south, leaving Nola in the dust. For me the journey was a triumph. I might not have been riding a reindeer-driven sleigh, but perched on top of all my booty in the back of the open pickup cruising along at sixty miles an hour, I felt as if I were flying. I had ninety-three pairs of underwear and forty-nine T-shirts; I was sitting on a sack of sixty sheets; my feet rested solidly on a crate of fifty machetes; there were thirty-three sarongs, each twenty feet long. One bag bulged with twenty-five pairs of flipflops, forty-eight pairs of socks, and two pairs of sneakers. I had thirty-seven bowls, fifteen tin plates, and four deluxe cooking pots with covers; there was a box with thirty-nine knives and a plastic bag with thirty-one necklaces. I had one hundred balloons, and tucked safely away in my shirt pocket was the pair of earrings Mbina had reminded me about several times.

Also on board were the American park director, who was driving; the Central African codirector, sharing the cabin; and the Winstons, a father-and-son team of scientists from Zambia on their way to study the duikers in Dzanga-Sangha. They planned to spend three weeks in Bomandjombo to assess the possibility of starting up a duiker husbandry program. Poaching of elephants and gorillas had been largely stomped out in Dzanga-Sangha, but plenty of snare-hunting still went on. Illicit hunting had increased dramatically since the closing of the sawmill, when most of Bomandjombo was left without jobs. Some of the meat was consumed locally, but most of it was trafficked out of the reserve and sold in the markets in Nola, Berberatti, and even Bangui. If duikers could be raised domestically it would relieve pressure on the population. It didn't seem to matter to the Winstons that blue duikers gave birth to only one young at a time and that a full-grown duiker weighed less than the average dog and was worth a mere eight dollars in the local economy. The Winstons intended to plough ahead with their study in Dzanga-Sangha, despite the practical objections. Winston senior, a jovial, portly man, was squeezed into the cabin with the two directors. His son, an avid butterfly collector, rode in back with me.

For a few hours we passed through patchy rain forest. Little villages dotted the roadside, most with houses of bamboo and mud. Toward noon we reached the savanna, which had been colonized by Mbororo cattle herders from the north. We turned onto a sandy track marked by a small Bayaka camp. Four miles later we arrived at a major Bayaka settlement, Belemboké. It seemed a strange place for Bayaka to live, this wide-open space. There was a bare wooden church and a small concrete hospital.

Belemboké, like Monasao, was a Catholic mission for Bayaka. For the past eight years the mission had been run by Father Joseph, whose main activity was administering medicines to the sick and treating the injured. His clients were Bayaka, *bilo* from nearby villages, and Mbororo who lived in encampments of grass huts scattered through the savanna. I had written to Father Joseph from Amopolo asking if I could buy medicines from him to treat the Bayaka. He had sent word through the grapevine that I was welcome to buy whatever medicines I needed. His hospital had one of the best-stocked pharmacies in the country. I loaded up on penicillin, antimalarial pills, injectable quinine, syringes, needles, eye medicine, bandages, and alcohol. Father Joseph fed us lunch and we resumed our journey.

My reunion with Amopolo was only two hours away, and I practically trembled with elation. This time I felt sure I would not disappoint the Bayaka. I had blown half of my remaining funds during my shopping spree in Bangui. I would explain to everyone that the money for the purchases had come from their music. If they knew that their music tradition was highly valued by the outside world, they would be encouraged to preserve it. Besides, I didn't want them to think that I was some kind of sugar daddy.

ONCE BACK IN THE *mbanjo* at Amopolo, I deferred the opportunity to plunge into the river to wash off the fine layer of bright red grime that had accumulated during the journey. I wanted to relish the excitement my hosts were expressing over my arrival. The men carried the sacks into my hut and stacked them in a corner, commenting on the probable contents of each, which they tried to divine from the shapes of the bulges. The women watched.

"Flipflops," Biléma announced as he heaved one heavy sack onto his shoulder and headed for my hut. "Flipflops," echoed the women, impressed, though unlike the men they were not really interested in footwear. "Sheets," Balonyona said with deep satisfaction as he hauled off another sack. "Sheets," said the women, the word passing from group to group in a wave of whispers. "Clothes," said Engulé as he hoisted the sack of sarongs. "Clothes," murmured the women in a ripple of excitement — they knew the sarongs were meant for them.

We stood for a moment and admired the heap. It took up nearly a third of my hut. Then we repaired to the *mbanjo*, acting as if all were normal with the world. The Bayaka showed commendable self-control. For a while we ignored the treasure in my hut and made small talk. Mabuti told me that earlier in the day Simbu had had a sudden flash that I would be arriving and had ordered my hut swept. What Mabuti failed to mention, but which I noticed later, was that nobody had actually done the sweeping. I pulled some bills out of my pocket and sent a couple of teenagers into town for coffee and sugar. As for cigarettes, I now had a massive stash. Mobo and Joboko each set about preparing his big pipe (Joboko's was bigger than Mobo's), piling up the fluffy stuffing called *musimbu*, pouring water through the pipe and over the stuffing, wringing the stuffing out, and finally putting it back in the pipe. It would cool the smoke on its way through. After coffee and a hefty smoke-up, silence descended on our group. The men looked at me. The women, sitting in groups in front of the nearest huts, were looking at me too. The time had come for me to speak.

"I'm going bathing," I said and went to fetch my soap.

IT WAS GETTING DARK. I had made it clear that I would not hand anything out until the next day. I was exhausted from my journey and needed to recuperate. The Bayaka were very understanding. Of course, they agreed, I should get a night's sleep first. After all, I was tired. It was only reasonable to assume that I wanted to rest. I was surprised by their magnanimous tolerance. Besides, I added, it was too dark to start now. Much too dark, they replied at once. How could I hand things out in the dark? they rhetorically asked one another. Why, it would be sheer chaos, giving things out left and right, looking for machetes with my flashlight, trying to find the flipflops, handing out the wrong sizes. It was too dark! Furthermore, I said, I wanted to distribute everything a little bit at a time. I didn't want crowds shouting, "Give me! Give me!" You see? the men in the *mbanjo* cried. Really, the Bayaka were just a bunch of savages. Always "Give me! Give me!" They ought to leave the *mondélé* in peace. A little bit at a time — it was only reasonable.

We sat around drinking coffee. The women had brewed their own supply. I was hoping the coffee would stimulate everyone to hold a night of music, but obviously they had other things on their minds. "No dance tonight?" I finally asked. Certainly not, they replied. I was too tired. Tomorrow there would be a dance.

As I returned to my hut to get another pack of cigarettes a shadow slipped inside and glided up behind me. I shined my flashlight at it, saw the prison stripes, and knew it was Balonyona.

"*Oui?*" I said a little curtly, wondering if he had just seen the huge cache of cigarettes. Miraculously, they had been carted into my hut without being identified.

"Monsieur Louis," Balonyona began, then paused to remove his hat. He had at some point bartered his cowboy hat for a black beret, which was much more practical but had a large hole directly over his scalp wound. "Me, I am *geedalist*. I've worked well for you, since long ago. But my wife, Matangu — I am married to Matangu, a beautiful woman — she can't sleep with the cold. Now if she had a sheet . . ."

"I'll give the sheets tomorrow," I interrupted. "Don't worry, there's one for you."

"Tomorrow there will be too much noise," he said. "'Oh, Monsieur Louis! Give me! Give me!' It's not good! Me, I am not like that. I've done good work for you. I'm your foremost *geedalist*."

I fell back to my second line of defense, that if I gave him a sheet now everyone else would want one. Balonyona responded with an unexpected variation on the predictable formula: I should set his sheet aside for the time being, hide it in my bed. He would come by to pick it up later, when everyone was asleep. Under his gaze I pulled out a sheet and tucked it between my reed mat and the log mattress. Satisfied, Balonyona turned to go, then paused in the entrance. "Louis." He faced me again with a smile, then lowered his voice to mutter, "Flipflops."

"*Na kutu!*" I cried. "Tomorrow!" Balonyona darted from the hut.

I was on my way out when Mobo suddenly appeared in the doorway. "Do you have my sheet?" he asked quietly.

"Yes," I replied, "but I'm not handing out anything until tomorrow."

"Momboma," Mobo continued, unflustered, invoking the name of his baby daughter of whom he knew I was fond, "the mosquitoes bother her too much. She never sleeps at night. 'Papa,' she says, 'the mosquitoes bother me too much. Ask Louis for a sheet. Then I can sleep well.' Momboma, she said to me." Momboma was only four months old and clearly incapable of speaking a word. But I found Mobo's ruse so endearing that I gave him his sheet. He concealed it in his knee-length baggy shorts and made a silent exit.

The women in my courtyard — old Esoosi, Nyasu, and Mamadu's mother, Bessé — kept an eye on my every move. Their senses now alerted by the two visits in rapid succession, they suspected that something was afoot. I heard Nyasu's query: "Did he give?" And then, "What did he give?"

"Sheets," came the reply from sharp-eyed Bessé.

The murmurs grew louder. Instead of leaving my hut, I backed into the darkness. Two heads, outlined against the moonlit sand, peered into the entrance from around the corner. I could almost feel their eyes straining to penetrate the murk. Something gave me away and they advanced boldly into the hut: Nyasu and Bessé, with Esoosi bringing up the rear.

"Listen," Nyasu demanded, "where's my sheet?"

"It's right here," I said, digging out three sheets as fast as I could, hoping to get rid of them before others came in. But even as I surrendered the sheets, my hut began to fill with people. The trickle was turning into a deluge.

Within seconds more than thirty people were in the hut. Those with flashlights considerately pointed them at the ground so that the air was bathed in diffuse light. I saw Dimba and Simbu, Doko and Joboko. I saw Biléma, Mamadu, and Lalié. Ekumu towered above the others, his head in upper darkness. There was Wadimo's wife. Akété's mother, Belloo, looked cross and determined; the chief's first wife, Eloba, looked equally grim. I recognized the faces, but their individuality seemed to merge into a kind of collective identity as they pressed slowly forward, arms reaching out, their cries for attention rising in volume. "Give me!" "Where's mine?" "Louis — over here!"

I was dealing out sheets with the speed of a card shark, retreating all the while until finally I stumbled backward over the sack of flip-flops. Just then Singali struggled through the dense crowd and stood protectively in front of me. He yelled at everyone to give me room, then turned to me and asked for three sheets. The whirlwind session went on for a few minutes more until, inevitably, I ran out of sheets. With an angry cry of "Aw!" the crowd began to file out, hurling back incriminations: "You didn't give me one!" "I don't have a sheet!" "Tonight I sleep in the cold!" As they left I saw that even teenagers and the older children had been in on the assault.

A deep calm settled over the camp. Probably everyone was eager to try out their new sheets. I was crawling into bed myself when I heard footsteps approaching. A dark form loomed in the doorway and entered my hut. It was Balonyona. "Louis," he whispered, "my sheet." I pulled it out from under the mat and gave it to him. Carefully tucking it under his shirt, he crept to the doorway, looked both right and left, and tiptoed off like a spy.

AT FIRST LIGHT a bitter voice — Esoosi's — competed with the madly crowing roosters, chastising, complaining, deriding. The voice ranted on, a cranky lament addressed to the dawn: what had happened to the Bayaka that they had become such savages? Leave the *mondélé* in peace! IN PEACE! Had they lost their heads? "Give me! Give me!" — It was savage!

Other, more distant female voices began to babble: why did the Bayaka behave so atrociously? Let the *mondélé* give from his heart. By sunrise the men, congregating in the *mbanjo*, joined in. It sounded as if a thousand arguments were raging at once. But in fact everyone was saying the same thing, berating themselves for their behavior of the night before. It was encouraging, and I listened for a while from bed.

Soon the sheer energy of the voices drew me out of bed. I dressed quickly — shorts, socks, and sneakers — and, deciding that the camp mood was amenable to an orderly distribution of sarongs, emerged from my hut with a sack of twenty. A second sack of thirteen remained in my hut as emergency supplies. There was bound to be some fallout from the women who didn't get a sarong during the first round. A momentary hush greeted my appearance. I dragged the sack out to the *mbanjo*. Nearby, the women who could see what I had started to migrate over. Then women from the farther reaches of camp, seeing the excitement, began to flock over too. The farther away their starting points, the faster they came. It was like an inverse model of Hubble's expanding universe.

When everyone was assembled I explained that each sarong was enough for three women — I would distribute each one to three women at a time, and they could divide it up later. Singali helped with the distribution, advising me on who could best share with whom. The session proceeded in an orderly fashion until the sarongs ran out. Knowing I had a reserve stash, however, I listened sympathetically to the women who had missed out, and told them to visit me later in my hut. I regarded a few claims with suspicion, especially those coming from mothers whose daughters had received a sarong. Surely, I insisted, their own daughters would share with them? Not at all, the mothers maintained.

There was a respite while I ate mongoose for breakfast. Afterward Singali told me to give a machete to Mindumi at once, before there was another rush. Mindumi still didn't have one, and he was the mayor. I readily agreed, for I knew that Mindumi had not taken part in any of the onslaughts. It wasn't right that the more aggressive ones should hog all the gifts. The opposite sort of behavior ought to be encouraged. So I pulled out not only a machete but a knife as well. The Bayaka didn't know about the knives, which had slipped past their keen powers of observation. Made in China, the knives had wooden handles and came with a leather scabbard. At four dollars apiece I considered them a sensational bargain, and they would certainly be useful.

"Give me one," Singali immediately said when he saw the knife. He admired his for a minute in the privacy of my hut and said, "A genuine knife!"

Mindumi, sitting in the *mbanjo,* accepted his gifts with a shy grin. But by giving them in the open, I signaled the start of another frenzy. I had intended the machetes for the men, but I was taken aback by the forceful demands of many of the women. Obviously I had not bought enough. As for the knives, they were gone in a flash. A period of disgruntlement followed, and another session of vociferous self-criticism. Then came a lull. Simbu brought over a meal of crocodile.

And so the day unfolded. When Bwanga walked off with the first pair of flipflops, an urgent mutter passed through camp, "He's giving out the flipflops!" After the stampede, the flipflops gone, I was fed again. We moved on to socks, the balloons. Several men were not ashamed to ask for a balloon. Bowls and plates followed. When it came time for the T-shirts, I made sure the children got their share. Esoosi started the avalanche for underpants. One pair of sneakers went to Singali because he was *makunji* (chief), the other to Balonyona because he was *geedalist.*

When evening rolled around, the huge treasure trove that had lent my hut such a festive air was exhausted. Even the big nylon sacks had been eagerly snatched up. Peace reigned over the camp, and by silent consent, including mine, an early night was called. For some time I lay in bed unable to sleep. It had been a remarkable day for me; I did not yet realize what a powerful impact it had made on the Bayaka as well.

The next morning, Amopolo was a hive of activity. Men filed their knives to razor sharpness. Everywhere machetes were being sharpened: the men heated the blades in fire, then hammered them against what looked like a short piece of railroad track, though there are no trains in the Central African Republic. The women enlisted my help in dividing the sarongs. As they unfolded them for the first time and stretched them out, they realized how long they were. There was a great deal of laughter as we took the scissors to them, cutting each one into three pieces. Men and boys proudly sported their flipflops. The new T-shirts assailed the eye with a kaleidoscope of colors: blood red, sea blue, sky blue, leaf green, butterfly yellow, cherry-blossom pink. Men wearing knives frequently unsheathed and admired them.

I still had the necklaces, though they were nothing to write home about, just colorful plastic beads. They had been surprisingly difficult to find in Bangui. By chance on my last day I passed a stall at the central market that had a supply. I bought the entire stock of blue, yellow, white, red, and brown beads. Two deluxe pink necklaces were especially pretty; the beads were many-faceted and had a glittery golden sheen. One I intended for Mbina. Normally the other would have gone to Bosso, but I reasoned that the two sisters would want to exchange necklaces from time to time, so I decided to give Bosso a blue one.

In the early afternoon Mbina came and sat outside her grandmother Esoosi's hut, opposite mine. I called her over. When she entered my hut I handed her the pink necklace. She took it with an impassive expression but then flashed me a smile. "Where are my earrings?" she quickly asked, tugging an ear. I had them ready. They were slightly classier than what you'd expect out of a gumball machine. Mbina gave them a brief but sharp glance before cupping them in her hand and leaving. I braced myself for the inevitable stampede. The women did not disappoint me. My supply of necklaces was wiped out in three minutes.

Long after the last necklace had been snatched from my hand, a delegation of older women lingered in my hut. They wanted necklaces, and they were prepared to sit there until they got them. Little good it did to tell them the necklaces were gone — they refused to budge. It was as if they had some secret knowledge about the one remaining necklace — the pink one, twin of Mbina's. I had not yet decided whom to give it to, but I certainly wasn't about to hand it over to any of the old women scowling in front of my hut. One of them had lost all her toes to leprosy, and her stubborn presence and expression of fierce determination infuriated me. Maybe, I reflected as we sat there in a silent but earnest contest of wills, I wouldn't give the last necklace to anyone.

Hours passed. A couple of the old women finally gave up and left, but three or four remained, including the leper. I had no doubt she would outlast them all. In the meantime, many girls and women had gathered in the courtyard, grooming each other and chattering happily. Suddenly I noticed that Mbina was delousing a beautiful teenage girl whom I had never seen before. I wondered how on earth I could have missed her. Who was she? Where did she come from? She sat in the women's typical posture, directly on the ground with her legs straight out in front of her, wearing only a pair of sky-blue underpants. She stared off into space, a faraway look in her eyes, while Mbina went through her hair pinching lice. Though she had evidently acquired one of the pairs of underpants, I was certain I hadn't directly given her anything. Nor had she asked. And surely her restraint was more deserving of a gift than were the obstinate old bats who occupied my hut. I began to despair that they would never leave. I hated them. Piss off! I thought with intense concentration, hoping to drive them away telepathically. Two of them got up abruptly and left. Only the leper and a woman who looked like her grandmother remained. They showed no signs of moving. Finally I decided that they were welcome to sit there all day if they liked — I was leaving.

I went outside and sat against the wall of Esoosi's hut. Now I had a close-up view of the girl, who seemed oblivious to my presence. Her skin was golden, her hair not quite black — there was something of the redhead in her. All at once I recognized her facial tattoos. It was the girl whose initiation dance I had recorded at the very end of my first visit. She had grown up!

I have no idea how much time passed while I gazed at the girl. When I finally glanced back at my hut it was empty! I saw my chance and went to fetch the pink necklace. There was no point in discretion now; even at the risk of provoking another onslaught I would give the necklace to the girl immediately, before she vanished once more. The women in the courtyard watched as I held it out to her. Still lost in her reveries, she made no move to accept it.

"Oka!" one of the women exclaimed. "The mondélé is giving you something. Take it!"

"Me?" the girl said, looking up in surprise.

I placed the necklace in her hand. When she saw what it was, she gasped as though I had given her a string of pearls.

BY EVENING it was clear that the day's high spirits would spill over into a dance. The drums had been sounding since early afternoon, and now the young girls sat in clusters and sang. One by one the women, their cooking duties dispensed with for the night, came over and joined in. For a while I waited to see if the eboka would be just another false start and turn into elanda. But tonight everyone wanted to dance. I strung my recorder around my neck and strolled over to watch.

The moon, nearly full, illuminated the clearing with silver light. A new song began, very yodelly and full of joy. I stationed myself in front of the most vocal group of singers and started to record. But I was not concentrating on the music. Despite myself, my mind kept wandering to Mbina. She was bound to be participating in the eboka, but where was she? I strained my eyes, searching through the faces in the group before me. I listened for her distinctive voice. At the same time I was confused by my feelings. It was only natural that I should enjoy the presence of such a lovely girl. Yet Mbina was not just any lovely girl to me. Ever since the dance during which I first saw the forest spirits, she had seemed special to me. That posed no dilemma as long as she was a child, but those days would soon be history.

Since Mbina was not in the group in front of me, I would have to look for her elsewhere. Perhaps she was among the teenagers chasing each other at the perimeter of the clearing. I looked in their direction. One of the girls pushed a boy and started to run away.

He grabbed her, and as she broke free her pink necklace flashed in the moonlight. It was Mbina! I felt a surge of jealousy that startled me. Then I realized, with considerable relief, that it was not Mbina after all. It was the nameless beauty, flirting with the boys. She *would* be a flirt, I thought with amusement. Watching her, I was struck by her extraordinary exuberance. Even Mbina's spririt was no match for it. I felt rather glad, too, because it occurred to me that seeing Mbina flirt like that would leave me most agitated.

As the *eboka* developed, the singers, both men and women, danced in a circle in front of the drums. On any other night I would have been disappointed, for the circle dance usually meant that the *mokoondi* would not appear. Tonight I welcomed it as an opportunity to locate Mbina. I stood next to the drummers, microphones directed at the circle. As the dancers passed before me, I looked for her in vain. Mbina was not at the *eboka*.

I was soon distracted from my musings by the erotic dancing of the flirt. Wearing just the sky-blue panties and the pink plastic necklace, she was simply ravishing. Each time she came around to my side of the circle, she leaped out and, arms stretched above her head, skipped forward with wild energy. I was mesmerized. Usually the men had a more flamboyant style of dancing than the women. Now I wondered that I could have been so blind. The girl with the pink necklace was the most fantastic dancer I had ever seen.

THE NEXT MORNING, I was catching up on events in my diary when a bush taxi puttered past on its daily run to Galabadja, the village at the end of the road. A few seconds later there came an explosive crash. I wondered what there was to crash into on this stretch of road. Soon camp was in an uproar as people rushed out to the road. For a few minutes I went on writing, unperturbed, about the girl with the pink necklace.

Biléma stuck his head into my hut. "Accident!" he informed me in a tone of awe, then disappeared.

"Mm-hmm," I grunted and kept writing.

A minute later Mamadu's head popped in. "A village woman crashed the car!" he exclaimed in happy excitement before running off.

"A woman driver?" I said absently and wrote: *During the eboka last night she danced up a storm.*

"Louis," Balonyona urged, pausing in the entrance, "bring your hospital! People have been badly hurt!" I decided I had better go take a look. I grabbed a bottle of iodine, a bundle of cotton, and some bandages. Akété joined me as I headed up the road.

"A bad accident!" he was saying with a big smile on his face. "Lots of people died!"

"People died?" I echoed in alarm.

"Lots!" Akété assured me.

We quickened our pace. The accident had occurred at the bridge. As we came into view I could see the mini-van at the side of the road, its back end smashed into a giant log. A crowd of Bayaka stood around, staring at the wreck. The passengers were lying here and there in the grass along the roadside. Beyond the bridge the road, deeply eroded, rose steeply. The bush taxi must have stalled on the way up, then rolled backward until it hit the log. It was not surprising that it had not braked — many bush taxis have no brakes.

As we drew nearer I noticed through the open door of the van a woman's leg sticking out from the front seat. I dreaded the spectacle I might be confronted with: bloody gashes, eyes blinded by glass, decapitation. What good could I do with my bag of cotton? The sight of the other victims strewn about in the grass was not reassuring. How many were dead?

Then the legs sticking out of the van moved. The woman sat up, poked her head out, and wearily watched me approach. The bodies in the grass began to move too. A man shifted his position. A woman next to him peeled a banana. Not only had no one been killed, nobody had even been scratched. The Bayaka looked relieved, despite their excitement moments earlier, when they seemed to greet the disaster with such relish. And when the woman driver decided it was time to resume the journey, they volunteered their services and pushed the taxi back onto the road.

THAT NIGHT the elders smoked the big pipe around my fire. Discussion was lively, and it wasn't long before the music started. For a change it was not the *geedal* but the *mondumé* (harp-zither) that was brought out. I was delighted to have the opportunity finally to make some decent recordings of this delicate instrument. Mobo began plucking in the midst of the conversation, now and then singing in a smooth high voice that had a story-telling quality. Eventually Mabuti asked for the *mondumé*. My previous experience trying to record Mabuti on the harp-zither did not inspire confidence in his performance now, and on the pretext that my batteries had run out, I switched off the recorder as he began to play. Thirty seconds later, not caring what the Bayaka would think of the contradiction, I turned it on again: Mabuti's playing was incredible. He proved to be a master of the *mondumé*, as Balonyona was of the *geedal*. Later an elder named Momboli came over with an open-ended four-holed flute called a *mobio*. I had read of this instrument, which is also found among the Mbuti of the Ituri forest, but I had never seen or heard it at Amopolo. When I tried to play it, I couldn't get a squeak out of it. Momboli, on the other hand, played in three octaves, the notes following one another so rapidly that at times it sounded as if two flutes were playing simultaneously.

The session was brought to a premature end by the arrival of Dr. Winston senior. He was mildly distressed. Part of his mission, he explained to me, was to examine the parasites of all species of indigenous duikers. He had been hunting with the Mosapola Bayaka, but all they had gotten were dozens of blue duikers; at the very least he wanted a couple of red duiker specimens too. Up until now he'd been spending most of his time cleaning blue duiker skulls. He wanted to try his luck hunting with the Amopolo Bayaka, and he was willing to pay handsomely for red duikers.

"How much?" I asked.

"As much as the Pygmies want," he replied. I relayed his offer to the Bayaka, and they agreed somewhat reluctantly to take Dr. Winston and his son hunting the following morning. They would be ready to go at seven.

The Winstons didn't show up until eight, but the Bayaka were far from ready. Their already lukewarm enthusiasm for the venture turned positively chilly when they saw that the Winstons had brought along two *gardes de chasse*. Suddenly everyone was ill.

"Monsieur Louis, my head hurts too much," Balonyona said. He removed his beret and pointed at his scar. "Today I can't go hunting."

"Worms," Singali told me, tapping his stomach, "today they're biting me in the stomach."

Biléma claimed his foot injury eliminated him from the outing. For proof he indicated a scratch on the inside of his left foot.

"But that's tiny!" I protested.

"It really hurts," he replied, looking me straight in the eye. Bwanga simply refused to participate.

The Winstons were getting impatient. I was increasingly embarrassed. When Biléma showed some signs that he might take part, I quickly offered him a thousand francs to lead the hunt. I was immensely grateful when he accepted. In the end a small hunting party was rounded up.

We set off. Once in the forest, the guards hacked with a vengeance at the undergrowth where Bayaka had passed without effort. Biléma and I sped ahead of everyone else and paused for a smoke. Biléma then continued on his way while I waited for the Winstons. One by one the other members of the hunting party passed me, first the men and then the women. One of the last was the fabulous dancer. As she appeared down the trail, an empty carrying basket on her back, I thought: it's her! Our eyes met as she passed. A little farther on she glanced back, as if to see if I was still looking. I was. Just before she vanished around a bend, she glanced back once more.

The day's hunt proceeded without notable incident. The scientists ran back and forth to verify each kill, Winston junior nimble and tireless, Winston senior stumbling, perspiring, huffing and puffing. Blue duiker after blue duiker fell to the nets, but no red duikers were even spotted. The Winstons were thrown into a brief paroxysm of excitement when a yellow-backed duiker zipped past directly in front of them, knocked over the net — and bounded off. But soon they became dispirited again. The guards chopped their way hither and thither, looking purposeless, miserable, and lost.

"What time do the Pygmies return from the hunt?" one of them finally asked me.

"Between four and five," I replied.

The guard checked his watch. "It's ten past two now," he said hopefully.

At one point I followed the Winstons to one of the kills. The animal (a blue duiker, of course) had fallen to Akunga's net. Akunga and I had had little contact, but I was intimidated enough by his deep gruff voice and humorless face to hand him two ciga-rettes every time he showed up at my hut, before he even had a chance to ask for one. Akunga was standing at his net with his wife, Awoko. With them, I was happy to note, was the flirtatious dancer. Might she be Akunga's daughter? She leaned against a tree, her lovely legs crossed, one arm behind her back, the other hand grip-ping the duiker by the neck so that it dangled along her side. She looked at me unabashedly.

Winston senior, seeing the opportunity for the photo of the cen-tury, fumbled hastily with his camera. The girl was too quick for him, however, and in a flash had dropped the duiker and sat down. Dr. Winston's camera clicked at the bare tree trunk.

OVER THE FOLLOWING WEEKS my relationship with the Bayaka began to undergo a subtle transformation. For one thing, I was no longer the completely dispassionate observer — not that I ever had been, but now I sensed an even deeper emotional involvement with the Bayaka. And they seemed to be up to something, to be conspir-ing in the execution of some elaborate plan. I began to detect un-dercurrents in the daily life we all shared, as though my mind were tuning in to a stream of subliminal thought that flowed through camp. I got the feeling that the Bayaka, in their own complex way, were encouraging me to rethink our relationship.

One afternoon Balonyona called me into his hut. Several men were there, including Singali, Bwanga, Mowooma, and Sombolo. "Okay," Balonyona said, "light it."

Mosombo produced a piece of *vaka*, a hardened tree resin that resembled a chunk of glass. *Vaka*, the "lamp of the forest," burned with a bright steady flame and was prized for its effectiveness in illuminating huts at night. Sombolo lit it, and Mowooma, waving his hands over the flame, which fluttered in one direction and another, began to "read" it. The gist of his interpretation seemed to be about me. I had come from far away. I would never leave, because although I was a *mondélé* my heart had found its home at Amopolo. My heart heard the *mokoondi*. I would bring the Bayaka many things: clothes, machetes, sneakers, knives, pots, medicine, coffee, marijuana, scissors, flashlights, a hospital, a school. I belonged to Amopolo.

That's a tall order, I thought to myself, but I was moved by the ritual. Pleased with the reading, the men abruptly called an end to the session. Sombolo extinguished the *vaka* and we dispersed.

Another time, when I was bathing in the Amopolo with Simbu, Mobo, Bwanga, and a few others, they began asking me about my marital status. It was not the first time, but on this occasion the questions were more pointed. Did I have a wife in America? What about children — didn't I want to return soon to take care of my children? The men looked at each other when I swore for the fifth time that I had no children. Would I, Simbu wanted to know, ever marry a *bilo* woman? I knew the answer to that loaded question: not on my life. They laughed approvingly. I should marry a Moaka, Simbu went on. After all, Yono had married a Moaka. Why didn't I marry one, too? There were plenty of women at Amopolo to choose from. There were chuckles when Simbu made his suggestion. Could he be serious? I certainly liked Bayaka women, I replied noncommittally. "Bayaka women are great!" Bwanga said enthusiastically, smiling at me. He should know — he had recently moved in with Doko's lovely daughter Mowa, after a very affectionate courtship. The two were obviously deeply in love.

One evening I joined Mbina and Yombo (Wadimo's daughter) in chasing one of Wadimo's chickens. It actually belonged to a *bilo*. During my stay in America a disease had wiped out most of the chickens in Bomandjombo, but for some reason it hadn't struck at Amopolo. Consequently many *bilo* had turned over their chickens to the Bayaka to look after. Our chicken-chasing antics caused general laughter. Later a small group of women gathered in the clearing and sang to the drums. There was no dancing, but the songs were lovely.

I posted myself in front of the women and recorded. Before long I became aware of the most extraordinary singing by one of the women just below my left microphone. The moon had not yet risen, and in the dark I could only guess who it was. The style reminded me of Bosso, yet the voice was not quite the same. It had an enthusiasm and energy I had never heard from Bosso. The sound was bright and joyful, and I considered it among the most remarkable singing I had ever heard. Several songs into the *eboka*, the moon, now at half, began to lighten the sky as it rose over the trees. Soon it gave me enough light to make out who was who among the dark forms of the singers. To my astonishment I realized that the singer whose voice had so captivated me was Mbina, her voice no longer in a child's high register. It was solidly in the middle register, and she sang with the full confidence of womanhood.

The next night another *eboka* was held. It lacked the intimate chamber-music quality of the previous night dance — in fact, it was the biggest dance I had yet seen at Amopolo. Practically everyone except Simbu took part. The women sat in a large circle, an unusual arrangement, and the singing had a vast, vigorous oratorial sound. It was impossible to record it all at once, so for each song I moved to a different location. Yet as the music grew increasingly intense, with a polyphony of stunning complexity, my mind wandered to thoughts of Mbina. Earlier in the day, when everyone was off in the forest and camp seemed empty, I had played through the songs of the night before. Mbina's splendid singing had filled me with a soaring sense of optimism. Then suddenly Mbina herself had appeared and sat down in my hut. During the playback she looked at me steadily and so intently that I could only sneak an occasional glance back at her. At the end of the tape she simply got up and left.

Now I couldn't help but wonder: had Mbina been trying to tell me that she was a woman now, no longer a girl? That had been my distinct impression. But maybe I was deluding myself, reading significance into meaningless incidents. The subtlety of Mbina's message argued against its being intentional. What did I know of the intimate undercurrents of daily life among the Bayaka? I should concentrate on the music, write my diary, and mind my own business.

The faraway cry of a forest spirit brought me back to reality.

Eventually a single large bush broke through the circle of singers, scattering them before it, and began to spin right and left, pausing occasionally to beat the earth rapidly. Men and women regrouped and danced slowly around it. Doko, usually restrained in his dancing, was plastered on *mbaku* and danced like a man thirty years younger, shaking his behind, swiveling his hips, and in general causing such hilarity among the women that his presence was almost a disruption. But the *eboka* had an irrepressible energy and focus that overrode even Doko's wild antics, swallowing them into itself.

Then I noticed her — the fabulous flirtatious dancer. The moon had risen, and as she danced, her necklace and her underpants, bright in the moonlight, marked her every move. I couldn't take my eyes off her. Her energy was magnetic, and I marveled that everyone else wasn't looking at her, she seemed so obviously the center of attraction. As if in reponse to my thoughts, Doko made a lunge for her. She ran away, her underpants bobbing off and finally merging into the distant shadows. But she was soon back and bolder than ever, dancing right up to me, then retreating into the circle of singers.

At the height of the *eboka* the bush spirit suddenly split into two, and during the remainder of the night's celebration the two halves seemed to grow bigger and bushier with each song. The dance was still going strong when there came a burst of light from a far corner of camp. Huge flames shot up. A hut had caught fire. There was a moment of confused wonder. Then, with cries of excitement, everyone sprinted off. The girl with the pink necklace, I fondly noted, was an incredibly fast runner.

THE FOLLOWING WEEK the camp was all stirred up. With just a half-hour's warning, the president was going to arrive — the president of the World Wildlife Fund, that is. She was visiting to check up on the progress on the Dzanga-Sangha Dense Forest Reserve. The authorities in Bomandjombo wanted to give her a reception befitting her esteemed rank. In ancient times the Pygmies had been called upon to dance for the pharaohs; now they were being asked to dance for the president of the WWF. The mayor's guards ordered the Bayaka to report in ten minutes to the yard in front of the reserve director's house, where the president would be having lunch. The mayor was counting on me, the guards added, to make sure they showed up.

The Bayaka were not pleased by the arrangement but decided to make the best of it. They dressed in their finest clothes, and we all headed over to the director's house. Bomandjombo's notables were gathered, waiting for the arrival of the auspicious guest. A folklore group from the village — two drummers and five dancers who looked as if they had dressed for a parade — was already in action. The plan was that the Bayaka should perform at the same time, some twenty feet away. Charles Ives would have approved.

The women sat down at the base of an immense clump of bamboo. Bwanga and Kukpata began to hammer away on the drums, which they'd carried over from Amopolo. Soon they were competing with the two village drummers. When the women added their voices to the contest, the village drummers redoubled their effort in retaliation. Sombolo, always the foremost Moaka to be called upon by the villagers for such occasions, started to dance. Bwanga and Kukpata did their utmost to drown out the village drums. By the time the convoy of luminaries drove up, it was pandemonium.

The president of the WWF stepped out of the car, smiling politely at the reception. Bottles of wine were uncorked, and the village authorities quickly joined the Americans in claiming their share. The Bayaka men watched thirstily. At first the Americans gravitated toward the highly coordinated dance of the village troupe. Sombolo, however, dancing like a clown, was more popular with the *bilo*, who crowded around to watch. Seeing his opportunity, Sombolo gyrated over toward the mayor, knelt on one knee, and while shaking his shoulders and head to the rhythms of the drums, beseeched the mayor for his glass of wine. The mayor handed it over reluctantly. Mabuti and Mobo, seeing the benefits of participation, hurried into the act, cadging glasses of wine from the gendarmes and police. The Americans moved over to watch the Bayaka.

The village troupe, taken aback by the lack of an audience, momentarily abandoned their performance. Clearly piqued by the victorious cheer from the Bayaka, however, they launched into another attempt. The Americans wandered up the stairs into the director's house for lunch, followed by the higher village officials. The Bayaka were really going now, and a number of men were dancing in a circle. Sombolo, Mobo, and Mabuti had managed to get fairly loaded. Mabuti's dancing resembled some sort of esoteric Oriental exercise. Mobo was unabashedly pestering the few remaining villagers for their drinks. Sombolo sucked in his cheeks and stomach, bulged his eyes, and moved forward in a kind of pigeon strut. The dance was rapidly turning into a joke. On the spur of the moment I decided to complete the charade, and I leaped into the circle of dancers. There was a scream of delight from the women as I passed in front of them, wagging my behind.

Eventually, when we were free to return to Amopolo, we walked back slowly in one big crowd. The village troupe, which had all but given up, once more jumped into action, now with an enthusiasm that seemed to announce their triumph. But it was a hollow victory, for there was nobody left to watch.

WHILE EXCHANGES of verbal violence were commonplace at Amopolo, the Bayaka rarely resorted to blows. When they did, you could be fairly sure that *mbaku* was behind it. A fight was invariably greeted with excitement, like some major social event. Teenage girls were an especially enthusiastic audience. It was always disconcerting when, with a cry of action that sounded like *heegalo!* they speedily flocked to the scene of battle, laughing and chattering. Each drunken punch provoked a cheer of amusement. Whenever a fist made contact, there was a cry of *wo!* as the crowd moved this way and that with the thrashing, stumbling contenders. At such times I felt most distant from the Bayaka.

One afternoon there was a colossal fight between Mowooma and Sombolo, who had gotten into an argument after returning from a village drinking binge. Mowooma followed Sombolo around, challenging him to a fight. Sombolo dismissed Mowooma's dares with an easygoing laugh. The two wandered from neighborhood to neighborhood, reenacting their charade like a couple of roving actors. Finally they arrived in my courtyard.

"Right here and now!" Mowooma was saying, tailing along behind Sombolo.

"Monsieur Louis," Sombolo said, "Mowooma wants to fight, but I don't like noise."

I replied that he was very wise and invited him to sit down. He continued to stand. A crowd of teenagers began to gather. Mowooma removed his shirt, hurling insults all the while. Sombolo turned his back on him. Mowooma grabbed Sombolo and threw him to the ground. Sombolo rolled in the sand and laughed.

"Aw, forget it!" Mowooma exclaimed, putting his shirt back on. "You don't even know how to fight." He started to walk away.

Suddenly Sombolo leaped up, furious and belligerent. "You wanna fight?" he challenged, pulling off his shirt and grabbing Mowooma by the arm. "All right, let's fight! Right here and now!"

"Forget it," Mowooma replied. "You're useless."

The fight began within seconds. Mowooma threw the first punch. On and on it raged, with no clear advantage to either man. Sometimes the older men and women managed to talk one of them into walking away. But then the other would follow and resume the quarrel. In this manner they slowly moved through camp. I was glad when they vacated my neighborhood. I withdrew into my hut, upset as always by this outbreak of violence. Nearly an hour later, however, they were back in my courtyard again. Mowooma now had a bloody nose, Sombolo a bloody lip. I could stand it no more and decided to intervene. With the help of a few men I managed to coax Sombolo, the less excitable of the two, into Mamadu's hut. Suddenly Mowooma went berserk.

"*Sombolo! Sombolo!*" he growled with menace, violently trying to lunge into the hut after him. Ewunji, Joboko, and others struggled to stop him. Finally, held down by half a dozen men, he craned his neck — the only part of his body he could still move — slowly out toward a woman who was standing in front of him as though to block his way. His face took on a horrifying grimace, his eyes bulged insanely, and he panted like a hungry dog as he focused his frightening glare on the woman. She immediately ran away.

Mowooma burst out laughing. The fight was over.

/ / /

I WAS LOUNGING AROUND with some of the boys in front of my hut going over some recent recordings when who should appear at Mokoko and Sao's hut but the fabulous flirtatious dancer, carrying a large wooden mortar. I still had no idea who she was, and I had been too busy to make any inquiries. I was thrilled to see her. She noticed my expression of pleasant surprise and held my gaze until she reached the hut, when she began talking to Sao. Soon she was pounding manioc. I could not take my eyes off her. What astonished me now was how frequently our eyes met — she was looking at me almost as much as I was looking at her.

For the rest of the day she remained at Mokoko's. Suddenly she and Sao seemed to be the best of friends. They chased each other, draped their arms around each other, and chatted and laughed. Mokoko was there too, as well as Sao's cousin Ngongo — one big happy family. Ostensibly Sao was cooking dinner, but it was the fabulous dancer who actually did all the work, preparing what looked like a fairly elaborate meal.

I remained at my observation post until it was too dark to see her eyes anymore, though her silhouette against the fire remained an enticing sight. As I went into my hut, I heard her call Sao and ask what she should do with "Looyay's food." She modulated her voice more than most women, so that her pronunciation of Sao's name rose through two octaves. Her lyrical voice was every bit as beautiful as the girl herself.

A few minutes later Joboko entered my hut with a meal for me. On his heels came Ngongo with another meal. When Ngongo saw me accepting the bowls from Joboko he quickly thrust the meal he carried under my nose.

"Eat this one!" he insisted.

"Louis is eating mine," Joboko growled. "Give yours to someone else."

"No!" I cried at once to Ngongo. "Give me, I'll eat yours." I handed Joboko back his bowls. "Who prepared this?" I asked Ngongo in an attempt to find out the girl's name.

"Sao," Ngongo lied.

I remembered reading a short section on courtship and marriage in a children's book on Pygmies that I had brought with me. It was written by the curator of the Pitt Rivers Museum — the man who was helping to finance my current field trip. That night in bed I quickly located the passage. Courtship was straightforward and simple: a man gave gifts to the woman of his choice. If the woman liked him, she accepted his gifts. After a while the two moved in together, generally erecting a hut in the man's camp. They were now married. A woman, the book went on to say, was attracted to a man who showed courage and skill in hunting and dancing. Well, I reflected, I was hopeless as a hunter, I couldn't dance to save my life, and my courage had never been put to the test. I might be a coward who didn't know it yet.

I filed the facts away for future thought, shut the book, and wondered vaguely what had prompted me to open it in the first place. Was I losing my marbles?

In the morning she was at Mokoko and Sao's hut again, cooking another meal. When our eyes met for the first time she smiled, then covered her face with a shy giggle. I was stunned by euphoria. Between cooking chores she clowned around with Sao and was hardly still for a moment, stretching, lying back, turning over, leaping up, twirling around, her laughter confident and contagious. In everything she did she seemed to be showing her extraordinary body. I was convinced that it was one of the natural wonders of the world. Now and then Sao or Mokoko caught my eye and gave a knowing grin. Eventually Mokoko brought over the meal she had prepared. She left as I started to eat.

"The man gives small presents to the woman of his choice." I thought hard now about that sentence from the Pygmy book. I had already given her the pink necklace, but only as part of my spree for the whole group. I desperately wanted to give her a second gift. It didn't necessarily mean I wanted her to be my wife, I tried to persuade myself. I just had this urge to give her something.

"I'm going to the village to buy cigarettes," I announced, standing up.

"Give me the money," Kukpata volunteered. "I'll go." Normally this was a task I entrusted to one of the teenage boys — the adult men being generally irresponsible with money — but now I insisted I would go into town myself. I set off.

All the Boamandjombo shops were run by Moslems, most of

them from Chad and related by blood or marriage. The only shop with more than a few tins of sardines, however, was run by a *bilo* named Ngunja. It was at the far end of town. As I walked, a villager tagged along for a while, complaining the whole time about the local Bayaka.

"In Cameroon," he claimed, "the Pygmies grow manioc, plantains, bananas, and coffee. They speak French. They even go to discos and dance normally. Here they're lazy, lazy, lazy! All they do is steal! They steal manioc, papayas, bananas, even meat they find in snares in the forest [snares were now illegal in Dzanga-Sangha]. They steal the fruit before it's ripe, they steal the snares themselves. Truly, Monsieur Jean-Louis," he continued, beseeching me with an earnest look, "you must civilize them. You must make Amopolo like Monasao or Belemboké, with a school. You must teach the Pygmies to be *normal*! It just can't go on like this!" I promised him I would do what I could.

After living at Amopolo, Ngunja's place struck me as a veritable cornucopia of goods. In addition to cigarettes, I bought two bars of perfumed soap and a pair of earrings with purple plastic stones. I pocketed the goods and started back, my pants bulging conspicuously. I exuded a powerful flowery fragrance. Back at Amopolo I quickly stashed the soap in my hut, but the scent lingered on. "*Savon de toilette*," several keen-nosed Bayaka deduced. There was no keeping secrets at Amopolo.

In the afternoon she appeared again, sitting with Sao, throwing more than the occasional glance my way. No one else was around, so I fetched the gifts and approached, suddenly very nervous. "Take," I said awkwardly, handing her a bar of soap and the earrings. She accepted the gifts as though they were her due. Sao was looking on, so I gave her the other bar of soap, hoping by that ruse to disguise my true intentions. Besides, I wanted to encourage Sao's friendship with the girl.

"Where are *my* earrings?" Sao teased, then laughed when I tried to stutter a reply.

MY MOODS WERE increasingly regulated by the appearances of the fabulous dancer. She visited Mokoko and Sao every morning before leaving for the hunt, if only for a few minutes. At the end of the day she returned, scantily dressed, sometimes decorated with bold strokes of a dark blue vegetable juice across her face and chest, or a sprig of berries in her ear, or a stalk of grass through her nose. Her sense of self-adornment was impeccable — everything she did seemed to highlight some aspect of her beauty that I hadn't properly appreciated before. If she failed to appear when I expected her, my mood would plummet; I would wonder where she was and worry that she might never show up again. Such fears were short-lived, however, for she always did arrive. As soon as she did, my mood brightened.

I began to take a more active role in the conversations around my fire. I listened carefully to what was said around me, trying to pick up clues. Were the other Bayaka aware of the attraction I felt for her? Did they approve? Were they all a party to it?

One night while she was at Sao's preparing a meal for me, the men's conversation around my fire seemed to concern her. Biléma said, "She's a *fine* woman." The others agreed. I got the distinct impression that they were matchmaking for me. But my rudimentary command of the language left plenty of room for doubt. That night, after she left Mokoko's, I asked Ngongo her name, pointing to her in the distance. He acted surprised by my interest and for a moment seemed not to know whom I was talking about. I thought it should have been obvious. Finally he told me her name was Goma, but his initial reaction threw me into depths of uncertainty.

A few days later I went into town and bought Goma a bottle of red nail polish. I handed her the gift during a moment when she was at Sao's alone and no one seemed to be watching. She took the present with a silent *ooh!* of admiration. It felt strange to please her so much with such trinkets.

Another afternoon, on my way to bathe, as I walked through Akunga's part of camp, I passed her sitting with a friend in the entrance to a beehive hut.

"*Elobayé!*" she called out in a quiet voice.

"*Elobayé!*" I softly replied. She giggled and covered her face. It was the first time she had spoken to me.

A COUPLE OF WEEKS earlier Singali and Balonyona, wearing their new T-shirts and sneakers, had set off on foot for Monasao, about fifty miles to the north. Singali had family there, and Balonyona had family at Belemboké, another ten miles north. Now they returned, full of stories of the marvels they had seen at Monasao, whose main attraction was that it had no *bilo*. Under the guidance of Father René and Sister Madeleine, the Bayaka there had started up their own plantations of manioc. There were grapefruit trees, mangoes, avocadoes; the Bayaka sold palm thatching and other products of their labor to their two *patrons*, then used the money to buy items from a shop run by the priest. What especially appealed to Singali and Balonyona were the subsidized prices at this shop for Bayaka only — a pack of cigarettes went for 150 francs, compared with 250 at Bomandjombo. The shop also had pots and pans, sarongs, vegetable oil, belts, machetes, strainers for manioc flour, kerosene lamps, and many other goods. Monasao was, in effect, a self-sufficient Bayaka community miles from the nearest *bilo* settlement — a Bayaka fantasy come to life. At its school the children were learning the rudiments of reading and writing. Singali was so charmed by the arrangement that now he was talking about moving his whole village there.

Singali and Balonyona were accompanied by Adamo, Singali's cousin. I remembered my encounter with Adamo on my first visit, and I didn't greet the news of his arrival with much enthusiasm. He had been overbearing enough on that occasion, and I expected now that his younger "brother" was chief, he would be insufferable. But I was wrong.

Adamo had brought his ten-year-old son. The rest of his family would follow in a week. Adamo was understandably proud of his son, who had learned to read and write. He was very serious for a ten-year-old, seeming to lack the spontaneity of character that the Amopolo children possessed almost to a fault. I noticed that he never participated in the music, and later I learned that all Bayaka who grew up at Monasao shared that reserved nature. As for Adamo, who had grown up at Amopolo but had lived at Monasao for ten years, he now harbored literary ambitions, which led to some extraordinary behavior.

Adamo immediately assumed it was his role to be my protector, and he lingered in my company with the attentiveness of a guardian angel. If I wanted to drink some water, he saw to it that I got water, often fetching it himself. If I went into the village, he sat in or just outside my hut to guard it, usually with a book. Though he had leafed through the children's picture book on Pygmies, he actually preferred to stare at the printed text of *Tristes Tropiques*, my copy of which had recently resurfaced. He could entertain himself that way for hours. He was the best mimic of literacy I ever met. He would frown in concentration as he stared at a page, now and then scratching his head as though pondering what he read, screwing his face into an expression of serious thought. These actions, combined with the Harvard sweatshirt he wore, were superficially most impressive and could fool the casual observer. He loved to watch me write in my diary and would sit next to me, his face inches from the paper, carefully noting the movements of my pen. Later, when he had some money, he went into town and purchased a school exercise book and a pen. Whenever I pulled out my diary to make some notes, he produced his own notebook and proceeded to fill it with line after line of what looked like illegible handwriting. Sometimes he would pause in his scribbling to review what he had just written, running his finger along the lines and making a sort of whispery sound: "*Pssswssswssswsss.*"

One morning I left for the hunt with Adamo. We went ahead of the others, but pretty soon Goma was behind us, a hunting net draped over her shoulder. Whose net was it? I wondered with a momentary flash of jealousy. The net turned out to be Adamo's. It was the first time I had known him to hunt, and since his wife was still at Monasao, Goma was helping him in her place. I was thrilled, for it meant I would spend the entire day in her presence. Occasionally Adamo found himself between Goma and me while on the march. Invariably he would find some excuse to step out of my way or her way, perhaps to scan the canopy, or to examine a plant, or even simply to take a leak. It all happened very naturally, yet I had the impression that he and Goma had arranged the whole thing.

After that I accompanied the Bayaka on their hunts almost every day. No matter whom I stayed with, Goma and I crossed paths many times. She would appear suddenly on the trail in front of me and walk along for a few minutes before turning off and vanishing in the vegetation. Sometimes she joined the trail directly behind

me. I didn't have to turn around and look — I could always tell
when she was there. We never made eye contact during these
hunts. Goma had other intentions now. She wanted me to see her
in action in the forest, and she wanted to watch how I handled
myself on these strenuous expeditions. I didn't want my style ham-
pered, so I always left my recorder and camera behind. Goma usually carried only a machete. Most women and girls at least had
carrying baskets and busied themselves with gathering, but Goma
was a totally carefree spirit of the forest.

On the night of the dark of the moon the Bayaka held an *eboka*
that was unforgettable. The sky was full of stars, and meteors
streaked across it, leaving trails of glowing smoke. For hours the
women and children sat and sang. Eventually they were joined by
Sombolo and Bakpima, who began the next song with a duet. Soon
the chorus was in full swing, overlaying the original melody with
such dense polyphony that it all but disappeared.

The piercing call of a *mokoondi* rose from the nearby jungle, and
the spirit entered the camp. The women greeted it with real rever-
ence. I had never seen anything like this *mokoondi* before — a
creature low to the ground, draped in raffia fibers. Its smallest
movements provoked exclamations of wonder, as though its very
presence were a miracle. By the end of the song the clearing was
dotted with a motionless legion of pale, faceless creatures wearing
conical hats. When the *mokoondi* shook, the rush of its raffia clothing was accompanied by the tinkling of a bell. It didn't speak, but
sang out in a high, off-key voice. Soft yodels echoed back and forth
among the women. Sometimes the most beautiful moments of an
eboka are those quiet episodes between song when the women half-
whisper fragments of melody, and the hush in the air grows all the
more palpable for their murmured music. Then the weird cries of
the *mokoondi* sound especially poignant, their element of dissonance seeming to come from another world.

Over the next few days my head reeled with melodies from the
eboka. It had been different from the dance normally held the night
before a hunt, during which the *mokoondi*, depending on how well
the women sang, gave them the food they would find the next day.
This *eboka* had had something to do with me, I was sure. Often

the *mokoondi* had come right up to me, its raffia skirt brushing against my legs while the attendant spirits hopped in a tight circle around us.

One morning Goma failed to appear at Mokoko's. When I still hadn't seen her by nightfall, I started to worry. All the next day she was nowhere to be seen. Only now during her absence did I begin to fathom the extent of my obsession. I craved her presence. Each day became an ordeal to be endured for the reward of sleep and oblivion at its end. I marveled at my happy-go-lucky pre-Goma days, which seemed a lifetime away, when I could sit contentedly for hours with whatever group of Bayaka I happened to be among. I longed for that carefree attitude now. But I knew that the turn of events that had driven me to my present distraction had taken me too far.

Several times I asked Ngongo where Goma had gone, but he didn't understand the question, or pretended not to. As the days passed I imagined every possibility. In my diary I usually referred to Goma as a girl, but in fact she looked older than a number of the married women. The Bayaka tend to marry young. Bosso and Bi-léma, scarcely more than kids on my first visit, were already married. On the other hand Singali's sister Sembé was probably older than Bosso, and she still lived, unmarried, with her mother, Esoosi. Had she not had any suitors (rather difficult to imagine) or had she not found one to her liking? Goma might already be betrothed to someone. I knew nothing of Bayaka practices in such matters.

Camp life continued to unfold as though nothing had happened, and I did my best to participate. Adamo's family arrived from Monasao: his wife, Sepé, and their baby boy, Tutu, as well as two older boys and a teenage daughter named Njongo, a dark, quiet beauty. Perhaps she was quiet out of shyness, for she had no close friends at Amopolo. She attended dances, though her presence and participation were restrained. Only once did I see her really show enthusiasm, during a night of musical games with the girls. Then she could hardly keep still for a second. Another day I heard her sing Tutu a lullaby to the tune of *Frère Jacques*, the most lovely rendition of that melody I ever heard. She was in every way the opposite of Goma, who with her wild dancing and bold taunts epitomized the "uncivilized" nature of the Amopolo Bayaka. Watching Njongo and even taking pleasure in her presence, I longed all the more for Goma.

One day, after nearly a week of skulking around camp, I forced myself to go hunting. I departed with the men and soon found myself alone with Akunga. We weren't walking particularly fast, but the others had dropped behind. Bwanga was not too far away. His voice rang out in gorgeous falsetto improvisations as we moved through the forest. For a moment I wondered whether Akunga had arranged for me to be alone with him. Maybe he was giving me the opportunity to speak about Goma. Should I say anything? I pondered furiously, trying to screw up the courage to ask where Goma was. I cleared my throat.

There was a loud snap in the canopy above. Akunga immediately covered his head and started to run. I covered my head and froze. A round green fruit, as big and heavy as a boccie ball, slammed into the ground between us.

I decided to keep quiet.

THE NEXT MORNING, as soon as I woke up, Mokoko called me over to Esoosi's hut. Mbina had had a raging fever all night, and they wanted me to take her into the Bomandjombo dispensary for an injection. I found Mbina sitting in Esoosi's, surrounded by several concerned women. She looked pale and tired. There were dark stains around her nose and on her chin. It's really serious, I thought with alarm. We set off at once for the village; Adamo came with me and Mbina walked a few feet behind.

When we reached the dispensary, I explained Mbina's symptoms to Bavone, the medic, and added my unsolicited diagnosis: malaria. Bavone took her temperature and questioned her in Sango. Since Mbina knew little Sango, Adamo acted as interpreter. Actually Mbina answered Bavone's questions in monosyllables — Adamo did most of the talking. Finally Bavone turned to me.

"Her temperature is normal," he said. "She doesn't have malaria — she was punched in the nose by her husband."

Her husband? I thought. When did Mbina get married? Now I noticed that the dark stains on her face were dried blood. Bavone gave her some water and a cloth to clean it off and told me to give her an aspirin when we got back to camp.

On our return walk, I decided that Bavone must have gotten it wrong about Mbina's husband. I questioned Adamo. He confirmed that it was her husband who had hit her.

"Who's her husband?" I asked, flabbergasted.

Adamo thought a moment and said, "Engulé." I knew Engulé. I had never witnessed the slightest contact between him and Mbina. How was it possible that they were married?

"When did they get married?" I asked.

"Tomorrow," Adamo replied.

By the time we reached Amopolo I was seething. How could anyone hit Mbina? I realized I had no right to interfere, but I felt too protective of her to let the incident pass without reprimand. Engulé was anxiously awaiting our return. I was gratified to note that he looked thoroughly dejected. I marched directly over to him even as he came forward to see how Mbina was.

"So you hit Mbina?" I shouted loud enough for everyone to hear. Engulé nodded sadly. "If you ever hit her again," I continued, shaking my fist, "I'll hit you and knock your teeth out!" Several women chuckled. On the way to my hut I heard them repeating my threat to one another and laughing with approval.

Mbina's marriage threw me into a pit of depression. It had happened so fast, without warning, and I had been completely unaware of it. Goma was older than Mbina. With my ignorance of Bayaka life, she could have gotten married right under my nose, and I wouldn't have suspected a thing. She had been gone for more than a week. Earlier I had had the reassuring impression that the Bayaka were cooperating in a plan to bring Goma and me together. That feeling now vanished completely, as if it had been an illusion all along.

EVERY DAY I had to deal with the Bayaka's requests for cigarettes, marijuana, money, soap, batteries, razor blades, peanut butter, and almost anything else they could think of. In my despondent mood I found their relentless bombardment heartless. Didn't they understand how I felt? Their demands for cigarettes, always so cocksure, annoyed me most of all, especially when they didn't ask, but merely made the gesture for smoking. I began to complain. My huge stock-pile of cigarettes had been reduced to a single carton in just two weeks.

One day I discovered that six packs had been stolen. It was the first theft I had ever experienced at Amopolo and I was shocked. I bitterly announced in the *mbanjo* that I would stop giving out ciga-rettes. The men agreed that things had gone too far. After that their demands for cigarettes dropped to zero and I was allowed to sulk in peace. Every couple of days one of the elders would hand me a pack of cigarettes without comment: first Dimba, then Mobo, then Bombé. The stolen packs were slowly resurfacing.

"Those cigarettes weren't stolen," Joboko confided one evening as he slipped me a pack. "You were being bothered too much. Sim-bu's behind this." Joboko tapped his head. "Simbu — he has very deep strategy."

Later that afternoon I returned from a nap in the forest to find Sombolo and Bakpima waiting in my hut. They had been waiting, they claimed, a long time. I gave them each a cigarette and asked what was on their minds. For a moment they looked at me curi-ously. Finally Sombolo rattled off a sentence in Yaka. It sounded like, "My daughter is going to be your wife."

I was taken aback. For one instant I thought: can he mean Goma? I had assumed that she was Akunga's daughter. On the other hand, aware of my propensity for misinterpreting the lan-guage in embarrassing ways, I merely mumbled, "Your daughter?"

"*Oui*," Sombolo replied. "My daughter Ngbali."

Now I was shocked. Who the hell was Ngbali?

"Do you understand?" Bakpima asked.

"No," I lied desperately.

"Ngbali is your wife," Bakpima enunciated carefully, leaving no room for doubt.

Thanks a lot, I thought sarcastically. "Huh?" I grunted, trying to look completely thick.

"He understands," Sombolo said with a laugh. Satisfied, they left.

That evening Goma was back. I saw her from a distance, but she knew that I saw her. For the first time the family resemblance struck me — how could I have been so blind? She was Sombolo's daughter. And I suddenly understood the mystery of the two names, for it was fairly common for a Moaka to have nicknames. Goma/Ngbali, running around and playing with some children with show-off energy, caught me watching her. She made a quick motion with her hands and mouthed some words at me, as if saying, *Well, what do you want?* Now I began to wonder too: what *did* I want?

Sombolo returned the next morning and asked me point blank: did I want to marry Ngbali or not? There were many practical objections to such a marriage, but I had scarcely begun to think them through. Now I tossed out the most obvious one: what would happen when I returned to America? Sombolo was ready: Ngbali would go with me — she wanted to. When I objected that she wouldn't like America, that she would be too lonely, he dismissed my concern with an easy smile — she would be with me, and if she didn't like America I would bring her back, of course. I knew I could never hope to explain the problems of passports, money, and language, nor how different a world America was. They were completely outside Sombolo's experience. He made everything sound so simple. Incredibly, as we talked, I felt that it really might all be possible.

"Well?" Sombolo asked, inviting any last objections.

I fought off the temptation to say yes. "Let me think about it," I replied.

Over the following days Ngbali avoided my neighborhood, though she remained highly visible in the distance with her wild antics. Often our eyes met, invariably provoking that motion of her hands that challenged me to make clear my intentions. There was no longer any doubt about her intentions. As for me, I knew I had fallen hopelessly in love with her. It didn't matter that we had never exchanged more than a single word — night after night she had danced for my eyes. Her slightest gesture was enough to reveal her presence to me among a chorus of women on a moonless night. She exerted a kind of gravitational pull on my consciousness. I still hadn't thought through the implications of marrying her, but the issue really boiled down to this: if I refused, I could lose her forever.

One afternoon on my way to bathe I noticed Ngbali sitting in the entrance to a beehive hut I was passing. I hadn't seen much of her the last couple of days, and it was beginning to worry me.

"*Elobayé*," I said with a smile, hoping to elicit a friendly response.

"Make up your mind soon or it's over!" she retorted with an angry wave of her arm.

That evening I got out the bottle of perfume I had bought weeks earlier in the village and slipped it into my pocket. It was nothing special, but it was the very best money could buy in Bomandjombo. The perfume would be my most lavish gift. Part of me knew that I was, in effect, about to propose marriage. I pretended to ignore that fact, however, as I emerged from my hut and walked toward Ngbali.

She was, unusually, by herself, climbing on the bamboo framework of Akunga's unfinished hut as though it were a jungle gym. Seeing her alone prompted me to action. I found it difficult to conduct private business under the public gaze of everyone at camp. I knew everyone was watching me now, so I walked nonchalantly, hoping to disguise my destination until the last moment. As soon as Ngbali saw me heading her way she got down from the bars, crawled under the lowest one, and sat in front of Akunga's hut, waiting. I handed her the perfume without a word. The whole village had fallen silent. She accepted with silent gravity. As I began to walk away, someone clapped. I turned and saw Simbu with a broad, approving grin on his face. He had been observing everything from his hut. Behind me, Ngbali was already sampling the perfume with her girl friends, who had appeared out of nowhere.

As darkness fell, the drums, which had been dragged over to Ewunji's small clearing, filled the night with a smooth pulsating rhythm. Now and then the scent of blossoms drifted over from the forest, a heady fragrance that I breathed in deeply. Women from Ewunji's camp massed together and sang. The music, softly sung in the middle registers, involved a lot of yodeling. I had not heard this particular music before and wondered if it was a specialty of Ewunji's group. A little earlier Sombolo had taken me on a brief tour of his neighborhood, pointing out the various members of his extended family. Ewunji was his father, which made this group of women the family I was marrying into. Ngbali was not among them, but I felt her presence keenly. From all around rose the scent of her perfume. It was cheap stuff, but tonight at the edge of the rain forest it smelled exhilarating and exotic.

The music began to fade around midnight. I had been hoping for at least a glimpse of Ngbali, but finally at Adamo's suggestion I got up to leave. We were making our way among a cluster of beehive huts when I felt a forceful tug on my arm. As I whipped around I heard giggles and caught a flash of Ngbali disappearing into a hut.

"She answers you now!" Adamo exclaimed.

"Answers what?" I asked, happy but puzzled.

"You want to marry Ngbali," Adamo explained. "Ngbali — she tells you *yes*."

SIX

The Bees of Mombongo

THE NEXT MORNING at first light Singali woke me and told me to pack my things — we were moving into the forest. I had read that the Pygmies moved into the forest seasonally, usually at the end of the dry season (which it now was), and that they were wont to make their move at a moment's notice. But I was unprepared for the suddenness of the decision. I hurriedly threw together my essentials: camera, recorder, microphones, a dozen batteries, a dozen cassettes, and my diary. Accessories like sheets, sleeping mat, spare shirts, and a change of trousers would follow later, carried by the women in their baskets. I entrusted my solar recharger to Simbu, who with several other families was staying behind to "guard" Amopolo. I reasoned it would be of little use in the rain forest.

Singali and I set off ahead of the others. As we walked south on the dirt road I tried to understand my situation. The facts were clear enough — I was betrothed to a beautiful woman, I was going to live in the tropical forest with the Bayaka, whom I must now regard as family in the literal sense — but I had not yet registered the emotional impact of these extraordinary circumstances. I was poised on the edge of a life that was almost too incredible to believe in.

Now and then Singali interrupted with remarks that I would ordinarily have found interesting but that I felt now as mundane disruptions of my high-altitude reverie.

"Elephants came out of the forest here last night. Ooh! That was one big elephant!"

"Mm-hmm," I replied with a glance at the tracks.

"Look! That's where they went back into the forest."

"Oh," I said.

After turning east and cutting across an overgrown manioc garden, we entered the forest. The transition between the bright outside world and the darkness of the forest was always impressive, but now the sense of leaving one world behind and entering another was heightened by the thought that I might not come out of the forest for months. The plan today was to go hunting until noon, when a group of us would break off from the main party to set up camp.

During the hunt I noticed that many women carried all their possessions in their baskets: aluminum pots, wooden mortars, bowls, even reed mats rolled up and sticking way out over the top. Some of the loads were larger than the women carrying them. The sight of Ngbali with her possessions reassured me, for no one had told me she was coming with us.

Around noon I left with Adamo, Joboko, and a group of women to establish the new camp. It had been agreed that we would camp near a stream called Mombongo. After wandering slowly along and arguing about prospective sites, we settled on an almost level piece of ground near the bottom of a vast slope covered in *bimba* forest. Fifty yards down the hill was the marshy fringe of the Mombongo.

Everyone set to work on what looked at first like a random attack on the jungle. Groups spread out and chopped down bushes and saplings. Using machetes, they scraped the forest floor clear of litter. While fallen leaves make a wonderful soft carpet to walk and lounge on, they are the daytime refuge of millipedes, scorpions, and the giant centipede, which is venemous enough to kill a small child. Large trees were left standing. Soon there were several small clearings joined by a network of paths. Women went off with machetes. The rustle of foliage and the sound of metallic blows filled the air.

They returned carrying bundles of *bimba* saplings, thin and supple, and started work on their beehive huts. Each sapling was forced into the ground and the top was bent over and twisted together with another one. The frameworks went up quickly.

Meanwhile the young men had collected their own *bimba* saplings. Now they began to make a large shelter that was open at the front and sides. It was our *mbanjo*, and here in the forest it would serve a double function: as a meeting place in the daytime and as a sleeping place for teenage boys, bachelors, and widowers at night. While some teenagers busied themselves tiling the roof with large oval *ngungu* leaves, others constructed the sleeping platforms. Mine was put up at one end of the *mbanjo*. About two feet of space separated it from what turned out to be Bombé's. The other platforms, narrower than mine, would be shared by three or four men.

Late in the afternoon the hunters arrived. The hunt had been a great success. There was lively conversation as the game was divided up between those of us who would remain in the forest and those who were returning to Amopolo. The layout of the camp was slowly taking shape; the *mbanjo* faced the largest cleared area, at whose perimeter a few huts had been set up. Beyond the surrounding bush were several small groups of huts. During the afternoon our presence had attracted huge numbers of sweat bees. These tiny insects had no sting, but they tickled as they crawled on the skin, looking for sweat, and their persistence in homing in on our eyes was maddening. They were soon joined by a slightly larger variety of bee, equally intent on sweat. I had encountered both types of bees many times during hunts. Today, however, I was about to make a new and formidable acquaintance: the honeybee.

As work on the campsite progressed, tens of thousands of honeybees invaded the area. Attracted by our activity as much as by the exotic smells we brought with us, the honeybees investigated every square inch of camp, including the people. They were slightly longer than American honeybees, thinner and darker, with a loud aggressive buzz that was matched by their boldness in action. A few flaps of the hand did little to discourage them, and their sheer numbers rendered any attempt to resist futile. The Bayaka generally let them have their way, so bees crawled on their backs and legs, up their arms, down their necks. They ignored the bees even when they hovered, buzzing furiously, an inch in front of their noses.

Sitting on a log next to Adamo, I tried to match the Bayaka's composure during the bees' onslaught. Earlier I had snapped a roll of film to document the rapidly transforming campsite. Now I was jotting down observations in my diary. The bees were holding a parade on my back. *Many people would be driven crazy by the bugs,* I wrote, and gloatingly went on: *Fortunately I'm not so bothered.* I paused to scratch an itch behind my ear. Immediately I felt a stab of pain. A honeybee, mortally wounded when its sting detached in my ear, wobbled off on its final flight. Adamo removed the sting and I rubbed some ash on the wound (a trick I had learned from the Bayaka), which quickly assuaged the pain. *I must admit, however,* I continued, *that they are a nuisance.* Zap! A bolt of intense pain shot through me, and I scrabbled wildly at my armpit. Another honeybee buzzed off. I rubbed ash on the wound, but the pain persisted for several minutes. The lymph gland where I had been stung started to balloon.

Writing was no longer possible. I put away my diary and watched the activity around me. Ngbali, visible through a chink in the foliage, cast a glance my way now and then. All at once my heart shifted into high gear, racing like an engine at full throttle. I knew I had every reason to be elated, but my heart's reaction was a little scary. I shifted my position on the log and concentrated on Ngbali. She was laughing as she talked to someone beyond my view. She hardly looked real anymore, receding into a dreamlike illusion. *Everything* was turning into a dream. With a start I realized that I was not feeling well. I jumped to my feet. My field of vision started to darken at the edges, to sparkle with flashes of bright emptiness. Sounds grew muffled. I was breathing, but no air seemed to reach my lungs. Suddenly I had a terrifying insight: *it was the bee sting!*

Both my mother and sister had potentially fatal allergic reactions to bee stings and had to carry emergency treatment kits wherever they went. If they got stung, they had to inject themselves with epinephrine to counteract the anaphylactic shock reaction. I had been stung by wasps, bees, hornets, and yellow jackets many times and had never had an adverse reaction. But a remark my sister once made came back to me with frightening clarity: the allergy could develop in anyone at any time — all it took was one extra sting to provoke it. Besides, weren't allergies inherited?

I paced around nervously, drawing in deep breaths to no avail. My heart was racing, and I could barely draw breath, but even in the midst of my distress I didn't want to alarm the Bayaka. I wondered what they would think when I suddenly keeled over before their eyes. I felt sorry for them — they would never figure it out. I wanted to explain, but how could I hope to begin?

Consciousness ebbing rapidly, I shuffled toward a pile of leaves on the other side of the log. It looked like the perfect place to lie down and die. As I tried to step over the log, my strength vanished and I collapsed onto the ground. My dying thought was *poor Bayaka!*

ADAMO AND JOBOKO were kneeling over me when I regained consciousness. I had been out for just a few seconds. As I sat up I broke into a profuse sweat, which further alarmed the two men. I remembered that the fatal allergy to bee venom was usually heralded by a severe reaction like mine; the next sting could kill me. And at the moment my back was crawling with honeybees. I sat perfectly still.

I tried to explain to the bewildered Adamo and Joboko the threat the bees posed for me. Adamo proceeded to fan and brush the bees off my back until a small swarm of enraged insects hovered around my head. I urged him to desist. I knew that the bees would return to their hives at dusk. Already the sun's orange light had left the ground and was splashed across the upper trunks and foliage of the tallest trees.

During the briefest of twilights the bees departed. With the onset of night came a profound darkness. The many campfires created pockets of light, illuminating the nearest branches and vines, but beyond lay impenetrable murk. From the darkness rose an astonishing conglomeration of noises — buzzes, chirps, croaks, clicks, and rasps — a dazzling electronic din. The Bayaka too seemed to be filling their small niche in the forest with loud and boisterous sound. I had the impression of a dark, timeless immensity pressing in around us. Our tiny community was so fragile by contrast, so transitory, that I found the thought of it too vivid to bear. I must be in shock, I realized. I had never had an allergic reaction — now here I was in the middle of the rain forest, barely recovered from a fatal brush with bee venom. Bees are more common than flies in the forest, rivaled in numbers only by ants and termites. They are the supreme commanders of all but the debris on the forest floor. And I used to love bees! Now they had become my mortal enemy. That I should develop the allergy on my first night in the forest with the Bayaka struck me as a great irony.

I thought about Ngbali. Should I go through with the marriage now, with such a debilitating handicap? I knew it would be unfair. Then again, how could I just give her up? I resolved on a compromise: I would tell Ngbali and her family about my allergy and let them decide whether to cancel the marriage.

Sombolo's enclave consisted of five huts. It was a small family grouping based on his wife, Yéyé's, relations, which I had just begun to piece together. The family I knew best, which had taken me under its wing from the very beginning, was Singali's, presided over by his mother, Esoosi. Through marriages her family included many important personages, from Simbu and Mobo (sons-in-law) to Adamo (nephew) to Dimba (grandfather of two of Esoosi's great-granddaughters) to Joboko (brother-in-law).

Ngbali's immediate family included her parents, Sombolo and Yéyé, and a four-year-old brother, Ayoosi. The wide gap in age between Ngbali (about sixteen) and Ayoosi almost certainly meant that siblings from the intervening years had died. Yéyé was several months pregnant. Though I was betrothed to her daughter, we had never exchanged a word. I had excellent relations with most of the women, but I had had no contact with Yéyé. She had not even taken part in any of those mad giveaway sessions.

As soon as I came into the family enclave, Yéyé slid a bowl of food toward me without comment. I found her silence, which at first I attributed to shyness, mildly unsettling. Sombolo, Mowooma (Yéyé's brother), and I chatted amiably while I ate, and Ngbali sat nearby and listened. There was a noticeable uplift in the Bayaka's spirits now that we had established ourselves in the forest. By contrast, I felt weighed down by private concerns, and I deliberated how, with my rudimentary Yaka, I would explain my problem with bees. Even if my language had been fluent, my predicament would strike the Bayaka as ridiculous. It was difficult enough to accept it myself. Each passing moment made it seem less real.

A lively racket had started up in the vicinity of the *mbanjo* — a percussion battery of pots and pans, since the drums had been left behind at Amopolo. The sound of the drumming gave no clue to the materials used to produce it. The deepest tones came from an empty plastic motor oil container handled by Kukpata. A number of children sang along in a chorus that had an unusually bright quality. By the time I finished my meal the music was in high gear. Girls and women had joined the children in what became a full-fledged *eboka*. In talking with Ngbali's family I had done no more than hint at my allergy, and now I realized it was too late to continue with my dismal story.

"Listen!" I said. "*Eboka!*"

"Let's go," Ngbali eagerly replied.

We picked our way through the dark toward the *mbanjo*. Ngbali joined the women sitting on the ground, and I lost sight of her. I stepped carefully over a sprinkling of glowing ashes and sat down with the men. The singing retained the bright sound I had noticed earlier, despite the contribution of many older women. Usually their participation lent an ambivalence to the *eboka*, tempering a mood of unmitigated joy with more subtle undercurrents. What I was hearing now, however, possessed little aural depth. From the children to the oldest woman the sound was one of unrestrained celebration. From song to song, the mood grew more powerful.

Despite my lingering emotional shock I was gradually carried away by the sheer exuberance of the music. Adding to my deepening pleasure were the movements of two dancers who emerged very slowly from the darkness. They were invisible but for the splashes of moonlight that reached them through breaks in the canopy. Their dancing was characterized by an economy of motion that contrasted sharply with the joyous energy of the singing. I thought it unlikely that anyone young would dance in such a manner. There was a kind of wisdom in the style as it related to the music that I found quite moving. As the figures advanced I wondered if they might be Bombé and Dimba, the two oldest men at Mombongo.

Then, with a start, I realized that there was no moon. The night possessed the thick and absolute gloom of a cave. The campfires had all been extinguished, and hardly a log continued to glow. Yet there on the ground around me lay the dappled pattern of moonlight — only now I saw that it wasn't moonlight but phosphorescence. The jungle floor was littered with speckles of silvery green light.

By now the two dancers had reached the center of the clearing. They looked like glowing skeletons. Each had a distinct face outlined in phosphorescent material — not the faint specks from the forest floor but bright solid bars. Additional strips of phosphorescence were cleverly arranged to suggest bodily forms. When the song that had lured them so far into the clearing ended, the two dancers scampered off. One retreated with a swift lurching walk; the other dropped down on all fours and pranced off into the darkness, its movements uncannily animal-like.

With each song the glowing *mokoondi* returned. Sometimes they ran off skittishly, only to come back a moment later, irresistibly drawn by the music. At other times they boldly moved right over to the singers. I grew aware of other glimmers of light moving swiftly through the darkness around the camp. They would vanish behind trees, emerge dancing with tiny movements so that they seemed to glide, then bound away again among the trees.

Only after the *eboka* ended, as I crawled into my bed in the *mbanjo* — Bombé was already snoring away on the sleeping platform next to mine — did I realize that I had neglected to record the music. I wasn't unduly upset, however. I knew that the night had been only a glimpse of the marvels to come.

SHORTLY AFTER DAWN the distinctive high-strung buzz of a honeybee woke me from my oblivious slumber. *Bees*, I remembered and opened my eyes. A few were already darting about. Occasionally one flew up to my face to check me out. They got up with the rising sun, and from now on so would I. Camp was already fairly lively, though I was far from the last one up. Groups of boys were still curled together on the sleeping platforms, five or six to a bed, each group huddled under a single sheet as though willfully denying the advent of day. I dressed hastily and tried to make myself bee-proof: trousers tucked into my socks, a long-sleeve shirt buttoned up to my throat. During my stroll around camp I noticed that bees went berserk over manioc flour. Clouds of them hovered around the mortars filled with it. Many buried themselves in the flour, emerging white only to dive back in again. Even a sprinkling of flour on the ground was enough to attract several dozen.

Eventually I learned to relax in the presence of the bees, though I always remained alert. As the days passed, their investigative frenzy abated and they focused most of their attention on manioc. They gathered the flour the same way they gathered pollen, but their mania for it struck me as unnatural. Sometimes individual bees would load up with so much flour to take back to the hive that they couldn't fly. They showed little interest in anything else. I discovered that I could pass through a swarm of manioc-crazed bees without distracting a single one from its purpose.

On that first morning at Mombongo, however, my chances for survival seemed slim. The danger lay not so much in the bees' aggressiveness, for they never stung out of malice, but in moments of inattention, when I might absent-mindedly scratch an itch that turned out to be an inquisitive bee. The bee might very well respond by stinging in self-defense. I had already been stung twice that way, and I was disheartened by the number of similar stinging incidents all around me. Adamo's baby son, Tutu, was stung on the eyelid, and the swelling practically closed his eye. It looked serious, but his parents showed only mild concern. I envied the casual manner in which adults reacted to stings, with no more than a sharp intake of breath at the momentary pain. Obviously bee stings were a fact of life in the forest. I was sure it would be only a short time before I would be stung again.

I spent most mornings at Sombolo's hut, which always seemed to be lightly dusted with manioc flour. Bees were everywhere. Ngbali would be busy pounding manioc in the midst of her own personal swarm. Sitting near her, I soon became a target of their attention, and they would collect in my hair. Ngbali rarely spoke directly to me, and whenever I spoke to her in my rudimentary

Yaka she would turn away and giggle. Her former boldness had given way to modesty, and I wasn't sure what to do. I engaged Sombolo and Mowooma in small talk and took comfort in the fact that Ngbali was always nearby listening.

After breakfast at Sombolo's, I would change into shorts and set off on the hunt with the men. The women would follow at their leisure. It was always a relief to leave camp in the morning. On the move in the forest we hardly ever encountered honeybees. I would pass most of the day near Sombolo's family, for I was anxious to be of some help. Though I was now adroit at moving through the forest, I was useless as a hunter to my new family, and painfully aware of my uselessness. Several times in those early weeks I rushed animals momentarily caught in Sombolo's net, only to be beaten to the catch by Ngbali herself. Even if I had succeeded in securing an occasional animal, the Bayaka would not have regarded it as much of a feat. A man's hunting skill was measured by his ability to drive game into his own net or spear it on the run. Securing game already in the nets was the work of women and children.

Once we came across an area strewn with *mayingoyo*, a large edible berry. The fruit on the ground was already too rotten to eat, but the branches above were heavy with additional clusters. When Ngbali saw me rummaging through the fallen specimens for an edible one, she called her uncle Zalogwé over to fetch me some from the tree. He grabbed two lianas, one in each hand, and swiftly pulled himself up them until he reached the fruit, forty feet above. I could not help but feel somewhat humiliated. Increasingly I wondered what kind of permanent role I could ever play in their society.

Aside from these private misgivings, I enjoyed our daily hunting trips immensely. In the mornings the forest dripped with the mist that still shrouded the canopy and concealed flocks of noisy parrots. Sometimes our approach sent black hornbills into flight with a loud creaky rush of wings, their bulbous beaks looking vaguely prehistoric.

Mowooma turned out to be one of the best hunters; it was not unusual for him to catch two or three blue duikers a day. Often it was his catch that fed Ngbali's family and me in the evening. Adamo was also a good hunter. One day, catching two animals in the first hour of the hunt, he came over to me full of excitement. "Hunting is great!" he exclaimed. "For ten years I grew manioc, and for ten years I was hungry. Now at last I'm eating meat again!"

The hunt began to wind down in the late afternoon. By the time we returned to camp there was only an hour or so of light left. A particularly successful hunt meant that the Bayaka could indulge, immediately upon their return to camp, in one of their favorite practices: eating meat *suya*. Prized items like duiker hearts and sirloin were rubbed in salt and chilies, roasted directly in the fire, and devoured. Porcupine was a highly regarded *suya* delicacy, as was the giant forest hog, rich in tender fat. I discovered that I could eat huge amounts of meat, and at Mombongo I ate like a glutton. Everybody did. There was no thought of saving food for the morrow.

AT MOMBONGO night was a respite from the bees, which retired to their hives at sunset, relinquishing their command of the air until morning. Another daytime plague, a yellow fly the Bayaka called *tuna*, which carried the parasitic filaria larvae, also disappeared promptly at twilight. With the arrival of night I was aware of one of the most precious blessings of the forest: no mosquitoes. Night was the time for crickets, fireflies (which the Bayaka called "stars"), and a host of katydid-like bugs that advertised themselves at high decibel level in the bushes and trees. The forest floor at night became the stomping ground of driver ants, whose raids occasionally rendered a corner of camp uninhabitable for several hours.

One night as I went to bed I placed my sneakers, contrary to habit, on the ground outside the *mbanjo*. I awoke in the middle of the night to a soft crackling noise that rose and fell from the nearby ground. A fire? I wondered. When I turned on my flashlight, I discovered that my sneakers were being pincered to shreds by thousands of termites. The crackling noise was the snapping of their mandibles, which they synchronized into bursts of collective chewing punctuated by silences. Even as they tore my sneakers apart I watched, fascinated. When I finally rescued my shoes, one of the soldiers bit my finger and drew blood. The damage to my sneakers was considerable: the canvas frayed, the rubber soles pockmarked by tiny bites.

The onset of night always had the same effect on me. Each moment became vivid and at the same time dreamlike. At first I attributed this sensation to my continuing fear of having a dangerous allergy. Later I decided it might be the result of the high oxygen content of the air. All day the forest produces oxygen through photosynthesis. At night the process is reversed — the trees absorb oxygen and release carbon dioxide. But just as the sun-heated ocean always seems warmest in the evening, even as the source of its warmth vanishes below the horizon, so in the evenings the forest air seemed heavy with oxygen, heightening my senses for a few hours, before acting like a soporific and sending me into a profound and dreamless slumber.

But at Mombongo night was rarely a time for sleep. It was the time of the *mokoondi*, pulsating, parading, dancing, and floating phosphorescent forms that flew through the air with reckless speed, a gallery of glowing faces, forest beings, animals, creatures, and dots. At Amopolo the women had to sing for hours to summon the *mokoondi*, and usually they did not come. At Mombongo a single yodel in the evening often drew the *mokoondi*, who would cry out from the surrounding forest. When everyone was asleep, they moved invisibly through the camp, popping leaves, thumping the ground, making kissing noises, and whistling tunes that might have been composed by Moussorgsky. If we failed to rouse ourselves for the music the *mokoondi* became demanding, their harassment violent and vociferous as they shook and pounded on huts, shrieking, "Push yourselves!"

And the Bayaka did. A full night's sleep was never guaranteed. Some nights the women were careful *not* to sing, indicating a collective decision to try to catch up on sleep. Nonetheless the *mokoondi* might strike at midnight, setting in motion an *eboka* that would last until four. Or they might raid the camp at three in the morning for an *eboka* that continued into the dawn, by which time the *mokoondi* would have transformed themselves into one or two large bushes.

As the weeks went by I began to recognize several of the spirits. The most vocal, whom the Bayaka called "the elder," was a large-headed creature of tremendous and inexhaustible vitality. It ran on all fours but danced upright, often in such rapid tiny movements that it seemed to glide or float. One was a dot that looped and whirled through the air like a fairy light, except that its energy was violent and unpredictable. One spirit had a long glowing penis. Their presence filled the camp with the pungent odor of damp, organic earth, a smell that would persist well into the next day. This was distinct from the fresh, leafy fragrance that the bush *mokoondi* left behind.

Despite the magical nature of the spirits, and my own willing suspension of disbelief, I could not help but form almost unconscious associations, not based on anything tangible, between certain spirits and certain of the men. Already at Amopolo I had begun to "identify" some of the *mokoondi*. On occasion I thought I recognized both Balonyona and Mabuti. Now at Mombongo, I began to "identify" a number of the phosphorescent *mokoondi*. The strongest of these impressions concerned the "elder," who unmistakably put me in mind of Adamo. There was some indefinable quality in Adamo's voice that I thought I could hear in the elder's piercing falsetto.

On some nights I counted more than twenty glowing *mokoondi*. Naturally they shunned light. Once, as someone lit a cigarette, the flare from the match sent them scattering among the trees. It took thirty minutes of singing to coax them back into camp. The speed at which they moved, not only through camp but in the surrounding forest, presumably ducking branches and leaping over roots in the dark, was uncanny. Whenever I moved in such darkness, I shuffled forward in tiny cautious steps with one hand out to protect my face. But perhaps the *mokoondi* were not quite as transcendent as they seemed. One night, during a particularly splendid ceremony that went on for hours, populating the camp with glowing forms, Singali came over and asked me for bandages. I rummaged through my pack and handed him some, but twice he returned for more. Finally the *mokoondi* broke off the ceremony abruptly and withdrew into the forest. Flashlights were switched on, and I was led behind a group of huts where Singali and others had been trying in vain to stop a bleeding gash on Engulé's head. He had obviously bumped it very hard.

Total darkness posed extra problems for recording these ceremonies, but it did not stop me. I learned to operate my recorder by feel. I devised a way to rotate the cassettes from pocket to pocket so that I would not record on the same cassette twice and would know in the morning the order in which they had been recorded. I was convinced I was hearing the most sublime music on earth. It no longer resembled "Pygmy" music to me — it no longer even resembled African music. It was beyond all such distinctions, a world unto itself. I recorded everything, not because I thought the opportunity unique (on the contrary, I believed I would have countless similar opportunities), but from an urge to preserve as much as I could from what I now regarded as the happiest period of my life. I will long for these days, I told myself while living them.

WITHIN A COUPLE OF WEEKS the population of our forest camp had stabilized at around sixty people. Joboko and Dimba, who helped establish the camp, returned to Amopolo after a few days. Others, like Mobo and his family, joined us later. Singali moved out to Mombongo with his third wife but constantly commuted between village and forest. Engulé and Mbina were at Mombongo, living together for the first time in a tiny hut whose entrance was no higher than my knees. Ewunji had brought out his entire group, including Sombolo's brothers, Zalogwé and Ndima. Bombé continued to sleep in the *mbanjo*, having once again split up with his wife, Balé. Balé herself occasionally showed up for a few days, but refused even to talk to Bombé. Bakpima, another of the original Mombongo pioneers, moved back to Amopolo after a fortnight — all too soon, for he was a marvelous singer who inspired the women when their energies were flagging or unfocused. Balonyona's absence disappointed me. I had no idea why he had stayed behind.

At Mombongo the Bayaka seemed to slide effortlessly into a more traditional lifestyle. It was gratifying to note the return of the beehive hut. I had read that the women constructed these huts in a matter of hours, but in fact the process was never quite finished. The women were constantly refining the designs — adding rooms, extending entranceways, leafing and releafing. Sometimes a hut was scarcely built when the woman, for reasons I could never fathom, tore it down and began again from scratch.

Even at Amopolo the women were usually engaged in traditional activities like basket weaving. But at Mombongo their traditional activities became more diverse. The men, on the other hand, were apt to stray far from the center of their cultural identity when they lived at Amopolo. The change in their behavior at Mombongo was all the more impressive. Gone was the gathering of raffia leaves for the villagers, gone too the frequent sorties in search of *mbaku*. Even idle moments were used to some purpose. While the men sat around and talked, their hands were constantly busy, sharpening arrows, stripping off the fibrous strands of a forest creeper to make *kusa*, rope for their nets. They accomplished these tasks with less apparent effort than it takes to knit.

The process of making *kusa* was laborious. First the vine was collected and cut into two-foot lengths. Then the bark was peeled off and the rest of the vine thrown away. Both these stages usually took place during the hunt. Back at camp the men separated the useful strands of fiber from the bark and allowed them to dry for several days. They would twist the fibers on their thighs into rope, adding piece onto piece, and slowly accumulating a ball of twine. Making enough rope for a seventy-five-foot hunting net took three months!

Some of the men underwent a transformation of personality so extreme as to be unrecognizable. A good example was Mobo. Though I had glimpsed his potential on hunts — he moved through the forest with a lethal silence — his usual mode of existence at Amopolo might be described as oscillating between the lazy and the dissolute. His favorite activity was lounging around in the shade and smoking massive amounts of marijuana on the big pipe, napping between each hefty toke. Now and then he would go on a drinking binge; being small of frame, he did not need much to get loaded. He obtained money for these pastimes through honest work occasionally, but far more often he used his considerable powers of persuasion to con money out of villagers for work or goods he never intended to deliver. Such was his talent that he could return to clients he had burned before and burn them again. At Mombongo, however, he was always the first to leave camp in the mornings, even before daylight penetrated the canopy, and the last to return in the evenings, when dusk had already settled in. Wearing only a loincloth, a large quiver of small poisoned arrows over one shoulder and a spear over the other, he would set off alone to stalk game with his crossbow. Rarely did he take part in the net hunt, for his extraordinary stealth was best suited for the crossbow. Sometimes, however, he left his crossbow behind and went to gather honey. Mobo loved honey.

Most remarkable of all was the change that came over Sombolo. The woman I had fallen in love with was the daughter of the undisputed champion drinker at Amopolo. Most of the older men were always ready to down a glass of *mbaku*, but Sombolo positively craved it. I had never seen him completely sober and could not imagine what he would be like without alcohol. With only a little drink in him he became a good-natured buffoon, usually beating the drum to get an *eboka* going. When he was moderately drunk his dancing grew more acrobatic and comical, and at this stage of inebriation he earned his reputation, especially among the villagers, as the best dancer in the region. When he was plastered, as he all too often was, his dancing degenerated into a struggle against gravity; he became the butt of children's laughter and a truly pathetic sight.

At Mombongo I had my first view of a sober Sombolo, and he turned out to be a formidable character. All trace of buffoonery disappeared. He seemed possessed by a controlled tension, like a tightly coiled spring, heightened by a sensory alertness that struck me as unnaturally keen. He was a marvelous mimic. I had already seen his gorilla imitation, a performance he was easily persuaded into whenever he was drunk, but now he directed his sharp powers of observation at his fellow Bayaka. One night he made us laugh until we ached with an imitation of Adamo's version of reading. He concluded with the telling remark that when he witnessed behavior like that, he really doubted there was any hope for the Bayaka.

My stay at Mombongo would not have had the same meaning without Ngbali. Something in her eyes seemed immeasurably distant, even unreachable, as though she were looking at me from across the gap between two worlds. When our eyes met, as they did often at Mombongo, I felt that I was in touch with a timeless aspect of the forest. Yet try as I might I could not define it. Although her exposure to village life was no less than anyone else's, Ngbali was one of the least acculturated inhabitants of Amopolo. She scarcely knew a word of Sango, and she obviously felt at home in the forest. It was something in her very nature, and it gave her a beauty I could not have imagined beforehand. Every time I looked at her she was more beautiful than I remembered, as though memory were incapable of containing it.

The sleeping arrangements at Mombongo suggested that Ngbali and I would not be spending any nights together. I slept in the *mbanjo*, the most public place in camp. Ngbali lived with her parents and little brother in a beehive hut. The apparent purpose of our being at Mombongo was to allow us to become acquainted under the best possible circumstances. This arrangement set up an indelible association in my mind between Ngbali and the forest. Through her my relation to the forest was personalized, and in time I could not imagine the forest without her, nor could I ever be content with a relationship to the forest that did not include her.

On the hunts now Ngbali had precious little to do. Sometimes she helped her father set up his net, but usually she left this duty to her mother. She rarely took an *eekwa* (carrying basket), though the younger girls routinely did — testifying to her special status as the bride-to-be of the "rich" white man. Her main task seemed to be carrying Mowooma's baby daughter, Etu, of whom she seemed particularly fond. She used her machete mostly in pointless activities, such as hacking sticks into little pieces or digging holes in the ground, that merely showed off her extraordinary energy. The only person with less responsibility on these hunts was myself. About the only thing I did was watch Ngbali, whose every gesture I found entirely captivating.

Ngbali no longer made an effort to remain near me as she had on the hunting trips before our engagement. She would move in and out of my view like some kind of elusive spirit. One moment she would be sitting on the ground a few yards away, but if I blinked my eyes or fanned the sweat bees from my face, I would discover that she had noiselessly disappeared. The one occasion when she spoke directly to me only made her more mysterious. We were in a lovely stretch of *bimba* forest, with little undergrowth. I was lounging with the men during a lunch break. The women were off a little ways, also lounging. Ngbali, sitting with Mimba, her uncle Zalogwé's wife, caught me looking at her. She began to speak to me, almost chiding me, it seemed, and gesturing emphatically with her hands. Her voice was so low that even had I been fluent in Yaka I would have missed her message. Nevertheless, I felt that I was meant to understand. Mimba, who alone might have heard what Ngbali was saying, motioned me to come over. But by then Ngbali's boldness had evaporated. When I asked her what she had said, she ignored me. Instead she faced away from me, busily digging a hole in the ground.

That incident left me feeling that things were not quite right. But it was not repeated, and with the many favorable incidents on each subsequent hunt, I let it go. Admittedly her glances were not as open and inviting as before. Sometimes I thought I could detect something slightly critical in them, as if I was not, after all, much to look at in the forest. But Ngbali seemed to enjoy my attention, and I took delight in observing scenes that had nothing to do with me. One time Ngbali probed a tree hole with her machete and aroused a sleeping colony of bats. They shot out of their roost in twos and threes, hardly more than flitting shadows as they vanished among the trees, while Ngbali and Mbina tried to knock them down with sticks.

Now and then I got a chance to show off. Conscious of the age difference between Ngbali and me (eighteen to twenty years), I availed myself of every opportunity to display my physical fitness. I was constantly cheerful on the trail. I bubbled with interest in the hunt, moving from one group of nets to the next, following the kills, chasing duikers that had escaped back toward the nets. Once one of these escapees actually ended up in Biléma's net, and that evening I proudly presented my earned share of meat to Ngbali.

One day at the end of the hunt a terrific storm broke out. Sombolo decided to run back to camp, and I ran with him. No matter how fast he went, I remained right on his heels. The forest glistened in the rain as if with silver streamers as we leaped over logs and trick roots, dodged branches and lianas, maneuvering with reckless speed along the twisting contours of the trail. There were cries of astonishment as we passed the rest of the hunting party, who dove out of our way into the jungle on either side of the trail; I distinctly remember Ngbali's cry of *wo!* as we flashed by her.

In camp after the hunt Ngbali's glances usually lost their critical edge, and she seemed once again as intrigued by me as I was by her. I spent the remaining daylight hours in the *mbanjo*, where the men smoked cigarettes and discussed the events of the day, accompanying their stories with gestures and a shared repertoire of sound effects. I could never figure out the meanings of the sounds, which seemed to be expressive rather than imitative. At nightfall I usually drifted over to Sombolo's enclave to partake as best I could of the intimate family scene. Mowooma was always talkative, stretched out in front of his hut, a bright fire nearby. Akunga preferred to lounge in his hut out of sight, though every now and then his gruff voice contributed something to the conversation through the hut wall. Ngbali was constantly doing little chores — chopping *koko*, fetching water or firewood. Although she pounded a lot of manioc, she did not prepare any meals unless she had earned a portion of meat on the hunt.

At some point during the evening Sombolo would draw me into the conversation, usually by asking me questions about America. In my rudimentary Yaka I would try to describe aspects of the land I came from. One night the conversation turned to airplanes, and I described everything from helicopters to jumbo jets to rockets. Another time I described the foods I knew the Bayaka would like best: giant watermelons as sweet as sugar, plums and peaches, nuts such as cashews and pecans, vegetables like carrots and sweet potatoes. There had been no hunt for two days because of heavy rain, and none of us had eaten much, so by the end of the evening I had worked up quite an appetite.

I told them about the seasons, and how a whole forest would lose its leaves for several months, only to grow them back with the return of warm weather. I described the cold that came, so powerful one had to wear "clothes" on one's hands; the houses that towered far above the tallest trees; the traffic that sometimes made it faster to walk than drive in a car. My fragmentary descriptions usually held the Bayaka spellbound, eliciting exclamations of wonder and disbelief at things completely beyond their experience. I often wondered what impressions I was conjuring up in their minds. Ngbali always listened intently, rooted to the spot. What could she possibly have been thinking about this strange world I was supposedly going to take her to?

One night her aunt Etu told a story that seemed inspired by my descriptions of America. Though I could scarcely understand the details, the basic plot was about a Moaka woman who went on a voyage to a faraway land where everything was different. Etu's description of the immense crowds was so effective it prompted Ngbali to cry out in wonder, "A *lot* of people!" The story went on long into the night when most of the camp was alseep, and in its course Etu repeated a little song from time to time, with Ngbali and the other women sometimes joining in. I could hardly understand a word, yet I was fascinated; to the Bayaka the story must have been truly enthralling. At one point Sombolo even urged Etu to hurry up and finish — he was tired and wanted to go to sleep. But the story went on for at least two hours more, and Sombolo listened to the end.

ONE MORNING I saw Ngbali and several women leaving the camp, each with an empty carrying basket, but no one told me where they were going. That afternoon, when I learned they had gone to the village and would not be back until the next day, I fumed. At least Ngbali could have told me she was going. When I complained to Sombolo and others, they told me that Ngbali and the women had merely gone to work for the villagers for a day in exchange for manioc. Mombongo had run out of manioc.

"What happened to the five sacks I bought?" I asked in consternation — everyone had assured me that five sacks would easily last two months.

"The Bayaka eat lots of manioc," Sombolo apologetically explained.

That evening at Sombolo's I felt Ngbali's absence keenly, and my distress mounted. I did not like the idea of her being exploited by a villager, especially doing such hard physical labor all day in the tropical sun. I still had some cash, so why didn't she just ask me for money to buy manioc? Wasn't I her husband-to-be? The fact that she apparently preferred to work rather than ask me tò help hit a raw nerve. The more I thought about it, the less I liked it.

Ngbali returned the next afternoon, her *eekwa* filled with a load of manioc I would have had difficulty lifting — she had carried it by a strap over her forehead for miles through the forest. I did not want her carrying heavy loads, and I decided to express my dissatisfaction by ignoring her. Ngbali figured out what I was up to in a few minutes and set out to break my resolve.

At first she tried to put herself constantly in my field of vision — whichever way I turned, she was soon there. Even without looking I could feel her staring at me unabashedly. Finally she resorted to a different tactic, ignoring me and picking up baby Etu. She lay down on a reed mat with Etu on top of her and began to play in a very suggestive manner. From the way she kept looking at me there could be no doubt that she was teasing me. Several times she caught me looking back, and soon I could not tear my eyes away.

Meanwhile, some boys behind me had spotted a giant millipede and were noisily urging it onto a stick. I saw my chance for revenge. Grabbing the stick, I made as if to jettison the millipede into the bush, then swerved around and rushed with it toward Ngbali. Amid cries and laughter all around, Ngbali dashed off into the nearest hut.

That evening when I visited Sombolo's, she was sitting alone in her parents' hut. When our eyes met, she gave me a lovely smile. The last trace of my anger and doubt evaporated on the spot.

WE HAD LEFT AMOPOLO at the end of *izibu,* the dry season. *Mboola,* the rainy season, was just around the corner. Already a couple of brief storms had soaked the chigoe-infested sands of Amopolo, and the sky clouded over with increasing frequency. In the forests, however, the distant rumbles we used to hear were full-fledged thunderstorms. Often the rain came in the late afternoon and lasted a couple of hours, but sometimes it rained all night and well into the morning. On such mornings the hunt was called off because the nets broke too easily when wet.

Early *mboola* was also the start of the honey season. Although honey was available all year round, during the first couple of months of *mboola* it was abundant. There were at least half a dozen varieties, each made by a different bee. One of the small, stingless bees made *kuma*, which had a sharp taste that reminded me of fermented maple syrup. The comb was dark, almost black, and resembled a rotten tree fungus. *Kuma* had a strong effect on the stomach and for that reason was rarely consumed by itself. The Bayaka mixed it with water to make a drink they called *njambu*, the "coffee of the forest." *Kuma* was found in large forest trees. Procuring it involved chopping the tree down and ladling the honey into pails made from *ngungu* leaves — the same leaves used to cover the huts.

Sako was a honey found in decaying trees and even in the ground. The tiny sweat bees that could be so maddening as they licked at the corners of your eyes made a honey called *bwangi;* I was told it was delicious but I had never sampled it.

The prize of all honeys, however, came in the form of the classic honeycomb and was the product of the *banjooey*, my mortal enemy the honeybee. Collecting this honey, *buuy*, is dangerous work, for *buuy* is invariably found near the tops of the tallest trees, the ones that tower above the canopy. A strip of bark is looped around the trunk of the tree and behind the waist of the climber. Using a homemade ax, the climber hacks foothold after foothold and very slowly walks up the tree. Reaching the hive can take the better part of a day. The climber smokes out the hive — the smoke has a soporific effect on the bees, so they rarely sting. Finally, he scoops out the comb into a bucket of leaves and lowers it to the ground by rope. Most of the *buuy* is eaten on the spot. Mobo brought back *buuy* the most frequently, but not far behind was Tété, known for his tree-climbing abilities. As a team, Sombolo and Mowooma also had an impressive record.

The Bayaka would consume large portions of honey in seconds. In the beginning I was more than satisfied with a bite-sized piece. When I overindulged I paid for it later, lying in bed with a queasy stomach. As I became habituated to a regular supply, my appetite for honey grew into an intense craving, even though it still made me sick. For a long time I believed I was the only one who paid for my gluttony, so I suffered in silence. Only many months later did

I learn that all the Bayaka got stomachaches after eating honey — it was just the price one paid for pigging out.

SOMETIMES WHEN the others hunted I went off by myself to make recordings of the forest. At dawn the forest was at its noisiest, a blend of monkey and bird cries. Although the monkeys soon fell silent, a few species of birds continued to call throughout the day. In the forest it was difficult to spot them — now and then through the foliage I would catch a glimpse of a yellow wing or a bright red beak or a startled-looking black eye ringed with orange. By noon the predominant sound came from the cicadas, large green insects that periodically filled the air with strident blasts. In late afternoon, as the sunlight left the ground, the first of the night insects began to pipe up, gradually altering the texture of the forest's sonic ambience with their electronic sound. At sunset came a final burst of monkey cries and birdsong, after which the chorus of night insects rose in earnest.

One of the most poignant sounds of the forest was the call of the tree hyrax, a call that will always evoke for me those months at Mombongo. A nocturnal tree dweller that looks something like a rabbit, the hyrax is actually one of the elephant's closest living relatives. Its cry began softly, a kind of warbly whimper, and rose in volume and pitch with each repetition, closing with a long, plaintive, flutey wail that could be heard a mile away. It usually called between nine and midnight and again in the couple of hours before dawn.

Though bees were seldom a nuisance while I was walking in the forest, I did have my share of encounters during the stationary hours I spent recording. The buzz of a single honeybee was surprisingly loud, seeming to slice through the tranquil ambience with its nervous energy. Soon the bee would appear, zigzagging low over the ground and finally coming to an aggressive hover an inch from my hand or foot. What impulse directed these mavericks to single me out, with the whole rain forest to choose from? Once prompted, only the threat of death dissuaded them from their purpose. I would wait for the bee to land, then flick it away with my fingernail. The stunned bee would lie among the leaves for a minute, then walk crazily in circles as if reorienting itself in a truncated version of the waggle dance. Finally it would buzz off urgently, this time in a beeline — perhaps, I mused, to tell the rest of the hive not to mess with me.

My return to camp after these recording expeditions was never without some anxiety. Fifty yards away I could hear the mighty resonating hum of the bees. Always in the daytime it was present: a complex chord of overtones and dissonances, as if the forest itself had enveloped our human intrusion with a pearl of sound. I often tried to record that hum, but it was too subtle to be picked up by a microphone. It was the combined hum of several species of bees and thus was probably unique to the forest camps. Nowhere else did so many species gather in such large numbers. The sound was never the same from day to day, varying with the ratios of the species present. On some days the honeybees were far outnumbered by one of the species of little bees. Sometimes the black bees predominated, sometimes the red ones.

On one of my recording forays I came across an abandoned and overgrown Bayaka camp. I spent a good thirty minutes in the middle of it before realizing what I had stumbled upon. The remains of a hut first clued me in. The sticks were black and rotten, and saplings were growing through the decaying framework, but there could be no doubt that I was looking at the ruins of a beehive hut. I cast around for more signs. Here and there a few telltale sticks still arched out of the ground, and I was able to trace the circle of what had been a small forest settlement. But there were no other signs marking the clearing where the dances were once held and where the *mokoondi* had pounded the earth and rushed frantically about. The forest was already well on its way to reclaiming it beyond recognition. No telling how long ago Bayaka had lived there — at least a couple of years, I guessed. In another six months the last signs of the camp would vanish entirely.

Finding myself in that abandoned camp put me in a wistful mood. It was just a spot in the forest, almost indistinguishable from any other, but it had once been the site of all the passions of a human community. It reminded me that one day Mombongo, now the scene of my own passions, a place of such deep significance in my life, would also be erased. And it made me imagine a time when there would be no more Bayaka, when the forest would be an empty, lonely place. Subsequently I came across other abandoned camps, and gradually they lost their saddening effect.

ONE EVENING when I returned from the hunt, I was nonplussed to discover three village women sitting in a small shelter that some boys had put up next to the *mbanjo*. They looked as if they intended to remain in camp for quite some time. Strewn about were several bulging bundles of manioc, in addition to a large supply of palm oil nuts. Cooking utensils were heaped up in a corner.

"Who are they?" I asked.

"*Bilo* women," Biléma answered.

"How long will they sleep at Mombongo?"

"I don't know" was Biléma's neutral reply.

And so I was introduced to yet another facet of Bayaka life. The three women were Sangha-sangha, and it was not unusual for Sangha-sangha women to join an established forest camp for a week or two. They brought village products — salt, peanuts, chilies, cigarettes, and marijuana — to exchange for meat. Manioc, always in short supply in the forest, was the primary item for barter. They smoked the meat they accumulated to preserve it, eating only enough to sustain themselves. When they ran out of exchange items, they returned to Bomandjombo to sell the meat in the local market.

I had been sending teenagers out regularly with money to buy cigarettes and other supplies in the village. Now, however, I was almost out of cash. I still had some traveler's checks, but I did not want to go all the way to Bangui to cash them. Naturally I had wondered what the Bayaka were going to do when I had no more money. So in a way the arrival of the villagers was fortuitous, since I wanted their cigarettes too.

In the beginning I found it difficult to relax in the presence of the villagers, but as the days passed I was amazed at how little difference the women made in the daily life of the camp. For one thing, they spoke Yaka and so were linguistically unobtrusive. (Sango tended to have unpleasant connotations — all too often it was the language used by villagers to boss the Bayaka around.) They kept mostly to themselves, cooked their own food, and sometimes went off on their own to gather *koko.* The only disruptions came when they harangued someone who had taken cigarettes or manioc days before on credit and whom they now suspected of withholding meat.

The Bayaka carried on as before, as if oblivious to the presence of the villagers. Somewhat to my surprise, the *mokoondi* still visited the camp at all hours of the night. And full-fledged ceremonies took place right before the eyes of the village women — had they cared to watch. Usually they slept through the proceedings. Occasionally one of them would raise her voice in protest if the *mokoondi* came into camp very late demanding an *eboka,* but invariably she would be ignored. Once a *mokoondi* even thrashed the villagers' hut in response. The single greatest drawback to the women's presence was that meat was no longer available in such great abundance.

These women stayed four days, and shortly after they left, others came, including the first wife of the Sangha-sangha chief, Biléma. All of them presented me with a gift upon their arrival. I gathered that the Bayaka had told them I was the "owner" of the camp. Not all of our visitors were Sangha-sangha. At Mombongo I first made the acquaintance of Bunduwuri and his wife, Jeanne, both originally from Nola. Bunduwuri, one of the few village men to visit Bayaka forest camps regularly, was careful to remain unobtrusive. When the *mokoondi* came, he was quick to extinguish his fire.

AMONG THE BAYAKA, when a man takes a wife he must pay a brideprice. Though not much by Western standards, the sum is considerable for the individual Moaka man and may take years to pay off. In fact much of the brideprice is paid in services rendered, not hard cash. It is a means of indebting a man to his wife's family. Typically, the newlyweds take up residence beside the bride's family. The groom will hunt with her family, run chores for them, and even babysit for his wife's younger siblings. Relatives of the woman's immediate family may eventually make claims on the man. A very effective unifying factor of the marriage is that the groom now "owes" a sister to his wife's family, usually as a wife for one of her brothers. These arranged marriages are not forced, but they often take place. Thus it was that Yéyé's brother Mowooma had taken Sombolo's sister Elia for his second wife.

Although Sombolo had asked for an immediate thousand francs (four dollars) at the time of the engagement, he and I had not really discussed the brideprice for Ngbali. I felt uncomfortable with the whole idea, and for good reason. The brideprice is not really about money, it is about allying two families. In my case, however, the system obviously would not work. Where was the sister that Ngbali's brother, Ayoosi, might one day claim as his wife? And instead of years of helpful service, I could dispose of the brideprice with a single cash transaction. I was glad Sombolo had not pressed the matter, but I knew it would come up eventually.

One day a village woman arrived with a gallon of *mbaku*. The sight of the lethal moonshine depressed me, but when the Bayaka returned from the hunt and saw what was on offer their eyes lit up. That evening there was little to eat as the meat was piled up on the villager's smoking rack. The *mbanjo* was deserted as the men gathered around the woman, taking turns drinking from the single cup she had brought along. When they exhausted the purchasing power of their meat, they persuaded the woman to pour them drinks on credit. They would bring her lots of meat tomorrow. As night wore on their voices grew louder. When I finally dropped off to sleep they were still going strong.

In the morning I heard stories about Sombolo's antics. He had gone off to take a leak, and when he hadn't returned after thirty minutes, the others went to search for him; they found him passed out on the trail. I knew Sombolo had come back empty-handed from the hunt the day before, and when he emerged from his hangover that afternoon I criticized him for drinking so much on credit. I was worried that if he owed the village woman a lot of meat, Ngbali might not get any to eat for days. Sombolo assured me he had not drunk a drop on credit. Others had shared with him. Also, he boasted, he had convinced the woman that she owed me, as camp "owner," a free glass of *mbaku*. Then he had claimed my free glass as his right as my father-in-law. Later the village woman herself asked me for two hundred francs. Apparently Sombolo had gone on to persuade her to sell him two glasses for which his "son-in-law" would pay. The woman really wanted only meat for her *mbaku*, but as a favor to me she had conceded to my father-in-law's wishes.

There was no hunt that day, for everyone was recuperating from their hangovers, but the crowd around the village woman in the evening was just as large as the night before. At Ngbali's I was the only man present, and I listened to Yéyé complaining to her sisters. Tonight Sombolo *was* drinking on credit. Ngbali was morosely silent. Later in the night Sombolo roused me from bed. The drinking festivities were winding down in the far corner of camp and he was on his way home. He just wanted to tell me how happy he was that I was going to marry his daughter, and he listed some of the things he expected in return: a pair of sneakers like mine, a belt, a watch, and a radio that used six batteries.

"Okay," I agreed, glad at least that he had not asked for money, "I'll give you all those things once Ngbali and I are married."

"And I also want a big house in the village," he added as an afterthought.

As he stumbled off to sleep, I began to wonder what I was getting myself into.

THE VILLAGE WOMAN hung around for several more days to collect on her debts. Rain was frequent now, sometimes forcing the hunt to be postponed. When there was a hunt, the *bilo* woman, anxious to return home, roamed around the camp on the lookout for meat, for she knew the Bayaka would hide what they owed her if they could. In the evenings her piercing voice rose in accusations until the Bayaka, for the sake of peace, surrendered the meat. When she left, she had still not collected on all her debts.

During her stay, hunger became a problem for the first time. The Bayaka always made sure I had at least one meal a day, and when they knew Sombolo had nothing to offer, they saw to it that I got something to eat in the *mbanjo*. But Ngbali depended entirely on her family for food, and she was hungry. One night in the *mbanjo* as I ate my one meal of the day, I asked where Ngbali was. I hadn't seen her since sunset. Zalogwé replied that she had gone to bed because she was hungry and there was no food. I was upset. Why hadn't anyone told me earlier?

I wanted to bring her the food I was eating, but it wasn't really mine to give. A meal served in the *mbanjo* was a meal for all the men who happened to be there. The men usually gave me a head start, but only because they ate so much faster than I did. On this occasion I knew that many of them had not eaten anything all day. So I took rather more than my share and carried it in my hands over to Ngbali. She was sleeping in her aunt Etu's hut that night.

"Ngbali!" I called softly into the dark. "Food! Take it!"

She was fast asleep and did not respond.

"NGBALI!" everyone in camp shouted at once.

She woke up with a start.

"I don't like you being hungry," I said. "I'm giving you my food."

Her hands shot out and grabbed the food with surprising force. As I walked back to the *mbanjo* I heard general laughter. When I asked what was so funny, her uncle Ndima told me, "Ngbali says it's only a little."

IN THE PREDAWN DARKNESS, just before the tree hyraxes fell silent, Bombé, the grand elder, would reanimate the fire next to his sleeping platform. After warming up over the blaze for a few minutes, he would begin to speak. At first his voice was no more than a mumble, but slowly it was raised in an address to the whole camp. I would drift in and out of sleep, carried along by Bombé's rambling discourse. Eventually Ewunji joined in from across the camp. The two elders talked back and forth, their voices gaining momentum. Finally old Esoosi got into the act, and by the crack of dawn a conversational fugue with twenty parts was well under way, each speaker reinforcing the words of the others, and everyone talking at the same time. Usually they discussed the forthcoming hunt or some incident from the night before.

On the morning after the village woman departed with her sack of meat, Bombé spoke about the Bayaka's abuse of alcohol and the hunger that resulted. Comimg from Bombé it was a surprising diatribe, for he was one of the worst offenders. As the grand elder he had pulled rank and drunk on the credit of others. I had to chuckle when I heard Ngbali's grandfather Ewunji chime in with supporting comments. He was an even bigger abuser than Bombé. Gradually, however, the focus of the discourse changed to a forthcoming women's dance, a *lingokoo*, and the need for lots of meat and *payu*.

When Ngbali's name was mentioned several times, I listened more carefully, now wide awake.

Lingokoo is strictly women's music. When the women sing *lingokoo*, the men are more or less confined to their huts. The women conjure up their own *mokoondi*, a deep hooting voice that sounds as if it is coming out of the earth. I had heard that sound on my first visit, when I recorded the ceremony for a woman who had died. Normally during a night of *lingokoo* the women wander around the camp. They also sing *lingokoo* for weddings, as they had back at Amopolo the night before Engulé and Mbina had first slept together.

Suddenly I realized I was listening to the plans for my wedding.

FOR SEVERAL DAYS Mombongo became a kind of textbook-model Pygmy camp, with everyone absorbed in the traditional way of life. Tété, Mobo, and Akunga spent long hours over smoldering embers, applying poison to the tips of their little arrows. Those who went net hunting departed early and returned late. In the early weeks the hunts had been conducted so close to camp that I sometimes could hear the hunting cries from my hut. But now a two-hour walk to the nets was not unusual.

I had never heard the music of the earth bow, one of the earliest of all musical instruments; now they were being constructed and played all around me. A piece of rope is tied to the top of a sapling, which is pulled over into a bow; the rope is anchored in the earth with a wooden peg. When the rope is plucked it has a deep, resonating sound.

My evenings with Ngbali grew more intimate. In the beginning I had felt inhibited by my limited knowledge of the language. I wanted to tell her what she meant to me, but in her presence even my simplest remarks came out garbled, and her shy giggles afterward didn't help. Now we seemed to have moved beyond that stage. One evening while doing chores Ngbali suddenly heaved a sigh and sat down next to me on the stick bench. After a few minutes Mowooma asked her to fetch water, but she remained at my side. He called her several times, but all she did was sigh again and snuggle up against me. Thereafter our snuggling became an evening ritual, conducted within a few feet of her parents. For Ngbali it might have been nothing more than a refuge from more chores; for me it was the highlight of the day.

One night, sitting in the *mbanjo*, Sombolo addressed the camp, telling everyone how happy his daughter had been since the betrothal. Apparently, before I met Ngbali, she tended to be moody and had rejected several previous suitors. Ewunji spoke out too, saying that his difficult child was finally content. The *mokoondi* themselves seemed to sanction our marriage. Early one dawn I awoke to the most beautiful yodeling a short way off in the forest. It was Yéyé, soon joined by the other women from her family and Sombolo — everyone but Ngbali herself. They sang song after song, a pure, rich polyphony unaccompanied even by clapping. In the distance the voice of a *mokoondi* urged them on. One of the songs I recognized instantly: Ngbali had danced to it at her *moyaya*, her initiation dance. I listened, spellbound. It was the first time I had paid attention to Yéyé's singing, and I thought she had the most beautiful voice in the world.

During those final days at Mombongo I experienced the most extraordinary feeling, the coalescing of some kind of force. The Bayaka seemed directed by an influence beyond the individual, beyond even any mere collection of individuals, something too strong, too deep and intimate, to be called social cooperation. It was not just a wedding that was going to take place. What was going on was almost supernatural.

Then one morning Simbu appeared silently at camp. He had left Amopolo long before dawn, he explained, and walked most of the way by the light of the waning moon. The urgency in his voice and his grim expression boded ill, but scarcely prepared me for the tidings: Akété, the gifted young harp player, had been killed in a hunting accident.

SEVEN

Villagers

I N A SINGLE STROKE Mombongo was abandoned as we prepared our return to Amopolo. The women loaded their baskets, the men shouldered their hatchets and spears, and with few words we set off along the trail in single file. I could hardly imagine what emotions the Bayaka were feeling. Perhaps they were consumed by grief over Akété's death. I confess that my thoughts were elsewhere. The unbearable sadness that had come over me in the abandoned forest camps now surfaced with the poignancy of personal loss: Mombongo, my Mombongo, was one of them. On my final glance back it was already a forlorn place, its magic wiped out forever.

On the walk back my mind raced in several directions at once. How would Akété's death affect my wedding, which was supposed to take place very soon? Did Ngbali feel the same regret as I, or were her thoughts wholly on Akété? Was someone with thoughts as selfish as mine worthy to marry into such an open-hearted people?

Out on the road the temperature was a good ten degrees higher than in the forest. I had forgotten how hot it could be, and as we approached Amopolo I could feel the misery that was awaiting us there. The strains of a powerful *élélo* reached us even before we crossed the Amopolo bridge. Upon entering the camp, the women dropped their things and went directly into the bamboo house where Akété had lived. It was already packed with women in the full throes of lament. I joined the men in the *mbanjo*, where a heavy silence hung.

Bayaka men do not tend to live long, and there are far fewer old men than women. The death of a healthy young man like Akété, who had not yet married, was an especially devastating blow to the community. The *élélo* was frightening — one long, anguished dissonance that rose and fell and seemed to shake the hut. Relatives kept at it full time, and other women joined the wailing in shifts. Traffic in and out of the hut was continuous. As some women emerged to tend to chores, others arrived. At one point I saw Ngbali leave the hut with some girlfriends. Our eyes met briefly, then we both turned away. Had I known that it would be our last mutual glance for months, I might have wondered what she was thinking about.

AKÉTÉ'S DEATH was violent and bizarre by most standards, but not unusual for the Bayaka. It was days before I heard the final version. Even the Bayaka seemed confused. The first word was that he had been attacked and killed by an *ebobo*, which normally means "gorilla" but is sometimes used to mean "villager." To clarify matters I asked, "You mean a *villager* attacked him?"

"No," the Bayaka replied, "a *gorilla*."

Next I heard that he had been shot by an *ebobo*. "You mean he was shot by a *gorilla*?" I asked in amazement.

"No," they replied, "by a *villager*."

Eventually I learned that both accounts were true. Akété had been out in the forest with a *bilo* man, who had hired him to help on an elephant hunt. It was illegal to hunt elephants in the reserve, but a few of the Bayaka still did, for elephant meat was one of their favorites. In the course of tracking down an elephant, the two men had encountered a family of gorillas. They shot at the gorillas in fright and provoked an attack. Akété was caught by one of them, and when the villager shot at it, he hit Akété instead. The bullet passed through his chest and shattered his right hand. It took the villager two days to carry Akété to the nearest village. He died in the back of a bush taxi on the way to the hospital in Nola.

The *élélo* for Akété went on all day, through the night, and into the morning. There was something truly distressing about the grief, a sustained surge of emotion that seemed to blot out the world. The men kept a fire going in the *mbanjo* all night. Now and then a heated discussion broke out over the compensation they would demand from the villager. Joboko insisted that the *bilo* must give them his gun. The Bayaka had always wanted a gun, and now they saw their chance.

Akété was buried the following afternoon. His mother, Belloo, threw herself into the grave and had to be dragged out. Ndoko, his father, watched the proceedings silently, looking hollow and exhausted. I spent the last of my cash on cigarettes, coffee, and sugar. Just after dark a large fire was built in front of Akété's hut. While the coffee brewed, the drums began to sound, and soon an *eboka* was under way. Before midnight, however, it was already fragmenting as people drifted off to bed. I retired during its final stage, when only a handful of men remained.

Soon the drums fell silent. A few men remained talking. I could hear Ndoko's voice among them. Sometimes one of them sang a brief phrase. Then the low voices would resume their discussion.

At some point during the night I became aware of an unearthly music. When I reached out a microphone to record it, I woke up, my hand in mid-air. Outside, the music continued. The men, many voices now, were wandering slowly around the settlement in their version of *limboku*, which they called *so*. The rhythms, tapped on sticks, were fast and sometimes frenetic. As they neared my hut I could hear, beneath the bright polyphonic texture of yodels, stranger voices. One talked and sang out like a kazoo. Another, rough and deep, like the voice of someone possessed, punctuated the songs with shouts and screams. But it was the third voice that really fascinated me: a resonating, breathy bass that sounded like a bullroarer. I went out to look.

The men were dancing around a central figure, shielding it from view with their arms. Mindumi hopped about the perimeter playing a homemade kazoo. But the bullroarer voice, now panting in a tense rhythm, rose from the center. Though the group sometimes danced in place and sometimes moved backward, its general direction was slowly forward. At one point the tight circle opened, giving room to the man in the center. From behind I got a view of a broad, powerful back. As the man danced, bent forward at the waist, elbows jutting out, feet stamping the ground, the bullroarer voice seemed to emanate directly from his heaving chest. The effect was electrifying, and I wondered who he could be. And then I recognized him — Adamo.

The *so* continued until dawn, when the men, still singing, uprooted a palm tree, then sang and danced their way to the Amopolo bridge and jumped into the water.

As LIFE RETURNED to normal and I readjusted to Amopolo, I saw little of Ngbali. In the intimacy of Mombongo, paying a visit to her family was a natural act. But Amopolo was big, open, and sprawling, with many more people, and all sense of intimacy was lost. I found myself contriving reasons to visit, bringing over small gifts like peanut butter or soap, which I was now scoring on credit at Ngunja's shop. Ngbali was never at home. She was always off visiting girlfriends and relatives, and I found it impossible to keep track of her. So I would end up giving the gifts to her mother or her grandmother or one of her aunts.

When I did see her, it was invariably from a distance. She played a lot with little children and often teased her brother, Ayoosi. He had become something of a cry-baby as a result. She spent long hours of the day in the company of her maternal uncle Mindumi and his wife, Zabu. At those times I had the closest view of her from my seat in the *mbanjo*. I watched her for signs of recognition, but she always acted as if she did not know me. Judging from the time she spent with him, Mindumi had a great deal of influence over her. Now I wished that I knew him better. Instinctively I liked him, but I had no idea what he thought of me. He never came around to ask for cigarettes, and we had had little contact.

Sometimes Sombolo would bring over a meal that he *said* was prepared by Ngbali, and I would wonder why he did not call me to his house, where Ngbali could give me the meal herself. Aunts and cousins came by and asked for things in her name: "Ngbali calls for peanut butter"; or "Ngbali calls for chilies." Later a meal with peanut butter or chilies was delivered, and I had to assume, since nothing was ever said, that Ngbali had prepared it.

And yet I found comfort in the fact that everyone referred to her as my woman. I loved to hear that phrase, and often when they said something to me about Ngbali, I would act dense and ask, "Who?" "Ngbali — your woman," they invariably replied.

"TONIGHT *LINGOKOO*," I heard my neighbor Nyasu announce.

"Yes, *lingokoo* tonight," Bessé replied.

It seemed that my wedding day had finally arrived — at least, so I surmised, for no one said anything to me about it. But all day I heard talk of the "women's dance," and I could think of no other reason for holding a *lingokoo* now.

The music started in the evening, when the men were still milling about. The teenage boys held an *elanda* in a far corner of camp in an act of defiance, but the women more or less steamrolled through it and scattered the participants. A short time later all the men had disappeared, so I withdrew into my hut as well. It was a high-spirited *lingokoo*, with ululations rising above the singing and frequent laughter. At some point I dropped off to sleep. When I awoke, the *lingokoo* had gained considerable momentum, and it was taking place outside my hut. One after another of the women danced into the hut and out again. It was too dark to see who they were, but I heard Ngbali's name called out and suddenly recognized her silhouette in the entrance, where she paused for a few seconds to gyrate her hips before dancing on.

In the morning I arose, presumably a married man. No one congratulated me, and the day unfolded as if nothing had happened the night before. Ngbali appeared briefly in the distance, but her behavior was subdued and she cast not so much as a single glance my way. Nevertheless my hopes rose high that evening when the usual gathering of men around my fire began to disperse earlier than normal, with remarks like, "Okay, let's go. He's waiting for his woman." From bed I listened to the conversation between Nyasu and Bessé, who habitually built their fire next to my hut. I could pick up only an occasional phrase or two from the incomprehensible flow of Yaka. But I heard encouraging words: "She's coming to-night"; "She's waiting until late"; "When everyone's asleep, she'll come." Eventually I fell asleep waiting.

I woke up a disappointed man. The roosters were crowing like mad and it was already growing light. I moped in bed long after everyone else got up. As if by tacit consent I was left undisturbed for quite a while. Finally Nyasu brought in a meal of plain *koko*.

"Did Ngbali come and sleep last night?" she quickly asked, the motive for the meal now apparent.

"Never!" I vehemently replied.

"Wo!" Nyasu cried in surprise. She hurried out to report to the others. Soon there was a low but excited discussion among the women in my neighborhood.

Ngbali did not come to my hut the next night, either, or the night after that. Sombolo dropped by, and when I ventured to ask him why she had not come, he explained that there was too much gossip at Amopolo, and as a result Ngbali was too ashamed. But Sombolo was an unreliable informant. Upon his return to Amopolo he had reverted to his village mentality and had taken to drinking in the village on credit — my credit, since he was now my father-in-law.

Over the next weeks I kept trying to make contact with Ngbali. I passed her hut every day on my way to bathe, and I would wait until I saw her before setting off. I always carried a small present. And yet these momentary contacts only deepened my distress. Ngbali would never look me in the eye, and when I offered her the gift she would hesitate. Sometimes she waited so long that the others who were standing around and watching would shout, "Take it!" Then she would accept my gift.

In the evenings I went to visit her without any gifts at all. If she was there with her family, she always contrived to remain out of view behind someone else, and if I sat down next to her she would find a reason to shift her position so that her back was to me. When I spoke to her she never replied, and even her shy giggle was gone.

"Doesn't Ngbali like me?" I would ask her female relatives.

"She likes you," they assured me. And often they added, "She'll sleep with you tonight."

But she never did. Instead, she virtually disappeared. I learned that she was hanging out with some less than immediate relatives whom I scarcely knew and therefore was unlikely to drop in on. The women in my neighborhood gave me advice: I must simply grab her arm and drag her to my hut. I made an attempt to do that one night, after confirming with her family that she was, after all, my wife. I waited near her hut, and when she returned late that night I grabbed her by the arm and said we were going to bed. She broke free of my grip and ran to a distant part of camp, where she joined an *elanda* that was going on. Thereafter she danced *elanda* frequently — and this was a period when *elanda* was danced so often that the adults began to complain. Always *elanda*, they sighed. What ever happened to *eboka?* Sometimes Ngbali herself was the instigator of an *elanda*. Sometimes two dances went on simultaneously in different parts of Amopolo. Ngbali would go from one to the other, and I gave up even trying to keep track of her. But I knew that *elanda* encouraged flirtation, and I remained in a state of perpetual agitation.

I found some solace in the fact that I was not the only one with woman problems during this period. One of the biggest surprises upon my return from Mombongo was that Simbu had taken a second wife. One day he pointed to a lively young beauty whom I had already noticed. "My woman, Saki," he said proudly. Mandubu, his first wife, seemed to take the development in stride. In the evenings they would sit together in front of Simbu's hut. Mandubu, I noticed, did the cooking and most of the chores, while Saki lounged around and giggled. Simbu was a venerable elder. Always serious, he never drank *mbaku* and never danced. I could not help but feel that in Saki he had taken on more than he could handle. Saki had a most vivacious personality and simply loved to dance. Like Ngbali, she was always dancing in *elanda*, and I had heard rumors that so far she had refused to sleep with Simbu. His jealousy, as a consequence, was said to be quite dangerous.

Simbu's troubles seemed to lessen the degree of my own; my problems weren't unique. Formerly I had compared my so-called marriage to Engulé and Mbina's, which had proceeded without a hitch — except that Engulé had given Mbina a bloody nose. Maybe marriage problems weren't so rare after all. On the other hand, I felt uncomfortable comparing my situation to Simbu's, and I hoped others did not do so. I was far from being a venerable elder, and though I could hardly dance, I clowned around a lot and generally found myself in the company of the younger men.

One day I came back from the village with some rice, which I dropped off with Ngbali's grandmother, Sopo. Sombolo hadn't been hunting and I knew her family was short of food. In the evening Nyasu came into my hut to ask for some rice (by now everyone knew that I had brought some back from the village).

"I don't have any rice," I replied. "I gave it to — "

"Your wife?" Nyasu interrupted. "What wife? Does she sleep with you? Does she cook you food? Does she bring you water or sit with you? She doesn't like you!"

"She doesn't like you!" Bessé echoed, coming into my hut.

"Sombolo is tricking you," Nyasu continued. "You're wasting your money on Ngbali, giving her soap and peanut butter and rice and sardines."

Other women had also crowded into my hut, Sao among them.

"Is it true?" I asked Sao; since she had been so instrumental in bringing us together, I considered her an expert on the matter.

"It's true," Sao replied. "Ngbali doesn't like you!"

So that was that. No wonder the betrothal had always felt un-real — the whole thing had been a charade! And I had fallen for it!

Numb from shock, I marched over to Sombolo's neighborhood. Most of the women were sitting around a fire in Akunga's unfin-ished bamboo hut, which he was building directly over his beehive hut. They were brewing some of the coffee I had given them the day before. Ngbali and her mother were not there.

"I just found out that Ngbali doesn't like me!" I blurted.

The conversation had sounded cheerful as I arrived, but now the women sat still and silent, except for Ngbali's aunt Etu, who burst out with a peal of laughter.

TRULY DISMAL DAYS followed, days during which I floated in a region between fury and despair. I wanted to leave, but I realized that I could not: Ngbali had become too much of an obsession. Sombolo still visited me occasionally, assuring me that Ngbali *was* my wife. I clung to the straws he offered, but his motives were now highly transparent, especially when he'd end his little speech with a request for spare change.

The consensus in my neighborhood was that I should forget Ngbali and think about taking another wife. Joboko's daughter Ngassa liked me and would make a good wife, I was told. Joboko himself told me that Mamadu's mother, Bessé, had not had a man in years and would welcome a lover. One evening around my fire Adamo told the others, in my presence and in a simple Yaka I was bound to understand, that if I married his daughter he would be very happy. Sao came into my hut one night to tell me that Bowanja was interested. I didn't even know who Bowanja was.

Their offers and advice only depressed me further. I tried to explain that I could not just turn around and marry someone else — my heart was still with Ngbali. I wondered if they could even understand what I was saying. Did they love the same way we did? I had assumed so — relationships were often stormy, but the flare-ups of jealousy and the fact that most of the marriages were long-lasting had seemed to prove the similarity. But now I began to have my doubts. The men in my neighborhood seemed to think I was being impractical. The women would respond to my explanations by saying to each other, "He likes *Ngbali!*"

Just as Sombolo's testimony was no longer reliable, there were also reasons for doubting the counsel of the people in my neighborhood. They were all part of Esoosi's extended family — the family that had adopted me from the start. Now I was hoping to marry into Ewunji's family. Esoosi's family was clearly afraid of losing influence over me and all the things I would presumably do or buy for them in the future. Ewunji's family, and Sombolo in particular, would monopolize me. It was dispiriting to think of the Bayaka feuding over me because of my relative wealth, but I could not deny that this was a factor.

One evening I decided that if anyone knew how Ngbali really felt, it would be her mother, Yéyé. When I saw her sitting alone I went over to talk to her. I had never spoken to Yéyé before, and I was fairly nervous. When I sat down near her fire she slid a bowl of food over to me. I pushed it aside and said that I had not come to eat. Then I launched into my lament: I really loved her daughter, and I had believed she loved me; now she avoided me and people were saying she didn't like me; they were telling me to take another wife, but I couldn't because I was too much in love with Ngbali; but I had to know the truth. Did Ngbali no longer love me?

I had wanted no one but Yéyé to hear what I said, but Mindumi, sitting in front of his hut nearby, was obviously taking in every word. Yéyé replied that she did not know her daughter's heart. All she knew was that Ngbali no longer prepared me food and no longer sat with me. I should stop giving money and gifts. Ngbali didn't want the gifts, and Sombolo drank with the money. But as for what was in Ngbali's heart, she didn't know, because her heart was different.

When I heard Yéyé's words, my last hope was extinguished.

LATE ONE NIGHT when everyone was in bed, Singali and Mindumi returned from a *mbaku* excursion in the village. They were still a long way off, but their voices could be heard, bellowing out a song in the manner of drunks the world over. As they got nearer I recognized the melody, though I had not heard it in years. It was from the *eboka* during which I had seen the *mokoondi* for the first time. And I thought that melody had vanished forever. Just hearing it now made me feel better.

When they reached Amopolo Singali said, "Goodnight, Mr. the Mayor," and Mindumi replied, "Goodnight, Mr. the Chief." I heard Singali enter his hut, mutter to one of his wives, and begin to snore. There was a moment of silence, and then I heard Mindumi talking to someone whose voice was too low to identify. "You're my sister," Mindumi said, "and she's your daughter. I'm telling you he's her husband." More discussion followed. Suddenly Mindumi erupted.

"Go to your husband's hut!" he hollered. "Go now!" Low voices again. "I said go to your husband's hut!" A pause. "Okay, I'm having you arrested tomorrow." Another pause, more talk. "Go!"

There was a sudden violent thrashing sound — Mindumi was ripping his way into Sombolo and Yéyé's hut! A child started to cry, presumably Ayoosi.

"I'm taking you to your husband's hut right here and now!"

A brief scuffle ensued, followed by the stomp of running feet. The encounter ended with Mowooma, in whose hut Ngbali had obviously taken refuge, speaking in rapid voice to his brother Mindumi, calming him, explaining that Ngbali would follow her heart. Finally, somewhat to my disappointment, Mindumi shuffled off to bed.

The incident was not mentioned the next day, apart from one brief remark by Mobo about "the noise last night," but I knew I had gained an important ally in Mindumi. He was a major figure at Amopolo, and he was Ngbali's senior uncle. Obviously *he* regarded our marriage as real. And Ngbali's behavior up through the wedding *lingokoo* had seemed sincere enough. Why had she gone through with the wedding if she had no intention of honoring it? Had her feelings for me changed drastically overnight, or had some other problem arisen? From these doubts I gained a renewed sense of hope, and I set out to find out what had gone wrong.

At Amopolo I had received visitors rather than visiting others. My fire was usually the most lively in the evenings. Now, however, I roamed the sprawling settlement, sitting now at Joboko's, now at Mobo's, then on to Sombolo's and Mindumi's. Pretty soon nobody bothered to build my fire anymore. The *geedal* sessions in front of my hut that used to enliven the nights became a memory as I wandered in quest of information. Direct inquiries yielded conflicting opinions as to what had happened. I was told that Sombolo had been deceiving me all along, that Ngbali's mother did not like me but that Ngbali did, that Ngbali's mother liked me but Ngbali did not, that Ngbali had been teased by her friends until she wanted to back out of the marriage, that Ngbali was simply a bad woman. The only conclusion I could draw was that either no one really knew or everyone knew but wasn't telling me. So I adopted the more productive method of eavesdropping. Everywhere I went I kept my ears on the alert, tuning in to conversations a hut or two away.

During this period my understanding of Yaka improved dramatically. At first, alerted by the mention of Ngbali's name, I heard some astonishing things, but I was never certain if I had heard correctly. Most of the talk about "Ngbali" seemed to be about a very tumultuous relationship complete with fights. Eventually I learned that these conversations usually concerned Bakpima's daughter, also named Ngbali. Her marriage to Engbeté was a stormy one. As my language improved I discovered that *my* Ngbali was often referred to as "the daughter of Sombolo." Later it seemed as if, in an effort to keep me in the dark, the Bayaka began to call her "the daughter," and finally simply "the woman."

One day Mokoko called me over to his hut. With an air of conspiracy he unwrapped a leaf to reveal a small mound of ground bark. It was "medicine," he said. I was to bathe well and then rub the grounds over my body. When I went to visit Ngbali she would be overwhelmed by a desire to sleep with me.

"That medicine is zero," I replied, upset that Mokoko should think it necessary for me to resort to such hocus-pocus.

"It *works*," said Sao, who was looking on. "What do you think Ngbali used on you?"

As MY MARRIAGE became less and less a current affair, I grew afraid that it would disappear altogether. Perhaps the Bayaka believed that with the passage of time I would forget all about it. Every now and then, to keep the subject alive, I would bring the subject up, complaining that I still did not know whether I had a wife or not. But during the next couple of months other concerns became the focus of attention at Amopolo.

One day the village chief, Biléma, paid us a visit. This was a rare occurrence, but, he explained, he had something important to tell us. Rumor in the village had it that Bakpima's wife, Ajama, who had been ill for some time with an inflamed leg, had died days ago but that the Bayaka had not yet buried her. There could be only one reason why not, and Chief Biléma, thinking he had figured it out, had come to deliver a stern warning: if the Bayaka were thinking of raising Ajama from the dead, they had better give up the idea at once. Were they such savages that they were willing to live with the dead? They must learn to accept death normally, like civilized people. Raising people from the dead was evil!

The chief turned to me with an appeal: "Monsieur Jean-Louis, you have come from far away to civilize the Bayaka. Truly you must teach them to accept death. Using sorcery to raise the dead is barbaric! They must bury Bakpima's wife!"

I replied that Bakpima's wife was still alive and was recovering with some penicillin I had given her.

"*Merci*, Monsieur Jean-Louis," Chief Biléma said, showing only mild surprise. "Truly we hope you can make Amopolo like Monasao, with a school and a hospital, where the Bayaka are *proper*."

On the spur of the moment I told the chief that the process of civilizing the Bayaka of Amopolo had already begun, and that we were planning to dig latrines as our first step.

"Ah *voilà!*" the chief cried with approval. He shook my hand and left.

Chief Biléma's remarks about civilizing the Bayaka were a typical refrain from the villagers. Although my papers authorizing me to live among the Bayaka referred only to musicological research, most of the *bilo* seemed to believe that my real mission was to introduce the benefits of civilization to Amopolo. The Bayaka themselves fostered this belief. One day around this time Mabuti, Singali, and Balonyona returned from the village full of excitement. They had been spreading stories in the village to the effect that they were turning Amopolo into a genuine village for "Monsieur Louis," that I was the "owner." "Everyone in the village knows," they said. "We told the police, the mayor, the gendarmes — *everyone!* We're making our village for Monsieur Louis."

I was not happy to hear the news. Amopolo was a monstrosity, and if they were making their village for me, I had best leave immediately. After all, the Bayaka had settled here because of the now defunct sawmill. Amopolo had existed long before my first visit, I reassured myself, and its slowly changing character was part of a process that had begun before my second visit.

Another potent reason for not accepting this so-called honor was fear of the possible consequences. Should I overstep my bounds as a music researcher, I was sure to get into official trouble sooner or later. During my first visit I had several times taken the law into my own hands by evicting drunken villagers who had come to Amopolo at night to "participate" in an *eboka*, although I knew that was risky. I had heard stories of a German researcher who had preceded me by a few years, whom both villagers and Bayaka called "Makola." He had so antagonized the villagers that eventually they made his life unbearable by continuous harassment. Makola was arrested several times, official reports condemning him were sent to Bangui, and in one story the gendarmes who controlled the barrier that used to exist at Bomandjombo's northern entrance had refused to allow him to leave for three days. In the end he left for good.

Gradually, however, it became clear that the role the Bayaka proposed for me, far from endangering my stay, actually seemed to strengthen my presence in the eyes of the villagers. I grew to tolerate, then accept the role they had cast me in — that I had come to "civilize" the Bayaka. I realized there was an element of shrewdness in the Bayaka's decision to promote such a belief, so I went along with it. When papers arrived from the mayor's office for me, they were no longer addressed to the "musicologist" but to the "agent for the integration of the Pygmies."

In keeping with my new role I decided to try to accommodate the *bilo*. Makola's experience showed me that arousing their animosity could do no good. Besides, I enjoyed chatting with the villagers about my marriage. The gossip was that Ngbali and I were happily married, and I found some emotional release talking frankly about the situation with the villagers, often asking their opinion about what could have gone wrong. I was touched by their genuine sympathy.

Another favorite topic was my "work" to civilize the Bayaka. I discovered that by openly discussing my difficulties and sufferings in carrying out my work, I would entertain the *bilo* for hours. I also heard some interesting stories in return. Bernard Koy, a policeman who befriended me, told me how when he first arrived from Bangui and was living alone, two Bayaka visited him one day. They introduced themselves as Sombolo and Mowooma. Upon discovering that Bernard was new in town, they described the wonderful relationship they had had with his predecessor, exchanging forest products for money and commodities from the village. Finally they talked Bernard into giving each of them a sarong and five hundred francs. Sombolo promised to bring him an antelope the next day, and Mowooma described the large leaf-wrapped bundle of honey he would deliver. Bernard did not see them again for two months. Another villager summed it up: "Even if you give a Pygmy a thousand dollars today, tomorrow he will ask you for a cigarette." He went on to deliver a prediction: "We in the village have tried for years to understand the Pygmies, and now we are truly exhausted. Now it is you who are trying, but one day you will become exhausted too."

ONE DAY THE ADJUNCT MAYOR visited Amopolo to make an announcement. There was too much "medicine" in Bomandjombo, he said. He meant, I slowly gathered, that there had been too much sorcery. Certain elements, he continued, had used this bad medicine to close the sawmill, and now Bomandjombo was suffering as a result. It was time to remedy the situation. As acting mayor during the mayor's absence, he had taken measures that he hoped would resuscitate the local economy. A dance would be held in Bomandjombo that night, and every man, woman, and child was hereby ordered to attend. A special group of dancers from Nola would use *nga-nga* (a form of divination) to discover the culprits responsible for the shutting down of the sawmill.

When evening came I was not inclined to go to the dance myself, but many Bayaka were curious and left for the village, where the *nga-nga* drums could already be heard. They returned late that night, full of outraged talk. Apparently the dancers had identified both Mowooma and Mobo as guilty of using sorcery against the sawmill. The implications of the identification were not yet clear, for both men had returned to Amopolo.

The following afternoon the adjunct mayor returned and ordered everyone, including me, to attend a second *nga-nga* dance. Soon we could hear the drums, but the Bayaka, unimpressed by what they had seen the day before, decided to stay at Amopolo. The mayor's guards, however, came to round us all up and herd us into the village. I remember being struck by the incongruity of Simbu coming with us, for of all the Bayaka he avoided the village like the plague. On our way into town I wondered if, in the eyes of the diviners, I too might be a suspect. The prospect made me slightly nervous, for I was secretly happy that the sawmill had closed. Would the *nga-nga* dancers detect my emotional culpability?

In the village we found the dance under way. The large square next to the mayor's office was filled with spectators. Village notables such as the adjunct mayor and Chief Biléma were seated, but the rest of us stood. In the center of the square a young man, disheveled and wearing a leopard skin over his head, tottered slowly along the line of spectators. Presumably he was dancing to the rhythm of the two drums, but from his bloodshot eyes it was obvious that he was either drugged or drunk, and his dance was nothing but a stagger. He carried a small mirror, which he gazed into from time to time. Two women followed him, lighting and handing him the cigarettes he chain-smoked. Now and then he would fall into someone's lap — presumably an accusation — and everyone clapped. It seemed a harmless enough charade, and pretty soon I was clapping too.

Among those accused were the former mayor and Chief Biléma. Suddenly, after a glance into his mirror, the diviner stumbled backward into Bombé. When Bombé was pulled into the center, the Bayaka began to murmur. One of the *nga-nga* women hit him on the head, and then several villagers dragged him away behind a house. The Bayaka looked on aghast. I tried to go after Bombé, but found my way blocked by a dozen *bilo*.

"This doesn't concern you," one of them snarled.

"You'd better not interfere," another warned.

"You have no idea what the consequences could be," a third hinted ominously.

Bombé reappeared, stripped of the tattered shirt he had been wearing. He was being dragged off to the *gendarmerie*.

"What's going on?" I cried as I tried to push my way through the crowd.

"He has used sorcery against the sawmill," one of the villagers explained. "It is forbidden. Even the president can do nothing for him now."

"What sorcery?" I retorted. "This *nga-nga* is nonsense!"

"You use magic in America," the villager pointed out, "and now America is rich and powerful."

"No," I spontaneously replied. "We in America discovered long ago that magic is too inefficient, and now we use science."

There was a loud commotion behind me and I turned in time to see Mowooma being dragged off, followed by Simbu. Both had been stripped of their shirts. The Bayaka, previously too horrified to move, were now in an uproar. I remember catching a glimpse of Mobo, weaving unobtrusively through the crowd in the opposite direction. A few seconds later villagers were crying out, "Where's Mobo?" But by then he had vanished.

In a burst of rage I ran into the square and kicked the large *nga-nga* drum with all my might. My threadbare sneakers afforded little protection, and the shock of the impact seemed to shatter my foot. The drum itself, exceedingly heavy, wobbled, tipped over, and rolled a yard. I limped off toward Amopolo, despite calls from the villagers that the dance was not over yet. The Bayaka, furious, followed me.

FOR SEVERAL DAYS we lived in a state of suspense, not knowing what was happening to Bombé, Simbu, and Mowooma. Every night the *nga-nga* drums sounded, but none of the Bayaka were curious enough to go into the village, nor did anyone come for us. We could only wonder what was being done to the three men. My foot had become badly swollen, and I gimped around camp with a walking stick. I was convinced that I had broken a bone or two and fully regretted my impetuous act. Villagers who came by during the day noted my injury and nodded their heads to each other, as if remarking that the *nga-nga* sorcerers had taken revenge on my disbelief. It was frightening to see how quickly the villagers seemed to accept the *nga-nga*. Many *bilo* I had gotten to know well expressed their firm belief in the guilt of the three Bayaka. Only later did it occur to me that they were more frightened by the whole affair than I. And though I continued to rail against the irrationality of it all, I had to admit that in a way the *nga-nga* ceremony had been strangely accurate. The men accused of sabotaging the sawmill were all either Bayaka or Sangha-sangha, the original inhabitants of the area. For them, the sawmill had been a mixed blessing at best. The area had been quickly inundated by outsiders, and the traditional forms of authority had been subsumed by the new hierarchy of mayor, gendarmes, and police. To some extent they had lost control over their own lives.

Then one night, long after everyone had gone to bed, footsteps approached Amopolo rapidly, the long strides of villagers. They entered the camp and crossed over to Singali's hut. There was rapid, low conversation, and then the footsteps retreated back down the road. Soon voices rose from one hut to the next — emotional, excited chatter.

"Tell me!" I finally called out.

"They've dragged Singali off to the *nga-nga!*" Mokoko replied emotionally from his hut.

A group of us gathered in the *mbanjo.* The talk was rabid: now they were coming at night and dragging us out of our homes! What next? Thirty minutes later Singali returned — he had only been called away by the park guards, who were leaving on a mission and needed some information on the whereabouts of a poaching camp. Everyone breathed a sigh of relief and returned to bed.

Only once during the *nga-nga* affair was there even any oblique reminder of my marriage. I was sitting with the men when I heard Ngbali's grandmother, Sopo, complaining in a loud voice that her child "knew" clothes from the white man, but she did not. I asked the others what she was talking about.

"She says that you haven't given her any clothes," Lalié explained.

"Why is she bringing that up at a time like this," I asked angrily, "when her own son Mowooma is in prison in the village?"

"You see?" Lalié replied, as if my question contained its own answer, "that's how the women think."

One afternoon as I joined the men in the *mbanjo* Joboko told me that Mowooma had decided to cooperate with the *nga-nga* diviners. He had gone to the sawmill yard with them and, under the eyes of all concerned, had dug up an onion.

"Is that good or bad?" I asked.

"It's *good!*" the men said. The onion, evidently, had been part of the fetish that had killed the sawmill, and with its removal the affair would be drawing to a close. That night the *nga-nga* drums sounded for the last time, and the next day Bombé, Simbu, and Mowooma were released and returned to Amopolo. When I grasped Simbu's hand and welcomed him back, he shook his head and heaved a sigh more significant than any words.

/ / /

EVERYONE, NOT JUST the Bayaka, was glad to see the *nga-nga* diviners go. Much later I heard that several members of the troupe had landed in prison in Bangui, and it was reassuring to learn that their form of divination, contrary to what I had been told at the time, was not sanctioned by the government. The rampant paranoia that had gripped Bomandjombo and Amopolo quickly ebbed with their departure.

My foot took much longer to heal, and for a while I feared I might have a permanent limp. And yet the affair was not without its benefits for me. One evening Mabuti told me how impressed the Bayaka had been to see my genuine concern over the fate of Bombé and the other prisoners. Now they all knew that I really cared about them, he said. My status as "owner" of Amopolo was no longer a bluff thrown up to the villagers, it was real. The only comfort I found in Mabuti's remarks, however, was that perhaps now the Bayaka would take my marriage problems more seriously.

One day Sombolo visited me and said that "the problem is over."

"What problem?" I asked, just to be sure.

"The problem of my daughter," he replied.

That evening Ewunji came into my hut and said the same thing: "The problem is over." I was accustomed to Sombolo's empty assurances, but coming from Ewunji the remark had more force.

The next morning Ewunji returned with the same message — at least I assumed it was the same message. Ewunji had a peculiar way of communicating with me sometimes, using gestures instead of words. On this occasion he sat down and stared at me for a minute. "Ngbali!" he said, and tugged on my ear. Then he jabbed my chest with his finger several times, tugged his own ear, and finally pressed his finger into my forehead, between my eyes, so hard that it hurt. Did I understand? his eyes seemed to ask. Yes, I tried to convey with my own eyes, I understood.

For a couple of days I ruminated over the meaning of Ewunji's cryptic reassurance. I was hoping for some outward sign to confirm it, but Ngbali remained as invisible as before, and with each passing day the significance of the incident seemed to lessen. Finally I decided on a drastic course of action. I had no idea what the "problem" was supposed to have been, only that both Sombolo and Ewunji had agreed that there *had* been one. So one night I steeled myself and went to visit Ewunji. His corner of Amopolo was still all beehive huts, as though they might leave for the forest at a moment's notice. After an appropriate pause I plunged into my speech.

"I know what the problem is," I lied, "but now it's over. I still want Ngbali as my wife."

I went on in this manner for several minutes. Ewunji and his wife, Aboya, listened impassively. When I finished, Ewunji nodded his head slowly. After another pause I got up and left, still with no idea what effect my speech might have had.

In the morning there seemed to be a subdued excitement in the air. Dawn began with lots of talking. Later in the day Aboya visited Esoosi in her hut, and soon Sopo joined them. They were infrequent visitors at Esoosi's, and they were obviously holding a meeting. I assumed it was about Ngbali and me.

For several days the concept of my marriage enjoyed a kind of revival. Even those people farthest removed from Ngbali's family, such as Joboko, referred to her as my wife. Once Simbu pointed to her and said to me, "Your woman." "I know," I replied, but the truth was that I was still far from certain. Ngbali's behavior remained unmodified, and she continued to spend an inordinate amount of time with the young children. Except for people's attitudes, I could detect no real change in the situation.

One evening I went to Mindumi's. He probably knew what was on my mind, since lately I had talked of nothing but Ngbali, but I was beyond the point of caring if my obsession bored or exasperated anyone. I reflected on how I used to be unable to display real emotion in front of the Bayaka; something always made me hold back. Nowadays I thought nothing of making a fool of myself in front of the whole settlement.

"Mindumi," I said, "I thought the problem between Ngbali and me was over. Why doesn't Ngbali come to my hut?"

"She's waiting for you to take her there," he replied.

"I don't think so," I said. "I think there's still something wrong."

"Why don't we ask Ngbali?" Mindumi sensibly suggested, and called out her name.

I had not expected a confrontation with Ngbali, and for a second

I got cold feet. Then I figured what the hell. Mindumi sent a boy to fetch her, and in a few minutes she walked over. She had been at an *elanda* in a far corner of camp. Mindumi told her to sit down, and she obeyed without a word. For a while he talked to her, explaining my grievance and patiently attempting to elicit a response from her. But to no avail. Ngbali remained silent.

"Okay," Mindumi conceded, "if you won't tell me, then tell your husband in his hut."

After several minutes of persuasion, Ngbali stood up and moved slowly in the direction of my hut. Mindumi and I followed. She paused briefly at the entrance, then at Mindumi's urging slipped inside and sat down in the sand. I joined her, and to my surprise Mindumi plopped down in the doorway.

I talked for hours. My latent ability to speak Yaka suddenly surfaced in a verbal explosion. I used words and phrases I'd never tried before, and as they poured out I realized I'd heard them many times, but only now did I know what they meant. Even as I spoke I astonished myself. I talked about anything that came into my head. I tried to address every doubt she might have had. At one point Mindumi interrupted to tell Ngbali to sit on my bed — sitting in the sand was bad. I took up the point, and eventually she moved onto the bed, turning her back to me.

Much of what I said was the sort of talk a man embarks on when alone with the woman he loves. But Ngbali and I were not alone; there was Mindumi sitting in the doorway. What could he have thought of my emotional blather? Beyond Mindumi was the hut where Bessé and Nyasu slept, only they were not sleeping now — they were listening intently and remarking on every word I spoke. I always knew when I scored a salient point by the way they repeated my words to each other. From time to time Esoosi and Sao had comments to add as well, each from her own nearby hut. Meanwhile Mindumi provided a running commentary on the action: "Now she's sitting on the bed and he's sitting in the sand." "Now he's moved in front of her but she's turned her head away." He also obligingly answered questions put to him by the neighborhood audience.

As I babbled on, Ngbali turned, in stages, to face me. Was she responding to specific remarks? I was talking about so many things it was difficult to know what was effective and what wasn't. She was a complete mystery to me. Mindumi had brought along his small kerosene lamp, and in its weak yellow glow she looked overwhelmingly beautiful. While her profile was turned toward me she began to sob quietly. Why? At last she faced me, and when I said that I was her husband, she lifted her eyes and looked into mine for the first time in months.

"*Mendo mumsa na molima wom*," she said, so unexpectedly that for a moment I was startled.

"What did she say?" I asked Mindumi.

"She says that there's no problem in her heart," he translated into French.

For an instant I was overjoyed, but when Ngbali stood up to leave I realized things were not so simple. There was no problem in her heart, and yet she was going.

"Will you visit me tomorrow?" I asked.

"*Ee,*" she said. "Yes."

With that reassuring reply, she walked out past Mindumi and into the night. My spirits were briefly dampened when I heard Nyasu remark in a tone of disbelief: "She left?" But Mindumi seemed to consider the night a success. He fetched his flute, and for several hours he sat outside my hut, playing long, lyrical melodies while the rest of Amopolo slept.

NGBALI DID NOT visit me the next day. Afterward, I wondered if I had really expected her to. She had a good reason, though it was probably coincidental: her mother, Yéyé, gave birth. I saw Ngbali with the baby a couple of days later. When I asked if it was a boy or a girl, she turned away and would not reply at first, but I knew she was smiling. "Boy," she finally said.

Meanwhile rumors in Bomandjombo had caught up with my marriage problems, and now the story was that Ngbali had found a man who danced better than I. That wouldn't be difficult, I reflected, since I could hardly dance at all. At Amopolo Ngbali was again widely referred to as my wife, and although I still had very little contact with her, at least she no longer made an effort to keep out of my sight. One evening I returned from the village to be told by Mabuti — who as Sombolo's cousin ("brother") had recently taken an active role in supporting my marriage — that Ngbali was waiting for me in my hut. I rushed over, only to find the hut empty, though the scent of the perfume I had given her lingered on. She must have gone to eat with her parents, Mabuti said. But she did not return that night.

DESPITE SUCH SETBACKS, I was sufficiently reassured about my marital status to contemplate a trip to Bangui to cash the rest of my traveler's checks. Word of my intention spread fast, and the Bayaka availed themselves of every opportunity to put in orders: machetes, sarongs, sheets, pots, bowls, and knives. By the time I left I calculated I would need three times as much money as I had to satisfy everyone.

In Bangui I went on another shopping spree. The shopkeepers remembered me and welcomed me back. For a couple of days I was a big man in the city. But during the return journey my elation began to fade. The Bayaka's expectations were bound to exceed my budget. I was particularly anxious over the big aluminum pots — they were expensive, and I had bought only five. There was bound to be a bitter backlash no matter whom I gave them to. I dreaded even thinking about it.

At Amopolo I made a speech about how the Bayaka must not swamp me with angry demands but allow me to give from my heart. The Bayaka agreed, then went ahead and swamped me with demands. One day when I returned from bathing I discovered one of the big pots missing. Later I learned that Ngbali had sent someone over to claim hers. It was a bold move, and I took it as a positive sign.

Night was my favorite time to distribute gifts. I would tuck an item under my shirt, even though the bulge did not escape the Bayaka's notice, and when I saw the intended recipient alone, I would walk up out of the dark and deliver it without a word. There was always a momentary surprise, and then the person took the item and spirited it away to the nearest hut. Once when I slipped Sao a sheet and was on my way back to my hut I heard Bessé, who had witnessed the transaction, mutter in a tone of awe, "He gives from his heart." I cringed, as if I were witnessing the birth of a new Santa Claus legend.

One day Sombolo came over to tell me he was leaving for Emona, a Bayaka settlement twenty miles to the south, where his second wife and baby daughter lived. He felt all right about going, he explained, because it seemed that my marriage problem was under control — Ngbali's heart was with me. The next morning he hitched a ride in the back of a WWF pickup that was going his way. As the truck drove away, Ngbali and several other girls chased after it shouting and laughing. Sombolo had told me he would be gone for a month, but it was nearly half a year before I saw him again.

BY NOW I KNEW several villagers well enough that they came to Amopolo expecting gifts of their own from my cornucopia of goods. I explained that my giving things to the Bayaka was part of my effort to civilize them and not simple philanthropy. The villagers accepted my explanation with good humor and returned to Bomandjombo empty-handed. But when, they always wanted to know, was I going to start work on those latrines? We were scouting out possible locations now, I told them.

In reality, however, we were planning something quite different. The *nga-nga* affair had convinced the Bayaka that we should all leave the road for the forest, as I had been urging ever since we abandoned Mombongo. The women were preparing loads of manioc, and Mabuti organized a group of young men to go start work on the campsite.

"Let's go really far into the forest this time," I suggested.

"*Oui!*" Mabuti agreed. "We'll go so far that no village women will ever find us."

One morning I handed Mabuti some large smoked fish I had bought from a Sangha-sangha fisherman, as well as a supply of cigarettes, and he set off south along the road with his workers. I promised to join them in three days.

Three days later I sent out additional supplies, but I stayed put, reluctant to leave Ngbali without resolving our marital status. With Sombolo gone, I could not be sure Ngbali and her mother would even join the forest camp. So each day I put off my departure, hoping that something would happen to dispel my uncertainty. Finally I realized I had to be content with a state of affairs best described as a hopeful limbo.

The Bayaka did not facilitate the departure for the forest. On days when I halfheartedly tried to encourage an immediate exodus they came up with all sorts of excuses to put it off until the next day. I always let myself be persuaded to wait. In the end it was simply guilt that prompted me to leave on my own. Mabuti and his crew were probably out of cigarettes and wondering if anyone would ever join them. One rainy afternoon I packed a few essentials and set off with Adamo. It was fairly disconcerting to learn that we would reach the camp by evening — I'd been expecting something like a two-day walk.

Several miles down the road we met Mabuti coming from the opposite direction. He was soaking wet and looked relieved to see us. We continued together until we reached our turnoff, which looked like a fresh trail hacked out from the jungle. Mabuti pointed proudly at the wide entrance. The work of his crew, he boasted. We proceeded along the trail through unusually dark forest. The undergrowth was dense, and scarcely a patch of sky showed through the thick canopy. My spirits lifted immediately — it felt good to be back in the forest. My procrastination of the last few days suddenly struck me as foolish — why delay such a delightful prospect? Ngbali or no Ngbali, I intended to remain in the forest.

We had hardly gone a hundred yards into the forest when Mabuti announced that we had arrived. In a tiny clearing carved out of the undergrowth stood half a beehive hut. Inside, Mabuti's crew was huddled together out of the rain.

EIGHT

Lost Dreams at Sao-sao

THE CAMP WAS NAMED Epoko, after a nearby stream. *Epoko* means "puddle" in Yaka, an apt description, for the stream was nearly stagnant, its water a murky orange. I was constantly mistaking bowls of it for *njambu*, that special mixture of honey and water. Beside the camp stood a tall tree the Bayaka called *bambu*, its immense boughs arching over us. The fruit, red and yellow and shaped like a grenade, was inedible. Every now and then a specimen would detach itself, hurtle through the understory, and smash into the ground. Within an hour of my arrival one landed squarely on my foot.

Epoko was a wet and lonely place. My disappointment at being within hailing distance of the road was augmented by the absence of the women. I could not help but dwell wistfully on the difference in circumstances between my first and second forest stays: Mombongo, with its promise of a whole new world, and Epoko, with its overtones of escape from recent tensions as well as my feeling that here my final attempt to win Ngbali would be played out. Mombongo had been spacious and airy; in the morning and evening the sun's rays slanted through the *bimba* forest and set the camp aglow. Epoko, especially now at the beginning of the heaviest rains of the rainy season, was somber and dark, so dark that even my nemesis the honeybees seldom disturbed us.

For several days there were only two dwellings: the beehive hut I shared with Mabuti, Adamo, and a couple of others, and the *mbanjo* (hastily constructed during a storm) where the younger members of the crew slept. One advantage of our small numbers was the almost complete tranquility of the encampment. The boys and men went hunting during the day, and in the evenings pounded their own manioc and prepared a collective meal. One night they even held a small *eboka*, complete with glowing *mokoondi*. Its only effect on me, however, was to make me more nostalgic for the wild nights at Mombongo, when my woman was among the singers.

After a few days Mindumi and his wife, Zabu, arrived. My mood brightened at once. Mindumi's presence suggested that I had not lost all contact with Ngbali. It also raised my hopes that she and her mother would soon join us. Mabuti frequently assured me that she would, and provided me with almost daily reports on the progress of her preparations: today she was soaking manioc in water, today she was drying it in the sun, today she was soaking more manioc. I knew he was only trying to make me feel better, but did he really imagine that I would believe he knew what Ngbali was up to at Amopolo?

The days stretched into weeks as our little pioneering group carried on with scarcely any word from Amopolo. Zabu, the only woman in our company, had taken over some of the cooking duties. The meals improved noticeably. I entrusted all the coffee and sugar to Mindumi, and the morning and evening cups of coffee he delivered soon became an essential ritual — a high point of life at Epoko, small luxuries being so rare and welcome in the forest. I began to enjoy a curious freedom from the anxiety that always plagued me when Ngbali was around. Always looking for some reassuring sign from her, trying to interpret her every action, eavesdropping on gossip to find out what she was doing — it was exhausting! And it limited my interaction with the other Bayaka.

Mobo and his family were the next to move out to Epoko. He brought word of an impending exodus from Amopolo. Over the next few days many more families arrived, and our niche soon filled up with huts, each one squeezed into the space between two others, until there was scarcely any room to walk. When Simbu came, he surveyed the situation and decided to start a second encampment fifty yards farther into the forest. Yéyé and Ngbali went directly to this new camp the afternoon they arrived. I visited it the next day and was immediately envious. The huts were arranged in a circle around a clearing that was perfect for dances. By comparison, my camp was a crowded and jumbled tenement. And besides, Ngbali lived *here*.

One night a lovely *eboka* was held with pots and pans for percussion since no drums had been made. The phosphorescent *mokoondi* came and promised lots of food. In the morning the hunting party left. Early that afternoon Mabuti returned ahead of the others to inform me that not only had the hunt, still in progress, been spectacularly successful, they had found a wonderful location for a big new camp. *Bimba* forest was on one side and a large stream on the other. The water was delicious.

Two days later we left Epoko. The women stripped the *ngungu* leaves off the huts and packed them into their baskets, to be reused at the new site. In some places we followed a freshly cut path, in others scarcely visible duiker trails. Adamo and I sped ahead. After a couple of hours at that pace we reached a major fork. Straight ahead the old trail continued and curved out of sight in the undergrowth. To the left a newly cut path descended steeply. On a sapling next to it hung a curious sign. A strip of bark torn from a tree had been nailed to the sapling, with the smooth white inner surface exposed. A row of symbols had been drawn in charcoal on this surface: backward *L*'s, upside-down *e*'s, reverse *3*'s, big and little *o*'s, a sideways *8*, and something that looked like the symbol for *pi*.

"What does *that* say?" I asked Adamo as we paused to look at the sign.

"*Sao-sao*," he replied without hesitation, "the name of our camp."

I continued to stare at the sign in amazement. Adamo noticed my fascination.

"Me," he finally added with a smile and pointed. "*I* wrote that."

SAO-SAO WAS A beautiful camp, and I should have been happy there. Yet never had my heart been so profoundly consumed by sorrow. The very beauty of the place deepened my sorrow, transformed it into a state from which no escape seemed possible. For the Bayaka, on the contrary, the camp was a reaffirmation of their traditional values. Only a handful of families had remained behind at Amopolo, and Sao-sao consequently became one of the largest forest encampments ever to arise in Dzanga-Sangha. The music at night seemed to come from an earlier age, as if the Bayaka had never known anything but the forest. But their joy, and every aspect of their remarkable renaissance at Sao-sao, only plunged me closer to despair. I was witnessing it all just when I felt their world slipping away from me forever.

I started out sleeping in the *mbanjo*, but very quickly my complaints put an end to the arrangement. I knew that if I lived in the *mbanjo* Ngbali would never visit, even in daytime. Besides, my mood just could not support the continuous presence of a bunch of boisterous young bachelors. Esoosi and Mandubu constructed a beehive hut for me, and within a week I moved in. It was my first experience of living in a proper beehive hut. The prospect of sharing such a cozy space with Ngbali filled me with excitement, but the thought that she herself had not built the hut dampened my enthusiasm.

In the early days, before my mood plummeted to a steady state of despair, my emotions were attuned to the most subtle — even imaginary — indications of possible attention from Ngbali. In Sombolo's absence Mabuti had taken it upon himself to be the principal agent of good tidings. Much of what he told me was patent nonsense, but in my state I was grateful even for illusions. One day Mindumi's wife, Zabu, brought a meal over to the *mbanjo* for me. After she left, Mabuti told me that Ngbali had prepared it, elaborating in detail on the trouble she had taken to obtain *payu* for the sauce, to find *koko*, to locate chilies. I was ridiculously elated for several minutes; then, toward the end of the meal, Ngbali herself came into view and ignored me so thoroughly that I lost my appetite. Either she really was unaware of my existence, I dejectedly concluded, or her behavior was calculated to discourage the faintest glimmer of hope.

Days went by when I scarcely set eyes on her. Curiously, I

achieved a kind of emotional equilibrium, sustained by nothing more than the occasional encouraging remark from Mabuti. I began to think that I could live without her after all. I spent more time in the *mbanjo*, taking pleasure in the men's company as I had in the good old days. Then I would catch a momentary glimpse of her, and my equilibrium would be shattered by the sheer force of my desire.

I spent a good deal of time napping. Consciousness had become a kind of agony. I never went on the hunt anymore, for it only reminded me of happier days. Once camp emptied out, I slept most of the day away, emerging only in the late afternoon. I devoted many hours to staring at the leaf-tiled ceiling of my hut, which was only several inches above my nose. I became acquainted with its every detail, visually tracing and retracing patterns along the ceiling and constructing imaginary triangles and rectangles.

The Bayaka must have been rather alarmed by my behavior, but they said very little to me about it. Sometimes one of the men would casually ask me what was wrong, and I would groan to myself, "As if you didn't know." Was it, I would wonder, really possible that they didn't? Perhaps pining away for a woman was so foreign to them that they simply did not make the connection.

One day Singali arrived from Amopolo with a telegram for me from Brian Eno. "Where are you?" it asked, and urgently requested that I send him the recordings I had promised for the New York Winter Festival before a certain date — already a month past. I had completely forgotten about it! I wrote back a note that could have been penned only by someone living in isolation in the jungle: *Sorry I missed the festival; no more money; send me an envelope with large-denomination French franc notes; I will meet you in London in December.* Often it would be weeks before a letter was taken to Bangui and posted, and no reply could be expected for at least two months. My remoteness from the outside world seemed particularly conducive to the writing of crackpot letters. It was as if no one would ever receive them anyway, so I might as well write whatever I damn pleased. I gave the note to Singali and told him to deliver it to the park director, to be posted on his next trip to Bangui.

Partly to escape from my misery, I usually volunteered to go to Bomandjombo for supplies when they were needed. The Bayaka called the work of running supplies *mbingo*. If I left at first light I could be back by nightfall. Often, however, I spent the night at Amopolo and returned the next day. Although I did not really like to leave the forest, I looked forward to my village runs because they took my mind off my unhappiness. Certainly *mbingo* work was preferable to vegetating in my hut all day. I also found a sort of comfort in the depopulated camp. It had a serenity and calm that Sao-sao now lacked. The only families that had remained at Amopolo were those of Joboko, Wadimo, Balonyona, Akunga, and Mowooma. Ewunji's group, though originally intending to move out to Sao-sao, never made it. Two of Ewunji's sons — Ndima and Zalogwé — had killed an elephant. When the villager who had hired them did not pay them for their work, they went to the police and squealed. As a result they were arrested and taken to prison in Nola. Zalogwé, the younger of the two, was later released. Ndima spent three weeks there. Finally, after being teased by the other prisoners that he would be executed for his crime, he escaped by jumping into a pirogue and floating downriver all the way to Bomandjombo. Afterward Ewunji and his group established their own series of camps in the forest, moving ever farther out and eventually entering northern Congo. Zalogwé returned after a month, but the others remained for more than two years.

It was always strange emerging from the deep shade of the forest into the wide, bright space of the road. I was pretty low on cash by now, so my *mbingo* runs involved not only making purchases in the village, but selling my own possessions — blank cassettes, medicines, pens — to raise money. It was the work of selling that I dreaded most as I walked along the road toward Amopolo. I had miles to cover, so there was ample time to calculate and recalculate the financial possibilities. I never knew beforehand how successful the run would be. Sometimes I raised my target sum in a few transactions. The villagers were poor, however, and usually I had to be satisfied with a minimum.

Once I had made my purchases and was on my way back to Amopolo, my spirits lifted considerably. I shared a portion of my score with the families at Amopolo; the men and I sat together in the *mbanjo* while Balonyona brewed the coffee. I took extraordinary delight in their company — it was like a refuge from my forest misery. But the mosquitoes were ferocious, and their ranks were now augmented by a tiny biting midge.

We often stayed up all night and held an *eboka*. Some of these dances were truly sublime. With so few participants the music had a quiet, soothing effect on me — sometimes it was almost whispery. On the occasions when the *mokoondi* participated, they rarely made themselves visible but instead cried out from the distance. When they did appear they were silent, crisscrossing the camp with mysterious purpose.

However much I enjoyed my Amopolo visits, I was always glad to set off for Sao-sao once more. It was during the long walks back that my spirits soared highest; in a sense they were my happiest hours during our stay at Sao-sao. *Mbingo* work is very rewarding in some respects. You imagine the people at camp bemoaning the lack of cigarettes and coffee, speculating on the moment of your return. The weight of the goods you are carrying assures an enthusiastic reception; for an hour or so you will be a hero. In addition, unbridled by the constraints of reality, my mind would fabricate chains of reasoning that invariably concluded with Ngbali becoming mine; I would "prove" in diverse ways that of course she had to love me.

On one of these walks I grew so euphoric with optimism that I decided to have it out with Ngbali that very evening. My resolve was somewhat shaken when I caught sight of her briefly upon my return — her indifference seemed deliberate, as if she knew what I had in mind. But I decided that the time had come to confront her. Anything was better than those long naps that filled my days.

That night at Mindumi's fire I called her over. She came without enthusiasm, but at least she responded to my call. So did a dozen relatives and friends, sitting down around us with an eagerness that would have pleased me had it been shared by Ngbali. Looking at her morose expression in the firelight, I felt my heart sink as I launched into my argument: the time was fast approaching when I would have to return to America. I would work in America for five months before coming back to Amopolo. I had to know if she was coming with me. If so, she had to tell me now. All kinds of "papers" were necessary: from the mayor's office, from Bangui, from my embassy. These things took time! Also, the plane cost money and I had to know if she was coming with me so that I could "command" enough money for both of us to fly.

As I spoke I realized that I was losing my mind. Where was I going to find the money for us to fly to America, when I did not even have enough for a bush taxi to Bangui? And what work was I going to perform in America that would get us back to Africa in five months? The situation had become hopeless, and my only way of coping was to tell lies, which I rationalized .by telling myself that Ngbali would never understand the complicated truth even if I explained it to her. I reasoned that if Ngbali wanted to come with me, I would find a way to make it work.

Ngbali sensibly replied that she did not want to go to America.

Did that mean, I persisted as soon as I recovered from the shock of her refusal, that she didn't want me to go either? Or did she not care if I went? If I went, did she want me to come back? Would she wait for me to come back?

But Ngbali had spoken and would speak no more. After a while she got up and went to her mother's. I followed, lingering outside her hut like a crazed person. I heard her talking to her mother, raising other objections to our marriage. She was listing them to Yéyé, but as was so often the case with the Bayaka, she was really directing her remarks to me. What did the "white man" (as she referred to me now) know about finding food in the forest? Could he bring her honey? Besides, one day he would leave forever. Even Makola (the German anthropologist) had visited for years, but in the end he had left for good.

I returned to my hut, chastened by the validity of her arguments.

THE BAYAKA HAD promised me that no village women would follow us to Sao-sao, but shortly after my showdown with Ngbali they began to arrive. Several huts were left at their disposal, one of them directly in front of mine. I couldn't suggest any other way to replenish our manioc supply, so I had to suffer their presence silently.

One of them, who had a slightly crossed eye, I recognized at once. She had danced at Ngbali's initiation years before, and the irony of her arrival now that Ngbali and I were through was not lost on me. Her name was Claire, and she was the oldest daughter of Chief Biléma of the Sangha-sangha.

One afternoon she waited out a storm in my hut. We talked about Ngbali. Because of her role in Ngbali's initiation, Claire was her "mother." She quickly endeared herself to me by speaking wholly in favor of the marriage. She was baffled by Ngbali's reluctance. "Ngbali is very beautiful," she said. "They would love her in America." I felt a pang of regret; now that Ngbali was no longer mine, I hated to hear her described as beautiful.

I had, in fact, been trying to persuade myself that she was ugly, that the whole thing had been a fever of the imagination. To this end I had focused on her two missing teeth. Most Bayaka had their four top teeth chipped to sharp points for decorative purposes. I had never seen this being done, but the practice was widespread at Amopolo and was done at a young age. Another popular form of dental disfigurement was to chip one or two teeth down to stumps. Bosso had had one of her top teeth so reduced; Ngbali had had two, a front one and its neighbor to the left. The considerable gap that resulted was the sort of cosmetic detail that might have turned me off in years past; now, however, it made little difference. I even thought she was more beautiful because of it.

I told myself that Ngbali was not the only beautiful woman. I tried to find a woman to distract me, someone I could watch at dances, for I realized I had gotten into the habit of watching only Ngbali. I forced myself to look at other women—at Engulé's wife, Mbina, at Adamo's daughter, Njongo. But then the forest itself would sabotage me: the clouds would roll in, the trees would sway and whisper in the sudden wind, the air would be charged with electricity, and everything would glow in the prestorm light. Then, gazing at the lush and iridescent canopy, I would feel such a longing for Ngbali that my heart seemed ready to burst.

I made a point of not looking at Ngbali, which required enormous will power. Yet despite my caution, I was sometimes fooled. Once, sitting in the *mbanjo*, I caught a glimpse of a woman in front of

Mobo's hut. The chink in the intervening foliage allowed a view only from the waist to the shoulders, so I had no idea who she was, only that her breasts were a vision of loveliness. Who could she be, I immediately wondered, and why hadn't I noticed her before? Suddenly the woman stooped over and peered through the opening in the leaves — directly into my eyes. It was Ngbali, and I frowned in anger at having been caught admiring her.

THERE WAS A mysterious aspect to Sao-sao, as if the ordinary laws of astronomy did not hold. Perhaps it was only a symptom of my fragmenting mind, but I could have sworn that the sun and moon rose in different parts of the sky. The moon especially seemed to trace an eccentric path, rising to the south of the sun, then veering in an ellipse toward the north, crossing the sun's trajectory twice, to set once more to the south. I knew it was impossible, but I saw it happen time and time again.

One afternoon the sound of many popping leaves rose from the surrounding forest, and Simbu informed me that Ejengi had arrived to take up residence nearby. But Ejengi never appeared. Instead, each afternoon the leaves popped in his lair, while Mabuti — whose special connection to Ejengi I had yet to fathom — cried out Ejengi's thoughts. These usually were topical, concerning the need to pay back debts to the village women, or admonishing the hunters to make sure I had meat to eat that evening, or calling for a dance without noise. To my disappointment I never heard a reference to my marriage problems.

I began to record more actively than I had in months. Everything I was hearing, I thought, might be for the last time. When I woke up in the middle of the night to one of Mamadu's all-night solo harp sessions, I no longer told myself that there would be plenty of future occasions to record him: I roused myself from bed at once. Another night I awoke to a rare and extraordinary session of Mabuti playing the harp-zither. In the dark I slipped a cassette into my recorder and taped. The next morning I discovered, to my great distress, that I had accidentally recorded over the Ejengi ceremony at Yono's village.

Above all I recorded the *mokoondi*. No matter how deep in depression I might be as I sulked in my darkened hut while the rest of Sao-sao celebrated, the voices of the *mokoondi* always drew me out. And if I did not join the *eboka* right away, they scampered into my hut, screeching *Looyay!* and thrashing the hut apart. Once again I began to feel that the presence of the *mokoondi* had a real healing effect. During the course of an *eboka* my emotional burden would be lifted, and for a few hours I would share in the Bayaka's joy at the miraculous.

Many of the *eboka* at Sao-sao verged on theater. The half-hour intervals between songs were often filled with the antics of the *mokoondi*. Sometimes one of them would invent a silly tune and insist that the women sing it over and over, while it performed an equally silly dance. Once when the women refused, one of the *mokoondi* said, "Okay, no yams tomorrow." Chastised, the women instantly complied. Occasionally two *mokoondi* got into an argument, which would end with one of them going completely berserk for several minutes. Sometimes they made us all drum the earth with our hands. Once they danced uncannily like a Broadway chorus line, sending everyone into stitches. And one night, before my eyes, one of them turned into an antelope.

The full moon, halfway through its wacky orbit, hovered somewhere north of the zenith and bathed the clearing in bright silver light. After several minutes of clowning around, one of the *mokoondi* — a faceless albino creature—lolloped in a leisurely way across the clearing, pausing within a foot of me. I gasped, as did all the women: it was an antelope! For an instant I thought the Bayaka must have released a captured one, or somehow called one from the forest into camp. But then the antelope reached the side of the *mbanjo* and began to beat the ground — it was a *mokoondi* after all. I promised myself then that I would never again doubt what I had seen nor rationalize it away. Now, of course, I wonder.

EVEN IN THE midst of my despondency I had to marvel at my predicament. I was broke, my only hope of succor a long shot fired off to Eno. If the money ever arrived, I could get as far as Bangui. In the meantime it was my fate to endure the paradise of Sao-sao as a kind of personal hell. Physically I was falling apart. I had managed to catch scabies, which made life a continuous discomfort. My sneakers had disintegrated and now belonged in the same league as the most hopeless and laughable footwear ever sported by the Bayaka. My big left toe seemed to be rotting at the base; whenever I stubbed it the pain was so bad I would check to see if it had fallen off. Not that its loss would have bothered me — in my mental state it might scarcely have registered. I should have been lame, but, transformed by despair into a kind of superhuman, I performed incredible feats of walking. I became the *mbingo* man *extraordinaire* and thought nothing of an eight-hour excursion to the village and back for a single pack of cigarettes.

Increasingly, I stayed away from the forest camp. Strange that I should seek solace from the gorgeous world of Sao-sao in the mosquito nights of Amopolo. Once, driven by a desperate urge to escape from my own skin, I set out at the crack of dawn with scarcely an idea of what I was doing. I passed Amopolo without a second glance, reached the far end of Bomandjombo, and in exchange for a handful of aspirin caught a lift with the bush taxi as far as the turnoff to Belemboké, the Catholic mission and hospital for Bayaka. I walked the final three miles to the hospital, feeling like a ghost in the sun-blasted savanna with its stumpy twisted trees. The temperamental *père* received me with great kindness, perhaps moved to pity by the sight of me. He gave me medicine for my scabies and a thousand francs for a bush taxi back to Bomandjombo. I declined his offer to spend the night and set off once more, now on the trail to Monasao, the other Catholic mission five miles to the south. Once a shepherd-less herd of long-horned cattle blocked my way. Let them gouge me, I thought, and continued walking. At the last moment they veered out of my way to drink from a pool. Later I passed through an abandoned Mbororo camp — several large round grass huts that I came upon unexpectedly, so well did they blend in with the dwarf trees and tall grass.

The sun was a fiery orange globe low in the west when I emerged onto the main road; the vista of sky and wild hill was like a vision of primeval Africa. Gallery forest followed the streams winding between the hills. In the distance rose a column or two of smoke. For a moment I woke up and felt with a fierce clarity: I am in Africa. It was a new feeling, one I had never had in the rain forest.

I was approaching Monasao when a bush taxi drove up out of the dusk. It was the daily ride to Bomandjombo, running late as usual. I got in, and twenty minutes later we were back in the forest, the road muddy and treacherous and riven with miniature gorges, tendrils of vegetation lunging across from both sides.

Late in the night, after disembarking at Bomandjombo and passing through the village, I decided to do what the village authorities were always admonishing the Bayaka for doing: I squatted by the roadside for a crap. In the pitch black I figured no one would see me, let alone recognize me. Besides, there wasn't a soul about. But I had hardly begun when a vague form strolled up out of the dark and addressed me: "Monsieur Louis, we've been wondering where you were."

It was Balonyona. I finished my business, and together we returned to Amopolo.

FIVE DAYS LATER I went back to Sao-sao. I suppose I was still secretly hoping that my prolonged absence had provoked anxiety and brought pressure to bear on Ngbali. No such luck. My contribution of luxury products to the camp had been so meager of late that in a sense my absence had hardly been felt. However, the Bayaka were glad to have me back; they had begun to fear that I'd left them for good. The highlight of my return was a brief and puzzling remark by Baku to the effect that after I had been gone three days, Ngbali had expressed anger at my absence and said that if I did not come back soon, she would leave for Amopolo herself. The remark was so surprising that I assumed it was apocryphal. The momentary hope it might have inspired was quickly demolished by my first view of Ngbali herself, who appeared totally unconcerned with my recent absence.

Thereafter I frequently absconded, sleeping two or three nights at a time at Amopolo. During one of my visits Joboko asked me to read a note that had been delivered to him from Bobongo, a Bayaka settlement about ten miles to the north. Though composed and signed in the name of a Moaka, the note had been written by a village scribe. I had seen such messages before — the actual wording, which could vary from formal or florid to ranting and raving, was left to the imagination of the particular scribe, but the sentiments expressed were presumably those of the commissioning Moaka. I had transcribed several letters myself. My masterpiece was a menacing epistle I composed at Gongé's insistence. Addressed to a Moaka at Mosapola, it threatened dire retribution should the addressee murder Gongé's only sister.

The note in question was an angry demand that Joboko reimburse the fifteen-thousand-franc brideprice that the signatory had paid him for his daughter. It had been four months, and she still refused to sleep with him. I thought Joboko had a serious problem on his hands — fifteen thousand francs (about fifty dollars) was a fortune for a Moaka. Joboko, however, scarcely seemed fazed. He merely nodded his head as if he had expected the news and muttered, "We'll soon fix that." I wondered if I shouldn't send a similar letter to Sombolo.

The Bayaka adjusted to my itinerant lifestyle and soon I had an escort on each of my excursions. If I stayed the night at Amopolo, my escort stayed too. A certain camaraderie would arise between us, and some of my fondest memories are of those *mbingo* walks. Once my companion was a bearded fellow with a deep voice named Bokumbi. All I knew about him was that his wife's name was Ngbali, which predisposed me to like him. Our walk was memorable, with deep rolls of thunder threatening us most of the way, then a terrific downpour, which sent us sprinting the final half mile to the old camp at Epoko, where we took shelter in my abandoned hut. Another time I slipped out of Sao-sao alone, but that afternoon Mindumi arrived at Amopolo to conduct me back. Once Mindumi's young son Landi came with me. The final hour of our return was by torchlight, and halfway along the forest trail we came across Lalié and Bwanga, who had just felled a tree filled with the liquid honey called *kuma.* We feasted on the spot.

EVENTUALLY I STARTED TO spend more time in the *mbanjo* fraternizing with the young men, who had begun to grumble that I never hung out with them anymore. Now it was almost like the old days again. Occasionally my mood would darken — provoked by some memory of Ngbali, or by a melody from Mombongo popping into my head, or by a woman's distant yodel — but then the cloud would pass. The possibilities before me now seemed limitless.

Through all my emotional turmoil, Mindumi was always there, bringing me sweetened coffee every morning and evening. I loved the sight of him approaching, with his wry smile and splay-footed walk. Still the guardian of the sugar and coffee, he managed to stretch out each supply a day or two longer than I thought possible. Perhaps my new feeling of calm was due in large part to his presence, to the feeling that he would never allow my marriage to his niece simply to fade away. He had heard my declarations of love, and he had believed them. He, more than anyone else, seemed to understand.

One evening Omoo called me over to his hut for a delicious meal prepared by his wife, Tambala, one of my favorite cooks. While I ate, Mbina's little sister Metimbo visited Ngbali, who was hanging out in the hut of the other Ngbali (Bakpima's daughter). Metimbo and Ngbali grabbed each other, wrestled, splashed each other with water from puddles. It was strange to see their friendship blossom spontaneously out of nowhere. After supper, Mindumi made some coffee for me, and I drank and watched the small group of women who had gathered in front of Ngbali's hut. Metimbo and Ngbali leaned their heads on each other's shoulders. The group sang *lingokoo* songs, illuminated by the small bright flame of *vaka*, which they kept burning by adding piece after piece of the resin. Ngbali was in high spirits. She kept leaping up, running around, whooping, and yodeling. Carrying a piece of burning *vaka* on the end of a stick, she was always visible. At one point she actually patted her stomach and boasted that she was the one who would bear my children.

Finally Mindumi said encouragingly, "Okay, go."

Ngbali froze in mid-pirouette. For a moment I really believed she would follow Mindumi's advice. But then she abruptly rejoined the group of women and sat down. Omoo chuckled.

"Never mind," he said. "Today he's seen with his eyes. Tomorrow he'll sleep."

But that tomorrow never came. There were more close encounters engineered by third parties. Once Mosio got us both into the confined space of his hut. The thrill of being so near her was spoiled when she turned her back to me. I could tell she was smiling, but I was annoyed. Afterward I encountered Lalié, Adamo, and Mabuti sitting on a log. "She likes you little by little?" Lalié asked. Though I resented the phrase "little by little," with its implication of a long way still to go and plenty of time for Ngbali to change her mind (yet again), I replied that yes, it seemed that way. Adamo nodded with a big grin, and Mabuti added definitively, "She likes you a *lot*."

When I had meals at Omoo's and Mindumi's, Ngbali was always nearby and often openly flirtatious. Taken separately, each incident was full of encouragement. But considering that we'd been husband and wife for more than half a year, they were disappointing. One night I smiled at Ngbali, and she smiled back. What progress! I thought sarcastically.

One morning I awoke to the sound of her voice. It was unusual that I should hear her in my neighborhood; during our stay at Sao-sao, she had never once come near it. It was only a few words, but I never mistook her voice; it always had an electrifying effect on me. Suddenly Ngbali appeared in the entrance. She knelt (so gracefully!) and placed my morning bowl of coffee on the ground. Then she was gone.

I lay in bed for a moment, happily meditating on this sign of genuine progress. Bringing me coffee was the first thing Ngbali had done for me since we married.

AND THEN, just as abruptly as it had begun, the "honeymoon" was over. I suspected something had gone awry when Mindumi's son Landi delivered my evening coffee. The next day I ate two meals at Mindumi's, but Ngbali was nowhere in sight. After a couple of days I complained to Simbu and Mobo that if this situation did not improve soon, I was leaving for America — I could not stand the uncertainty anymore. The subsequent discussion spread among the Bayaka like wildfire, and soon camp was in an uproar. Various theories were again proposed: Ngbali was a bad woman; her mother did not like me; her mother did not want Ngbali to go to America with me. I had heard them all before, and the reiteration depressed me no end. I withdrew into my hut.

Soon one voice rose clear above the others. Yéyé, stung by the accusations, was shouting that from that moment on there was no more problem. *She,* at any rate, was not its source. Her voice grew louder as she approached my hut. From the whimpering that accompanied her, I knew she had dragged Ngbali over.

Various men gathered outside to give Ngbali counsel. Bombé, Tété, and Mabuti spoke in turn. Eventually they gave up, and only Adamo was left. I went outside and joined him in coaxing Ngbali into my hut. With great reluctance she entered and sat on my bed. I talked to her as I had talked once before, only now I added an important concession: if she accepted me, I would remain with her at Amopolo. I would not go to America more than once a year, and I would never stay in America more than one month at a time. I had no idea how I was going to keep my promise, but I meant it with all my heart.

Ngbali listened impassively. When I finished speaking she picked up my flashlight, handed it to me, and asked me to walk her home. I did as requested and returned alone to my hut. "Don't worry," several women consoled me. "She'll give you her answer tomorrow."

But no answer was forthcoming. After another couple of days I understood that Ngbali and I were through. My threat to leave, my final, desperate gambit, had failed to budge her. She was going to let me go.

On the third morning I announced that I was leaving. I scarcely believed it myself as I packed my things. Men and women gathered around me, lamenting, bemoaning, commiserating. But no one tried to talk me out of it. And Ngbali was nowhere to be seen.

"Are you going forever?" they asked.

"Forever!" I cried, deeply hurt, and hoping to hurt them too. But in my heart of hearts I knew my departure would have no lasting repercussions. The Bayaka had lived for many years without me. They would be inconvenienced for a while, and then they would adjust, and I would no longer mean a thing to them. I hated them for it.

During my final hour at Sao-sao almost everyone set off for the hunt, leaving me alone with my bags. Ngbali was one of the last to depart, carefree and laughing with her girlfriends. Bosso, who stayed behind, came over and sat on the bench next to me. Her back was to me, and she did not say a word, but she had never sat on that bench before, and I recognized her presence as a gesture of support. For a while we sat quietly side by side. Then I stood up, shouldered my bags, and left.

NINE

Ejengi

IN A SENSE my departure for America was like one of my *mbingo* runs, only on a more extreme level. I spent four nights at Amopolo. Several people from Sao-sao came out and joined me, including Simbu, Adamo, and Mindumi's wife, Zabu. Then to my astonishment a letter from Brian Eno arrived with the money I had requested. It was a fortuitous coincidence, and I interpreted it as a sign that I was indeed meant to leave.

I flew to Paris, then traveled by train and ferry to England. After a few days in London, where I duplicated some of my recordings for Eno, I flew on to New York, arriving penniless at the doorstep of two dear friends, Jim and Sara.

My stay in New York left such a dreamlike impression in my memory that sometimes I wonder if I was really there. All of me certainly was not. I arrived in winter, and the severe cold only heightened my sense of floating through the scenes around me like an astral body. Jim and Sara endeared themselves to me by putting up with the mere ghost of their friend. I was restless but purposeless, simply a presence that had to be nourished and soothed.

Dream logic prevailed. I learned that a proposal for a book about my experiences among the Bayaka, which I had submitted to a literary agent before I ever knew Ngbali, had been accepted by a publisher. The company was ready to sign a contract and pay an advance. I would have a year to write the book. At the moment the last thing I wanted to do was to write about Ngbali. On the other hand, the advance was enough to pay my way to Amopolo, and I realized that I had to get back as soon as possible. I sorely regretted having told the Bayaka I was leaving forever. If Ngbali really believed me, she might marry someone else as suddenly as Mbina had married Engulé. I grew frantic.

Only two weeks had passed since I'd left Ngbali, but already she seemed to inhabit a world immeasurably remote, like a memory from long ago. Yet the feelings she had aroused in me remained undiminished, and I clung to them as though they were my last link with her. My passion began to resemble a kind of madness in which I took refuge. Afraid of being drawn into the world around me, I refused to acknowledge its reality. To do so, I believed, would be to betray Ngbali, to relegate her to the status of mere memory. Something in me had changed irrevocably, and I realized I could never readjust to a life in the West. I resented everything about it, even having to speak English. The longer I remained, the more unhappy I would grow.

I signed the contract, explaining that I could write the book only in Africa and that I had to leave immediately. The publisher complied.

Ten days after arriving, I flew out of New York. Five days later, by a lucky sequence of connections, I reached Amopolo. Exactly three weeks had passed.

AMOPOLO LOOKED EMPTY and desolate in the gray light of late afternoon. The drizzle and chill in the air had driven everyone into their huts. My arrival seemed highly inauspicious. By the time I reached the *mbanjo*, however, I'd been spotted. A murmur rose through the camp, and the men left off napping and quietly gathered. The greeting was simple. "Looyay — he's come," said Bombé as he shook my hand Bayaka-style, no pressure to his grip.

We sat in silence for a few minutes. Some of the women were stirring about now, and I kept my eyes peeled for Ngbali. Soon enough I saw her. She did not look over, but she must have known I was back. I breathed a sigh of relief: perhaps I was not too late after all.

The group of men in the *mbanjo* was unusually large. People I had not seen in a long time were there: Mitumbi, Sosolo, Maliamba. I looked around at all the faces.

"Monsieur the mayor," Balonyona suddenly announced in his speedily stuttered version of French, "he hasn't come here because of the death."

It took me a few minutes to digest his words.

"Mindumi?" I asked in disbelief as the meaning began to dawn on me.

"*Oui*, Mindumi," Balonyona confirmed. "He has died!"

I uttered a cry of astonishment. I had thought much about Mindumi while in America. I had not brought back many presents, but I had remembered a pair of American sneakers for Mindumi. Almost more than anyone else, I had wanted him to know that I'd come back, that everything I'd told Ngbali about staying forever, about being lost when I was far from the Bayaka, about being in love with her, was true. I wanted him to know that his faith in my sincerity had not been misplaced. Instead, he had died thinking I had left forever.

I RAN INTO Mindumi's widow, Zabu, the next afternoon on my way to bathe. She was sitting in the tiny strip of shade along the side of Akunga's big bamboo hut. She was alone, and I paused awkwardly, then sat down next to her. She told me how Mindumi died. Shortly after I left, he had gone into the forest to help Bokia, who was high in a tree hacking away to get at a honeycomb. Bokia called out for Mindumi to stay back because a large branch was threatening to split off from the tree. Mindumi ignored his warning, and the branch fell on his head. He was killed instantly.

I tried to tell Zabu how much Mindumi had meant to me, and suddenly I found myself crying. I made an effort to hold back the sobs, which shook my body. Zabu was also crying quietly. Soon her sister Tambala joined us to weep. Poor little Tété, who was with us, finally burst into tears.

Mindumi's death really stunned Amopolo and left an immense vacuum. It was not just that there was no one quite like him but that, as Singali tried to express it, "There was so much of him at Amopolo." I would not realize how deep the shock was for many months, but I could sense that the community was not the same. None of us could have known then of the terrifying events to come, but already Mindumi's death seemed to mark the beginning of a new phase in the history of Amopolo.

I felt great comfort in Zabu's company, and she evidently felt the same in mine. She visited me frequently, sometimes with food, sometimes with her three children, and we would sit together and talk. I gave bananas, peanut butter, and other treats to the children. I provided her with anything she asked for. She was in advanced pregnancy, and I felt protective toward her. We both wanted the best for her unborn child.

One night she came over alone with some food and sat near me while I ate. Afterward, in a rapid mutter, she confided something very strange: that Mindumi had been murdered by *gundu*. The wife of Sosolo, jealous that I liked Mindumi so much and gave him the coffee and sugar to guard, had used *gundu* to kill him. She had powerful *gundu*.

I was taken by surprise, but I suppose I thought *gundu* was a kind of superstition — after all, Mindumi had been killed by a falling tree. It was only an accident. How could you murder someone by making a tree fall on him? But I did not know how to say *It was only an accident*. Instead I said, "No, Zabu, no one killed Mindumi. God called him. That's how it is." Later I wondered, what the hell is *gundu*?

A couple of days after my return Adamo arrived by foot from Monasao. He said his family would follow in a week. The next day Sombolo arrived from Emona in the opposite direction, news of my return having reached him by bush taxi. I was not sure whether I was glad to see Sombolo or not. I appreciated that he had kept alive the issue of my marriage to his daughter — often he was the only one who did — but most of his reassurances had been pure fabrications, designed to elicit spare change from me.

That evening Zabu came by to invite me for a meal. She had moved into one of the two beehive huts in Mowooma's huge, and

still unfinished, bamboo hut. Sombolo, Yéyé, and Ngbali lived in
the other beehive. Sopo slept in a corner, and Mowooma and his
two wives slept in one of two inner rooms that were under construction. When I arrived they were all present. Mowooma was lounging on a reed mat. He shined his flashlight at Ngbali several times,
telling me she was my wife. Ngbali finally turned her back and
giggled. Later she served me my food, but instead of handing my
bowl of water to me directly she put it on the ground and slid it
toward me with a giggle. When I returned to my hut much later
that night I was rather more cheerful than when I left it.

I coasted along in an upbeat mood. Women problems seemed to
be the order of the day at Amopolo, and I suppose I found some
comfort in being in good company. Engbeté and the other Ngbali
had finally, after months of turmoil, split up. I learned about it
when she came over and asked me for a sheet.

"But I gave Engbeté a sheet at Sao-sao for both of you!" I protested.

"Engbeté took it when he left," Ngbali explained, and I realized
that whoever I handed an item to was considered its ultimate
proprietor.

"Did Engbeté leave for good?" I asked.

"He left forever forever," she replied. I got her a sheet.

Then there were Bwanga and Mowa, who had once been like two
lovebirds. They were the most publicly affectionate Bayaka couple I
had ever seen. But those days were long gone. Recently they had
been having fight after fight, and Mowa had moved back in with
her parents. One day when Bwanga was sitting with me in my hut
Mowa came by and without a word dumped a bunch of his possessions on the floor. They included Bwanga's flashlight, which she
had smashed and crunched beyond recognition. Bwanga picked up
the wreck and with a shake of the head said, "Women!"

Old Bombé and Balé's relationship had recently intensified; they
were both living at Amopolo now and their encounters were frequent. One afternoon on my way back from the village I ran into
Balé coming from the opposite direction.

"It's over!" she announced without explanation, grabbing my
arm.

"What's over?" I asked.

"Me and Bombé," she said. "It's really over this time! I'm going to the mayor's office to tell them."

But that evening when I wanted to give some small thing to Bombé, who was off in the village, the men told me to give it to his wife, Balé. She would give it to Bombé when he got back.

"I thought they split up," I said.

"They did," Biléma and Engulé explained, "but that was this afternoon. They're back together now."

One day Sombolo stopped by to ask for some pills for Ngbali. "Is Ngbali sick?" I asked with mild concern.

"She's very sick," Sombolo replied, and from his description I knew she had a serious case of malaria. Naturally I grew very alarmed and hurried over.

I found her dazed with fever, but willful enough to make it clear she did not want me to see her in that condition. Physically Ngbali was strong and amazingly healthy, and seeing her with the force knocked out of her was particularly upsetting. She put up a fuss about swallowing all the pills I counted out for her — as I knew she would. One of the things I loved about her was her fierce resistance to all innovation. It was only by throwing a small fit myself that I finally persuaded her to take the medicine.

The next day she was sufficiently recovered to realize the benefit of my medicines, and she swallowed the aspirin I gave her without protest. After that I nursed her back to health, visiting every day and spending an hour or two with her family. They were pleasant times, especially the last couple of days, when Ngbali had fully recovered but seemed to enjoy stretching out her convalescence, lounging about and playing with her small cousins. That she actually appreciated my care was confirmed one evening when Zabu called me over for a meal. Ngbali fetched me water without being asked and handed it to me directly. Toward the end of the meal I heard Yéyé complain about feeling hungry, so I gave the remains of my food to her. As she ate, Ngbali appeared in the entrance to Mowooma's hut and began to speak in that quick soft manner she used when she only half wanted me to understand her. For a few seconds I did not even realize she was addressing me: "I'm just getting better from a bad illness. And now I'm hungry. Why do you share your food with my mother instead of with me?"

My immediate urge was to grab the food away from Yéyé and present it to Ngbali. Fortunately, I had no choice in the matter: Yéyé had quickly finished eating before Ngbali finished speaking.

AS THE NEW YEAR advanced and the dry season, with its all-powerful sun, established itself firmly, I realized that the Bayaka had not gone on a single hunt since my return. The world of Saosao had become like a memory of some long-past epoch. It was difficult to reconcile the personalities around me with those I had known in the forest. Hunger prevailed, yet everybody seemed content to let it prevail. The staple food was now manioc: the tuber was pounded, made into a kind of dough, and eaten with the leaves of the plant, chopped up and boiled. Though the fare filled our stomachs, it never satiated our hunger.

By day Amopolo was like a furnace, with no hope of even a brief shower to help us through the day. The chigoes thrived and multiplied, feeding especially on the feet of the children, several of whom reverted to crawling on all fours. By contrast the nights were often chilly, yet never chilly enough to deter the mosquitoes. Unlike the chigoes, whose numbers diminished significantly during the rainy season, mosquitoes were a year-round plague at Amopolo. Their attacks caused the Bayaka to sleep fitfully at night, so they were often tired during the day. Small wonder they were never enthusiastic about going hunting.

I realized more clearly than ever that Amopolo was a poor site for a village. Besides being next to a raffia marsh, where mosquitoes bred, its proximity to Bomandjombo only encouraged the men to trek into town at any time of day or night in search of that elusive free glass of *mbaku*. Invariably they returned to Amopolo with debts. To pay their creditors, the Bayaka gathered raffia leaves in the marsh, which brought them a hundred francs (the price of one glass of *mbaku*) for a bundle, half a day's work. If a man drank four glasses, he was indentured for two full days of work. Increasingly the men were employed in gathering raffia (they called this work *mbo*), so they were less and less available for hunting. It was a disturbing trend, and I complained about it loudly and often. The men agreed that things were getting out of hand, but they continued just the same.

I began to have serious doubts about the survival of the Bayaka should they remain at Amopolo. And now they had decided to entrench themselves further by heeding my advice about the need for latrines. Conditions in the surrounding bush were fast becoming untenable. When I stepped on a turd during one of my solo excursions I returned to camp in a rage. At the time my tirade had fallen on deaf ears, but now, all of a sudden, everyone wanted to build latrines. I had brought two shovels as gifts to the camp, and pretty soon there were ten-foot-deep holes all over Amopolo. Yet not a single latrine ever progressed beyond the digging stage. No sooner was one dug than the men moved on to the next. A stroll in the dark was hazardous to one's life. There was something desperate about the frenetic energy and dedication the men put into digging those holes, none of which would ever be used for the purpose it was intended. They could dig an average of two useless holes a day, but they did not have the strength to go hunting. I did not have the heart to dissuade them from digging — it might, I felt, be as dangerous as waking up a sleepwalker in midstride — but I did not encourage them either. That, I felt, would be tantamount to encouraging them to remain at Amopolo, which I did not want them to do. I watched them dig and was secretly grateful that no latrine was ever completed.

I also had to organize my own work plans. I had been given money to write a book, and I thought I should at least go through the motions of setting myself up to begin. I commissioned a carpenter in the village to build me a table and chair, and bought a kerosene lamp. During all my time at Amopolo it had never occurred to me to invest in a lamp. Now it quickly became one of my few essential possessions. At first I slightly resented its steady illuminating presence. It certainly made life easier, but in abdicating the evenings around a simple campfire I felt I was separating myself from the Bayaka. They had nothing but praise for my new setup: the large redwood table and chair, the kerosene lamp, and a small digital alarm clock. *At last,* they seemed to say, *our white man is starting to behave like one.*

Soon I had a routine established. As darkness fell I lit my lamp, sat in my chair, opened the notebook on my table, picked up my pen, and stared at the blank page until late into the night. My work was a source of endless fascination for the Bayaka. As soon as I opened my notebook, boys and men gathered around my table to watch and comment on my every move, their faces intent in the glow from the lamp. Some remained at their observation posts for hours. Others came and went. My hut became a kind of round table where all sorts of topics were discussed, often having little to do with me. Invariably I found myself listening in.

When, after a week, I finally wrote the first line, the men who were witness to its creation extolled its merits. When I crossed it out after a minute they glorified my supreme expertise. If I protested at the noise, the noise grew louder, as those already present tried to force newcomers to go away. Arguments erupted over who had the right to stay. Usually the biggest noisemakers prevailed, each celebrating his triumph with an eloquent soliloquy on my need for peace and quiet. Sometimes it was not noise but the silent observer who irked me. Once Etubu came into my hut and stood as quiet as a mouse behind me, looking over my shoulder. After fifteen minutes I told him I couldn't work with him watching me that way. He replied that he wasn't watching me — he was looking at my digital alarm clock. I let him stay.

My relationship with Ngbali seemed to be on an upswing. Every evening I spent some time with her and her family. Ngbali would sit with me, brew the coffee I had brought along, and we would share a bowl. She was always in a lively, cheerful mood, and fairly soon I felt encouraged enough to hint that it was time we moved in together. Finally one night she promised me, "Tomorrow."

Early the next morning a few loud voices rose in an argumentative lament. Soon the whole camp was involved in what sounded like a shouting match. Obviously they were discussing some problem, but I couldn't understand their excited chatter. I had other things on my mind, and nothing was going to spoil my mood. Eventually the talk subsided.

As the day wore on I grew unusually restless. I realized that I had not seen Ngbali since waking up. Often she would leave for the forest or the village before I was out of bed, and I would not see her until evening. But *this* absence was different: her mother, grandmother, aunts, cousins, and friends — anyone who might have gone with her — were all present.

When Sombolo came by for his daily cigarette I asked him where Ngbali had gone. To gather *koko* in the forest, he replied. When Mabuti, a distant relation of Ngbali's, stopped by for his cigarette I asked him as well. (By now I knew it was wise to corroborate all data.) To catch fish, he told me. The women's method of fishing was to dam up a section of stream and then to gather up the fish from the drained area below the dam. It required a large work force — who had Ngbali gone with? There were plenty of women she could have gone with, Mabuti replied somewhat cryptically.

By nightfall there was still no sign of her, and I knew something was wrong. Out of habit I was sitting at my table with the notebook open before me, surrounded by my usual audience, but I was not thinking about writing. I was waiting to pounce on the first member of Ngbali's family to appear. Eventually Mabuti sauntered into my hut, probably hoping for a second cigarette. I confronted him immediately with the lie he had told about Ngbali's whereabouts. Okay, so where was she?

There was a guilty silence. Then Singali spoke up: everyone had been deceiving me. Ngbali was gone. She had left before dawn with her uncle Zalogwé. They had gone to lay snares in the forest. No one knew when they would be back.

Suddenly I understood the commotion of that morning.

I DRIFTED THROUGH the next few days in a stupor of despair. I had become so absorbed in Bayaka life that I'd lost all sense of who I was in their eyes. I had tacitly assumed that I fit right in, that my expressions of emotion (my earlier shy reserve had long ago been worn away) so closely though unconsciously modeled on their own, would automatically be interpreted as a sign of our common ground. Now it occurred to me that such ideas were nonsense; more likely my sudden outbursts were, to the Bayaka, just one more peculiarity of a very peculiar white man. To Ngbali my relentless efforts at courtship may have seemed like the unwelcome advances of an ogre. Often when they talked to one another about me, the Bayaka still referred to me as "white man," even after all this time. I began to feel ashamed of my behavior: a white man who gave presents to the Bayaka and then expected to sleep with one of their women. I had turned into a kind of man I despised.

The following afternoon I braced myself and went to visit Yéyé. I found her alone in Mowooma's hut.

"I don't like noise," I said by way of opening, a phrase borrowed from Sombolo, who always used it on me. Yéyé looked at me, her expression inscrutable for all its apparent candor. Her eyes, large with wonder or fear, perhaps, were startlingly beautiful. It was the same expression that Ngbali had. For the first time I realized how closely the daughter resembled her mother.

I apologized for bothering her daughter and promised to leave her alone in the future. When I finished, Yéyé replied that she had talked and talked to Ngbali about her behavior toward me, but Ngbali just would not listen. Ngbali simply had a bad head.

Ngbali didn't have a bad head, I immediately responded (though in my heart of hearts I was beginning to agree with Yéyé). She was a good woman, and I was deeply in love with her. It was just that in her heart Ngbali did not love me. Talk meant nothing to the heart. Neither did force.

Yéyé's expression remained as unreadable as ever, but I thought I detected some subtle response to my words — surprise, perhaps? It was difficult to tell. Nevertheless, confident that I had made some sort of impression, I asked Yéyé to apologize to Ngbali for me. I returned to my hut, and for several minutes I felt deservedly proud of myself: that apology had been one of the most difficult I'd ever had to make. Soon, however, my relief gave way to fathomless grief: I had just given up Ngbali.

The next afternoon I was rather surprised when Akunga's young son, Mango, came by to tell me that Yéyé had prepared me a meal. One part of me had almost expected such a development, though perhaps not quite so soon. I was beginning to learn that when things seemed most hopeless between Ngbali and me, something always occurred to reverse the decline. I imagined myself caught in the sort of weird tests behavioral scientists dream up to measure emotional deprivation.

Yéyé was in a bright mood. She called me Looyay and told me

to sit down. She had never before addressed me by name. Then she served me a tasty meal of antelope while she, I noticed, ate plain *koko*. The meal was a touching but perplexing gesture. I might have believed that Yéyé was thanking me with a gift of food for letting her daughter alone, but while I ate she talked to her mother, Sopo, and some of her remarks were highly suggestive. "Her heart *is* with the man," she said, and I thought she must be talking about Ngbali and me. Later, bouncing her baby, Mbanda, on her lap, she pointed at me and told him I was his brother-in-law. I could scarcely believe my ears.

Yéyé continued to serve me meals, and sometimes she and her mother visited me in my hut for ten minutes. Despite Ngbali's absence, these visits cheered me up. Soon I felt confident enough to consider a long overdue journey to Bangui to cash some traveler's checks.

The day before my departure was memorable. I woke up to the news that Zabu had given birth during the night to a son, whose name was to be Mindumi. In the evening a small farewell *eboka* was held. I sat with the drummers and watched. First I noticed Mabuti's younger wife, Sakpata, who was an inspired dancer. Then I noticed Bosso, as exuberant as in the days before she'd become a mother. Finally my attention was riveted by Yéyé, who danced and sang so beautifully that I was moved to tears in the dark. She was singing my name.

ON THE SECOND DAY of my return journey from Bangui I became very anxious over the likely disenchantment awaiting me at Amopolo. By the time we reached Monasao I was so agitated that I decided to stop there. Better to live in the relative security of an illusion for a few more days — grim reality would have its hour soon enough.

Several families at Monasao knew me and many others knew of me. I had yet to introduce myself to Father René and Sister Madeleine, however, and as I walked toward their humble mud-brick houses I was nervous over my reception. They were missionaries and their mission was to convert the Bayaka to Christianity, an objective I was not comfortable with. Nevertheless, they had done some impressive things. Monasao, whose population was nearly fifteen hundred, was a self-sufficient Bayaka community. Traditionally, the Bayaka were dependent on the villagers mainly for manioc. At Monasao every family had its own manioc plantation, and they sold the surplus to villagers. To reduce the temptation of *mbaku*, René had founded Monasao away from other villages. The closest one, very small, was a mile away.

Monasao was spread out on either side of three miles of road. It was very pretty, with fruit trees everywhere, planted fifteen years ago by the *père*. The huts, more than half of which were beehives, were set far apart by Amopolo standards and gave a feeling of tranquil spaciousness. There was a school (the schoolteacher and his family were the only villagers in Monasao), two churches, a simple hospital, and two small stores, one run by René, the other by Madeleine. The Bayaka earned money either by working for René and Madeleine on projects for the community, or by selling manioc and forest products to villagers. Though the forest was some distance away, groups still went hunting.

René and Madeleine received me with sincere hospitality. The Bayaka helped by introducing me as one of themselves. René, the soul of Monasao, accepted me at once. Madeleine, the community's backbone, gave me one long penetrating look, decided in my favor, and thereafter was all warmth and kindness. I was given a mud-brick cabin (the old hospital) to live in and invited to take my meals with them. Otherwise I was left to myself. I intended to stay several days.

At dinner that evening René told me that once a month he spent a week on the road, sleeping one night and preaching the gospel at each of the Bayaka settlements as far south as Mosapola. Only days earlier, he had visited Amopolo for the first time while I was in Bangui. The *père* shook his head. He had never seen such bad chigoe infestation. And the mosquitoes at Amopolo were in a league by themselves (Monasao had none). In addition, a number of the men had been drunk. His method of preaching was to have a huge fire built, around which the Bayaka sat, and then to tell the story of Jesus, interspersing his sermon with prayer songs in Yaka to tunes he had made up himself. The Bayaka were encouraged to sing along.

At Amopolo, however, he had not had an opportunity to preach and had merely spent the night. Ejengi had arrived, and the Bayaka were keen to carry on with their dance.

"Ejengi is dancing at Amopolo?" I asked in surprise.

"Ejengi danced until nearly dawn," René replied.

I expressed concern that perhaps I should leave in the morning since I had never seen Amopolo's Ejengi.

"Oh, don't worry about missing Ejengi!" René said with a wry chuckle. "Ejengi's not going away in a hurry!"

They told me that once Ejengi danced at Monasao for more than *two years!* He danced at all hours of the day, and at night whenever there was a moon. If the moon rose at three in the morning, the Bayaka got up then and danced. They drank *mbaku* constantly, they smoked heaps of marijuana, they were totally useless for work. Madeleine finally put an end to it by driving her Land Rover directly into the middle of a dance in progress, opening the door, and ordering Ejengi to get inside. Then she drove him to the forest and told him to go home.

When I asked René if he planned to return to Amopolo to try again, he said no. It was not so much the adverse physical conditions at Amopolo that deterred him — though at his age (he was seventy-four) they were formidable — but rather the severity of the corruption. Amopolo was the worst-off Bayaka community he had ever seen. He had little hope that in their present condition the residents would even listen to one of his sermons, let alone consider it seriously. Perhaps, he added, my influence would eventually make the Bayaka more receptive. Certainly it was admirable that I continued to live among them. With all the parasites, he imagined, I must fall ill often.

In fact, I had been feeling weak and rundown since leaving Amopolo, and the next evening at the dinner table, as if to demonstrate the accuracy of René's remark, malaria fever struck me so rapidly and with such force that in the middle of a sentence I blacked out. I spent the rest of my stay at Monasao recovering.

After several days, feeling once more fit and healthy, I bade farewell to my hosts and caught the daily bush taxi to Bomandjombo. We broke down several times, once near the village of Yobé. On my last journey past Yobé I had stopped to give a bag of colorful plastic necklaces to the Bayaka women. This time the Bayaka were gone, their settlement abandoned. Several irate villagers approached our stranded vehicle and accused me of ordering "their Pygmies" into the forest. I denied the charge.

"You're the white man at Amopolo, aren't you?" one of them asked angrily.

"*Oui,*" I replied.

"*Voilà!*" he cried. "They said it's *you* who ordered them to go into the forest!"

Fortunately the repairs were now finished and I reboarded the bush taxi. As we drove away one of the villagers shouted, "Give us back our Pygmies!"

AMOPOLO'S EJENGI did not disappoint. All the energy and frenzy I had come to expect during his visits were there, but with an extra musicality. On that first night Ejengi came out at twilight. Many villagers were present. A few were Sangha-sangha, who assisted in the dance, running alongside Ejengi with sticks to protect the women from him, but the great majority were outsiders (not Sangha-sangha) who had come to watch. They formed a huge semicircle around the smaller group of singers. Most of them were clearly afraid of Ejengi and fled whenever he approached. After a couple of hours the Bayaka slowed the momentum of the dance to encourage the villagers to leave. When the crowd thinned out, the dance picked up again and went on until midnight.

The next morning I was called over to Mitumbi's part of camp to examine one of the men, Etundu, who was ill. He was one of the Bayaka I knew least, which meant that he was one of the shyer and probably gentler men. I found him sprawled on his back, gravely ill.

"How long has Etundu been ill?" I asked in consternation.

"A month," was the reply.

It was typical of the Bayaka to say nothing to me about his illness until now. I could do very little for him at this late stage. He wasn't conscious enough to swallow any medicine. I returned to my hut discouraged.

That afternoon the sound of popping leaves rose from Ejengi's lair (*janga*) in the nearby jungle. Soon there were cries of *oka!* as one of the men began to declaim Ejengi's thoughts. Ejengi was saying that out of deference to Etundu he would not dance that night. Later Mabuti stopped by my hut. Mabuti was the "proprietor" of Ejengi at Amopolo, although what this meant I had yet to fathom. He was slightly inebriated, and what he said made only partial sense. There was something bad at Amopolo, something horrible. People were dying. That was why he had called Ejengi, so Ejengi would make everything right again. Already Mindumi had died, and now Etundu had fallen ill.

Mabuti began to sob and moved off to cry by himself.

Etundu died in the early hours of the following morning. By daybreak the *élélo*, joined by all the women at Amopolo, was heartrending. He was buried in the afternoon. In the evening, as the drums began to sound for Ejengi, only his immediate family continued the *élélo*. The full moon rose and Ejengi appeared for a night of dancing. Yet before midnight the moon began to darken — a lunar eclipse, I realized — and as Amopolo was plunged into darkness Ejengi retired. At three A.M., the moon once more bright, the men emerged and performed their *so* ceremony for Etundu. It had scarcely ended at dawn when Ejengi emerged for more dancing. Etundu's death had made but a ripple in the proceedings.

SHORTLY AFTER MY RETURN I determined that Ngbali was back. Her presence gave me little peace of mind, but at least I could keep some track of her whereabouts. Sometimes I wondered if Ngbali had already been someone else's betrothed when I met her. Would the Bayaka, seeing my interest, have led me on to believe she could be my wife in order to keep me (and my presumed fortune) at Amopolo?

Meanwhile Ejengi danced — at dawn, at noon, at dusk, at midnight. Even when he had temporarily retired to the *janga*, his thoughts would be proclaimed by one or another of the men, always to the sound of popping leaves, as if the thoughts were crackling in from another dimension. Sometimes he ran around camp accompanied by the speaker. Every day the boys wore a different assortment of those strangely festive "framework" hats — wide-brimmed or brimless, helmet- or crown-shaped — associated with Ejengi, constructed out of pale yellow strips of palm curled into flower and snowflake patterns. Ejengi, I was learning, was the occasion for the initiation of boys, a process called "seeing Ejengi." All day men and initiated boys went up and down the path leading to the *janga*. It was forbidden to the women and the uninitiated, the cutoff point masked by a curtain of raffia fibers of the sort that made up Ejengi's clothing. For the first time I found myself relatively alone for hours at a time, the men preferring to lounge around in the *janga,* only occasionally sending one of the younger members out for cigarettes or marijuana. These requests were invariably made in Ejengi's name.

For the dances themselves, the singers — the women — lined up in a dense crowd in front of the *mbanjo.* The position exposed them to the equatorial sun until about four in the afternoon, yet they could sing and dance for hours with only an occasional drink of water or rest in the shade of the *mbanjo* for relief. Yéyé, one of the most dedicated of the dancers, was always present; Ngbali was there quite often. From my hut — in fact, from my table if I turned my head — I had a perfect view of the singers; I could watch Ngbali from the comfort of my own home.

She was still a fabulous dancer. Her moves were so imaginative, no one else attempted anything like them. During the *esimé* section of each song she really let loose, the extraordinary rhythm of her cries perfect to the nanosecond, the variations in her pitch accurate to the quarter tone. She was a marvel to behold. Had she been my wife I would have been immensely proud; instead I felt a painful longing, with raging jealousy lurking in the wings. On some days she looked toward my hut often, and occasionally she even spent the day on the closer side of the *mbanjo.* On other days, however, she seemed to ignore my direction altogether.

During the course of each dance many of the young women would pair off in intimate but temporary friendships, chasing after Ejengi together, seeking each other out if they got separated in the excitement of the moment, holding hands, and running back laughing to their place in front of the *mbanjo.* Several times Ngbali and Mbina spent a dance together this way. On other days Ngbali danced with Banda, a young woman who had recently come from the Mokala River in Congo with her husband, Eloi, her parents, and her brother.

In the beginning I enjoyed having Ejengi around. His presence told me something was going on. The collective spirit of the community was activated, and the mood was constantly heightened to one of expectation. Also I got to see a lot of Ngbali. But there were definite drawbacks, too. Sheer chaos reigned because the collective spirit of the community was wholly devoted to Ejengi. The lack of interest in hunting, the carelessness in regard to hygiene and daily living, the alcoholism, and the *mbo* labor for villagers all grew worse. But the most serious consequence of Ejengi's presence, the one that aggravated all the other problems, was the barrage of villagers who came day and night to watch Ejengi.

I had never properly appreciated the absence of villagers from nighttime musical events at Amopolo. Although the drums could be heard in Bomandjombo, the villagers had showed no interest in coming out to watch. Now, with Ejengi's arrival, at the first sound of the drums they thronged to Amopolo — not out of mere curiosity but out of an insatiable fascination. They seemed to realize that Ejengi represented a power that defied explanation, and they never tired of witnessing the demonstration of that power. Sometimes the Bayaka stopped a dance early so that the villagers would leave. Then, if there was a moon, they would begin again late in the night. Some dedicated villagers often returned to watch, even after midnight.

Many *bilo* turned the occasion into an opportunity for profit. They came with cigarettes, bundles of marijuana, jugs of *mbaku*. The Bayaka consumed all to excess in their zealous dedication to Ejengi. They fell farther and farther behind in their debts, committing themselves to weeks of *mbo* work. Villagers roamed the settlement at all hours to collect on their debts; frequently they confiscated items — a sheet, a machete, a cooking pot — and held them in escrow. Invariably the confiscated goods were more valuable than the corresponding debt. The Bayaka would protest — now and then a fistfight even broke out — but they always gave in and rarely made an attempt to recover the item. I watched in horror as all the gifts I had distributed slowly found their final homes in the houses and huts of the villagers.

I discovered that an Ejengi dance was a good occasion for writing. Absorbed in their ceremony, the Bayaka rarely bothered me for cigarettes, and I could begin a sentence fairly confident of reaching the end before someone interrupted. In the end, however, the arrival of curious villagers or the mounting heat would flush me out of my hut and into the fringe of the forest. I always carried my notebook with me, though I never wrote a word. And as I crossed the manioc fields, making sure no one saw me, I would feel an immense relief at having escaped the chaos. Behind me the sounds of the dance would seem to reach fever pitch even as they receded into the distance. By the time I reached my secluded refuge, the music was only slightly louder than the chirping of birds. I would flop to the ground, place the notebook under my head, and go to sleep.

When he wasn't dancing, Ejengi often joined the group of men I sat with. For long periods he would remain motionless in a crouched position while the men smoked and talked. Suddenly he would tap the inside of his raffia clothing, indicating he had a thought for translation. One of the men would shout it out. On one of these occasions, Mabuti brought Ejengi over to introduce him to me. Ejengi seemed momentarily confused, turning left and right and recoiling. Mabuti explained to the others that Ejengi wasn't used to my smell. Everyone laughed except me. Thereafter Ejengi frequently crouched down next to me, and I was told that he liked me. Small wonder, since I always catered to his ravenous appetite for cigarettes and marijuana. Friendship with Ejengi was expensive, but I felt I could hardly refuse a forest spirit. If during a dance I holed up in my hut, blocking the entrance against the prying eyes of the villagers, Ejengi would eventually come by between songs. His entreaties for me to join the spectacle were translated by one of the men. Since I did not want to hurt Ejengi's feelings, I usually emerged from my hut to watch. Once when I returned from a night at Belemboké, where I'd gone to buy medicines, Ejengi came over and shook my hand! A slit in the raffia clothing appeared, and I was told to slip my hand inside. It was grasped by a gnarled and calloused hand.

One day the men invited me to join them at the *janga*. We would have to be careful, though. None of the women or uninitiated boys must know about my visits there. I had to take a roundabout route, crawling a good part of the way through jungle on my hands and knees. Ejengi was never present during my visits to his lair, but dozens of his castoff raffia outfits were, like so many shed skins. They were as comfortable to sit and lie on as hunting nets, and I learned that one of the men's favorite activities was to nap in the shade sprawled out on Ejengi's old clothes. Now and then one of them shouted out a "communication" from Ejengi. The others quickly picked a bunch of leaves and popped them during the declamation.

During these pleasant idylls in the *janga* the men began to discuss initiating me. They never spoke about it directly to me, and at first I wasn't sure what they were talking about. But as they went over and over their plans in my presence I understood. Ejengi liked me, they said to one another. I was an adult, so it was time I saw Ejengi. The talk became more enthusiastic. It was decided that Joboko would be my "father in Ejengi." I would be given something to drink, but they expressed some doubt that I would drink it. "He'll drink it," Joboko declared with assurance. "He's a man, he won't be afraid. He knows we wouldn't kill him." As the days passed, the plans became more definite, and one day the men decided that my initiation would begin the following morning. I went to bed that night wondering what sort of concoction I would be expected to drink.

But the next day it was Biléma's son Elivé who was initiated. Elivé was not yet five years old and he was terrified. In the *janga* he was rubbed down from head to toe in a reddish oil and decorated with half a dozen plastic necklaces. What else went on in the *janga* I don't know, but several times during Ejengi's dancing Elivé was lifted screaming and kicking up to Ejengi's veil, which then parted and pulled him inside.

A few days later, on a Sunday, the ten-year-old son of Biléma, the Sangha-sangha chief, was initiated. He slept for several days at Amopolo, and on the day of his initiation his father attended, sitting in my chair, which had been requisitioned for the occasion. Usually

Sunday drew the biggest crowds of visiting villagers, but on this particular Sunday not a single outsider showed up.

Another time a whole group of boys was initiated together. While none was as young as Elivé, they all looked very solemn, and spent much of the day sitting still and staring at their feet.

But my initiation, like my marriage, never happened. For weeks the talk went on — so positive, so eager — but it had nothing to do with reality. I yearned to be initiated. To become an adult according to Bayaka custom could only enhance my standing in Ngbali's eyes. A traditionalist, she might have objected to the marriage solely on the grounds that I was still a child. But initiation was not something I could ask for. I had too much respect for the tradition to demand it. Besides, where had my imploring gotten me with Ngbali? And so I waited. And wondered: was all the talk about my initiation sincere, or was it another elaborate Bayaka charade?

One day I was sitting with some men when Ejengi joined us. After a few minutes he tapped on the raffia.

"Tell us," the men said to Sombolo, who was next to Ejengi.

"I don't hear anything," Sombolo confessed.

"I hear it," Bwanga volunteered, and leaped up to proclaim Ejengi's latest *pensées*.

The exchange triggered a train of thought that I had already been mulling for some weeks. The method of "thought transference" from Ejengi to his speakers had all the outward appearance of telepathy. It might have been just a clever simulation, but even so the idea was there. There were other mysterious elements to Ejengi, too. There was the way he grew in height and then collapsed into a small heap on the ground. Even more perplexing was that as he grew, he tilted to the side, at the same time rotating slowly and running. I once tried to stretch my arms out over my head, tilt at the waist, and rotate. It is an impossible maneuver, yet Ejengi made it look deceptively simple.

THE EJENGI DANCE more and more resembled an energetic death rattle. Villagers continued to swarm to watch the dance, to contract *mbo* work, to collect on debts. The Bayaka were being smothered, and their only escape seemed to be to lose themselves ever more deeply in the Ejengi ceremony. Only then was there respite from the grim realities around them. Hunger was rampant. Baku's wife, Bwangi, had bone cancer and was slowly dying. She had been well enough to join the encampment at Sao-sao, but since then she had deteriorated considerably. Now she looked like a skeleton, and when she had to get around she moved like a crab, on her hands and feet, her buttocks dragging along the ground. She was scarcely able to provide even minimal care for her five-year-old son, Baja, who was quite obviously starving. His legs and arms were like sticks, his ribs protruded through papery skin, his head looked too large and fragile. I gave him snacks of bananas and peanuts, but they were hardly sufficient to counter his malnutrition.

More and more often I found myself escaping from the Ejengi dances to the solitude of the forest. My old hideaway had long since been discovered — by Yéyé, of all people, who was collecting some firewood. She didn't see me until she was almost next to me, when I self-consciously cleared my throat. I made other hideouts, but each was uncovered by the Bayaka wandering in the forest. I was beginning to resent their inevitable intrusions, and in a couple of cases suspected them of deliberately tracking me down.

I liked Ejengi. He had a childlike and unpredictable disposition. I was proud of his affection for me. Therefore, it especially pained me to realize that Ejengi had been called from the forest to help Amopolo, and instead he was destroying it.

ONE AFTERNOON DURING the heat of a dance a villager tapped Ngbali on the shoulder and asked for some water. She obligingly left the dance to fetch it, and when she returned and handed him the bowl she smiled at him. Instantly I was seething. I knew my reaction was irrational — Ngbali was merely being civil — yet civility was more than I had gotten from her in months.

I slunk out of my hut like some shadow of silent fury and made for the forest. I did not stop walking until I was well out of earshot of the camp. I went to ridiculous measures to cover my trail — backtracking, making false starts at forks in the path — until I was certain I'd left nothing but confusion in my wake. Then I leaped off the trail into trackless forest and eventually settled down at a well-concealed spot. Perhaps my precautions were justified — at one point I woke up from my nap to the sounds of two voices proceeding along the trail. They advanced slowly, almost a sure sign that they were tracking, but to my delight they soon passed into the distance. A short time later they returned at a brisker pace, and I reflected with glee that they would have to report that I'd vanished into thin air.

My determination to spend the night in the forest was put to the test as darkness fell, activating my imagination. I would be a sitting duck for any passing leopard, though it was more likely I'd be stepped on by an elephant before the night was through. Nearby, crickets and katydids chirped and whirred and rasped away; more disquieting were the noises from the leafy floor: rustlings and an ominous murmury undertone. From the distance came the deep pulse of Ejengi's drums.

Late the next morning I made my way back to Amopolo. The drums were pounding erratically as I neared, and there was loud chatter and laughter. They were in a break between songs. My absence, I reflected as I entered the settlement, had gone completely unnoticed. Many Bayaka were gathered in the *mbanjo*. Without a word I sat down a little to the side. Ejengi, who was running around camp, soon came over and crouched down beside me.

You again, I thought to myself, full of resentment, but also comforted by Ejengi's attention — he seemed the only one who cared about my recent absence. It was a moment of emotional turmoil for me, and suddenly I found myself making a mental appeal to Ejengi, confiding a secret dilemma I had been grappling with.

To my surprise Ejengi leaned into me, pressing against my chest. It was a move of unexpected intimacy. When I stopped thinking, he leaned back.

Did you really hear me? I thought.

Ejengi leaned into me again. After a minute he stood up and began to move away. I felt a surge of wild hope. It was ridiculous, I thought, but was it possible?

My heart called out, *Ejengi!*

Ejengi stopped and turned around.

Can you hear me?

Ejengi came back, crouched down, and leaned into me.

At that moment, all my doubts vanished.

TOWARD THE END of the third month of the ceremony, two Ejengis appeared and danced at the same time. I was so struck by the novelty that I broke my recent vow to not record another Ejengi dance. I taped several songs, packing away my equipment only when a villager walked up in the middle of a recording and asked how much my "apparatus" cost.

More than a hundred villagers were present, an immense crowd. They had formed a wide half circle behind the much smaller group of singers and seemed to be settling in for a long time. The full moon guaranteed a whole night of dancing, so it was possible they would remain until morning.

Thoroughly discouraged, I withdrew from the scene despite my curiosity about the two Ejengis. I sat down at the side of my hut, where at any rate I had a clear view. Before long several elders joined me: Joboko, Simbu, Mobo, Doko, and Dimba. We watched the dance and talked, and pretty soon I launched into my favorite theme of late: that I loved Ejengi with one heart, that I loved his dance, but that he should return to the forest and wait for us there. It was bad for him to dance near the village. Just look at what was happening to Amopolo: hunger, drunken noise and fights, all the men doing *mbo* work. It wasn't Ejengi's fault, I stressed (though secretly I was beginning to think it was), it was simply that he always attracted villagers. Amopolo was overrun — there was no space for the Bayaka. Even in the middle of the night villagers roamed the settlement, and there had been numerous cases of theft. It was positively dangerous.

"Dangerous!" Joboko agreed emphatically, but his next words surprised me. "Ejengi is a *big* spirit! Something could happen to those villagers if they continue walking around like that!"

I knew that by advocating Ejengi's departure I was endangering the prospects for my initiation, which was still being discussed during our sit-downs in the *janga*. But my alarm over the conditions at Amopolo now surpassed any desire to be initiated. I especially did not want Ejengi to hang around expressly for my initiation, and to make sure that this was understood, I even told the Bayaka that I preferred to "see Ejengi" another time. Right now I just wanted to see the Bayaka regain their own space. I wanted to see them hunting and eating meat again. We should all move into the forest.

The elders agreed with me. But I had been saying the same thing for weeks, and while they had agreed with me on each occasion, our progress was zero, and I suspected them of humoring me once again.

Night was upon us, but the moon cast a kind of pale daylight over the settlement. The villagers, contrary to habit, were not wandering about. In fact they weren't even talking. They had become motionless, passive observers, their stares rigidly fixed on the wild movements of the two Ejengis in a collective expression of mute expectation.

An *esimé* was in progress, and the two Ejengis were dancing in turns. The old Ejengi could be distinguished by the darker color of his aged raffia clothing. By comparison the new Ejengi, pale yellow, looked fresh and vigorous. The drumming seemed to be approaching some sort of climax, with complex and disruptive cross-rhythms threatening to overwhelm the momentum of the dance. Suddenly the old Ejengi collapsed, leaving a lifeless heap of raffia on the ground. I thought perhaps my senses were fooling me, but it really looked as though whoever had animated those clothes had vanished into thin air. The pile of clothes was no more than a few inches in height — how could anyone fit under it?

The new Ejengi continued to dance for another minute. Then, a few yards from the old Ejengi, it too collapsed — not the ordinary drop I had witnessed hundreds of times but the lifeless collapse of a puppet whose strings have just been cut. The drums fell silent.

I was watching very carefully now. The elders with me had all turned to look, too. The villagers were frozen, many with mouths hanging open. The singers sat down and were quiet. The men who had participated in the dance retreated. In the silence a boy walked up to the old Ejengi, lifted the raffia clothes with the tips of his fingers, and threw them into the nearby bushes. Then in the same manner he picked up the raffia clothes of the new Ejengi and tossed them several feet into the air, closer to the center of the space partly enclosed by the villagers. He tossed the clothes several times, and his gesture reminded me of a magician demonstrating to his audience that there's nothing in his hat. Finally, apparently satisfied with the placement of the raffia clothes, the boy withdrew.

From the back of the camp a small group of men approached, sighing and clapping in simple rhythm. My attention was riveted as they neared the lifeless Ejengi. I thought I knew what to expect: when they got close, one of them would dive under the raffia heap to reanimate the spirit. That the Bayaka were capable of performing such maneuvers with lightning speed I had no doubt. Once I had watched Zalogwé "play" mokoondi during a children's eboka, dancing behind a shield of palm fronds, which he carried until the moment of release, when he made a kind of crawling leap over to the mbanjo, sitting down just as the fronds hit the ground. A second of inattention and one might never have known he had had anything to do with the dancing fronds. I was on the lookout for such a move now. But the men were still a good ten feet away when Ejengi leaped up and began to dance, and I was left staring in amazement, as flabbergasted as the villagers.

TEN

The Cry of the Mokoondi

D AWN WAS BREAKING, but I reckoned I still had several hours of sleep to look forward to. I had stayed up very late. Yet someone was entering my hut to wake me up. I opened my eyes to find Mobo.

"Hunger has won out," he said. "I'm going to sleep in the forest. Are you coming?"

His offer caught me by surprise. I needed time to prepare myself mentally to move into the forest. Besides I was dead tired.

"I'll follow later on," I mumbled.

"Later never," Mobo insisted. "*Now* is good."

In fifteen minutes we were on our way. Even as we left Amopolo, leaves were popping and someone began to declaim Ejengi's thoughts. Soon we entered the calm, silent forest. We were a small party; in addition to Mobo's family there was a group of boys, including a teenager named Mobila just coming into his own as a man. Others, I was told, would join us after the hunt.

Absorbed by conflicting thoughts and emotions, I remember little of our walk. I was not happy about leaving Ngbali behind at Amopolo, but my presence there served no purpose, and for my own sanity I had to get away. At one point my attention was called to a long pale yellow snake as thick as my calf that wound its way silently up the trunk of a tree.

We set up camp near the headwaters of the Mombongo. By now I was glad I had come, and Mobo gently poked fun at my attempted procrastination that morning. Before dark the hunting party arrived — Adamo, Yongo, Bokumbi, Bakpima, Engulé, and a dozen women — with four small duikers and three porcupines. That night we slept with full bellies for the first time in months.

In the morning honeybees invaded the camp. While the others departed for the hunt, I set off alone, wandering far enough to avoid the bees, and plopped myself down beneath a large *bimba* tree. I was going to spend the day writing my book. It struck me as ironic that having set myself up comfortably to write at Amopolo, I should now leave it all to pursue the task in the most basic way, my notebook on my knees. I discovered that the peaceful setting and isolation were highly conducive to concentration. I wrote more than I ever had before at one sitting. In the late afternoon, with a headache and a stiff neck, I returned to camp.

My arrival coincided with the return of the hunters. The camp was still overrun by bees, but I wasn't unduly worried. I had spent three months at Sao-sao without getting stung once and had become positively casual about the threat they posed. Besides, I now had a kit with an antidote, ready for action in a handy, trigger-action syringe.

By twilight the boys had requisitioned the pots and pans for percussion, and soon an *eboka* started up. As darkness swallowed the camp there came the sharp report of a popping leaf. The *mokoondi* were announcing themselves. I reached my hand into my pack for a bottle of aspirin — and withdrew it with a startled cry. A terrific pain shot up my arm. I switched on my flashlight long enough to see a honeybee frantically pumping me with venom. The men shouted angrily at me to switch off the light, and I sat there in the dark, sweating.

I had no idea where I had stashed the bee sting kit. For a moment I rummaged blindly through my bags while the phosphorescent forest spirits danced into camp. But it was no use: I had obviously stowed it away too cleverly to be found in my present panic. I monitored the pace of my heart — it was thumping away. I checked my breathing; I seemed to be getting dizzy, but was it from asthma or frantic hyperventilation? I reflected sardonically on the supreme irony of the moment: I was going to sit there quietly in the dark until I dropped dead because the *mokoondi* had arrived and I couldn't use my flashlight!

The song in progress, its melody a series of descending yodels, had reached the peak of its polyphonic density, its texture of yodels a kind of perpetual motion. Because there were so few older women, the music had an especially bright, joyous sound. Several *mokoondi* were screeching out in their version of a sing-along. I saw the "elder" among them, floating slowly backward. Another, with the large, close-set glowing eyes of some nocturnal creature, silently bobbed its head in rhythm and craned its face out toward the choir of women. Others were faintly visible moving through the *bimba* forest beyond the edge of camp. I had never seen so many *mokoondi* at one time before. Every man and boy at our small camp must have transformed into one. I had forgotten the powerful joy those glowing beings inspired, and now I felt a surge of euphoria.

Suddenly I realized that a good twenty minutes had passed since my bee sting, and I was still alive. My hand was swollen and hurt like hell, but if that was the extent of the damage, why had I been wasting all that time and energy agonizing over the psychology of bees? And to think that had I been able, I would have injected myself with a heart sedative! What a wonderful joke! The courage with which I had faced the deadly threat of the bees turned out to be nothing but eccentricity. I wasn't allergic to bee venom after all.

OVER THE NEXT WEEK I was stung practically every day, and one day twice. My right hand, which bore the brunt of the bees' anger, resembled a rubber glove that had been blown up like a balloon. Yet somehow I managed to write, with scarcely any visible effect on my handwriting, even though I could barely grasp a pen. The first few stings were traumatic, for I had yet to feel genuinely confident of my reprieve from the fatal allergy. Eventually, however, I endured each fresh sting with an indifference that amounted to impudence.

In the forest I was able to achieve a regular writing routine that was impossible in the chaos of Amopolo. Each morning I ate a filling meal, drank a cup of instant coffee, and set out for my writing spot even before the hunters left camp. In the late afternoon I returned, and another meal was always waiting for me. In the evening there was more food, often followed by an offering of honey.

Camp was filling up with new arrivals. Men were joined by their wives. Bombé arrived and installed himself in the *mbanjo,* where I also was sleeping for the time being. To my disappointment no one from Ngbali's extended family came. The only connection, a tenuous one, was the arrival of Eloi and his young wife Banda, who had become Ngbali's friend.

One night I was shaken awake and warned about an approaching storm. Wind was hissing through the forest canopy, and all around us the *bimba* trees swayed and creaked. Now and then came the loud crash of a falling branch. Bombé got up and stood at the edge of camp, facing the darkness. "Give me water!" he cried. "I'll give it to the children! If I die, bury me in the earth! But the children are thirsty! Give me water!" And so he continued until the wind subsided and the rain began.

A few hours later I was startled out of a deep sleep by a long wail of anguish. I listened. For a moment there was no sound but the patter of light rain. The air was cold and misty. Perhaps it was only the squawk of a bird, or a voice in a dream. But then came another cry of pain, and soon several voices talked excitedly. Someone called me, and my heart sank. Whatever the news, it was bound to be bad.

I was shocked into emotional numbness by what I found. The cries of despair had come from Eloi. He was sitting on the ground in the entrance to his hut, his arms around Banda, who slumped back against him. She was unconscious, and the gurgling that now and then rose from deep in her throat was a clear indication that she was dying. I could do nothing, and we were miles from any help. I remembered that in the morning Eloi had asked for aspirin for his wife's headache. I had caught a glimpse of her lying in bed when I delivered the pills, and she had sat up to swallow them with some water. There had been no reason to suspect anything more than a simple headache. For a terrible moment the forest seemed to loom and breathe like some vast, amorphous presence whose indifference was really a form of malevolence.

Banda died an hour later. In the gray light of morning Mobo set off alone to carry the tidings to Amopolo. The rest of us waited out the rain that had begun to fall with renewed force at dawn. When the storm passed, we broke camp and started back. Bokumbi carried Banda on his back, her weight suspended by a strap over his forehead. We were a grim procession. As we passed the decaying remains of our old Mombongo camp, reminding us of the joys experienced there, we were overtaken by Banda's brother, Musako, who had come in after us by another trail. He pulled his sister down off Bokumbi's back and began to lament over her body.

"Not here in the forest!" the others exhorted to no avail. "Wait until we get to Amopolo!" Bakpima's wife even slapped him with the flat side of her machete, but Musako did not feel a thing.

"Savage!" Bombé cried out in disapproval.

Musako was finally pulled away from his sister. We set off once more, but we had scarcely gone a hundred yards before Banda's father and mother caught up with us. Another agonizing scene followed. Adamo and I continued on our own and reached Amopolo around noon. The rest of the party arrived an hour later, and the *élélo* began in earnest.

ON THE AFTERNOON following our exit from the forest, Omoo, who was drunk, came tottering into my hut with a menacing glare. Why was it, he wanted to know, that every time I led the Bayaka into the forest, someone died? First Mindumi, now Banda. What did I have to say to that?

The others quickly jumped on Omoo's case for saying such "nonsense." I did not take the accusation too seriously, but I was shaken by the suddenness of Banda's death, and I had no intention of persuading the Bayaka into the forest ever again.

It was agreed that the problem that had led to Banda's death had begun in Congo. She had been having headaches ever since. Adamo told me that she had been a woman with powerful eyes. She had seen, even then, what was to come. Dimba remarked that he had noticed something wrong during Ejengi. Banda would dance awhile, then sit down, staring into the middle distance, lost in thought. She would dance again, then sit down and think. The others nodded knowingly. Yes, it had been coming from a long way away, and she had known. I didn't understand their reasoning, but I welcomed their conclusion.

Mobo had sworn that he would sleep only three nights at Amopolo before returning to the forest. True to his word, on the third morning he was at my hut urging me to get up, just as he had a week earlier. I was still reluctant to leave Ngbali behind. I'd heard stories of a virulent strain of cerebral malaria that was wreaking havoc in Cameroon. Fatal in less than twenty-four hours, it struck only in the brain. People called it *le marteau*, the hammer. I deduced that this had been the cause of Banda's death. The raffia marsh near Amopolo, with its hordes of mosquitoes, was probably a breeding ground for new mutations of malaria. The thought of leaving Ngbali exposed to such a danger made me extremely uneasy. At the same time I was angry at her for allowing herself to be eaten alive by mosquitoes. Had she any sense, I thought darkly, she would have moved in with me, if only to share my mosquito net.

Mobo persuaded me in the end. I had to tear myself away from Amopolo, away from Ngbali's presence, but as soon as we entered the forest I was once again happy I made the effort. In the forest my worries about Amopolo lost much of their impact, as if that sun-bleached world no longer existed, and in consequence my own sense of helplessness lost some of its intensity.

There were only a handful of us: Mobo and his family, Adamo, good old Bombé, and a couple of boys. We passed both Mombongo campsites, the old and the recent, and forged ahead until we reached the site of a third abandoned camp, a place I had admired since passing through more than a year before. The edge of a passing storm rumbled and crackled to the east, dropping a gentle rain on us, as we scavenged materials from the old huts to erect a temporary shelter. I pulled out a half-pint bottle of malt whisky I'd had ever since my visit to London. It seemed fitting to drink it now. As Mobo, Bombé, Adamo, and I took turns sipping, we ran through the list of Amopolo's horrors — mosquitoes, chigoes, villagers, sunlight, and so on — and by so reciting them reaffirmed the peace and beauty of our present surroundings. Given the option of living in the forest, how could anyone choose to remain at Amopolo? Again and again we dwelt on its horrors — imitating the hum of the clouds of mosquitoes, repeating in stern voices some of the villagers' favorite phrases when berating the Bayaka — until in the end we were laughing like lunatics.

IN THE MORNING Musako arrived with his wife, Ndoko's daughter, Mbutu. It was the first I knew of their marriage. I felt exonerated by Musako's presence, which surely meant that he did not blame me for his sister's death. Later in the day Wadimo and his wife showed up, and Engulé came without Mbina, who was preparing manioc and would follow in a few days.

For several days our little community was a haven of tranquility. There was a lovely expanse of *bimba* forest to the south, and I spent hours wandering through it scouting out likely writing spots. I selected two, one for the mornings until around noon, when the sun reached a hole in the canopy and shot a bright beam directly into my eyes, and another, darker spot for the afternoons, shielded from the sky by layers of foliage, so that no direct light ever broke through. Before moving from one to the other, I would return to camp and go down to the stream to bathe. The Mombongo was a single narrow channel here, and the creamy sand of its bed shone gold through the tannin-stained water. A wall of luxuriant vegetation tumbled down to the edge of both banks. The stray sun rays that filtered through filled the air with diffuse emerald light. Protruding above the shallow water, an elephant's collarbone provided a shelf on which to put my soap and toothbrush. A few feet away the skull lay under a tangle of aquatic plants. At times I felt like the most privileged man on earth, living in such a paradise.

One quiet night the deep tones of a drum came throbbing through the forest from a great distance. "Ejengi," Mobo remarked from his hut, and we lay there in the dark, listening to the faint tattoo that seemed to merge with the natural pulsation of the night itself. Soft as it was, rising above the sounds of the dripping forest, fading again and vanishing for a moment, it still managed to reach into the very core of my heart, to reawaken my agitation, as though

Ngbali's presence were being wafted along the sound waves. I tossed restlessly into the early hours of the morning, when the drums fell silent.

I filled my days with writing. At first, I had approached the task with dread and a touch of awe at the immense obligation. Now I was eager to be off each morning. I savored the exotic delight of writing about the Bayaka while still among them. Sometimes after an hour or two of deep concentration I would pause and look up from my notebook, marveling to find myself where I was.

During my hours of silent labor many animals passed me, scarcely ever aware of my presence. Monkeys swarmed in the canopy above; sometimes whole troops boisterously leaped from tree to tree, sending a shower of sticks and twigs down on me. Occasionally larger branches came hurtling to the earth with a crash, while the monkeys screamed in alarm or delight and I retreated hastily. Blue duikers browsing in the undergrowth would step delicately and pause within feet of me to munch on leaves. I began, for the first time, to see the birds I had previously only heard. Some of the matchups were surprising, such as the little brown bird that made a sharp, vicious whipping noise that set me on edge. Large black hornbills flapped noisily from treetop to treetop, squealing to each other in sad, ancient voices. Once I watched a column of big black ants march single file under my legs. Twenty minutes later they returned by the same route, each carrying one tiny green seed.

One day a number of men arrived from Amopolo to spend the night. They brought some disquieting news for Engulé. After an *elanda* the night before, Mbina had slept with Mowooma's oldest son, Mbunda. Apparently he had waited in her hut after the *elanda*, then sneaked away at the first crowing of the roosters. Engulé paced around in agitation for half an hour, muttering something about seeing whether Mbina had gotten pregnant, but on the whole I thought he received the tidings with remarkable calm. He didn't even leave for Amopolo the next morning. I might have concluded that jealousy was not a major factor in Bayaka relationships, had I not already seen terrific and violent eruptions of it between spouses on countless occasions.

Gradually our camp grew. Balonyona and his family arrived, including a baby daughter named Mbota. I was glad to see Balonyona. It would be our first time together in the forest. Engbeté and Ngbali (Bakpima's daughter), whose stormy relationship had ended in a "permanent" divorce, were back together now that Ngbali was pregnant. I remember feeling great satisfaction watching them work together on their hut. Bombé's wife, Balé, arrived and built a small hut, and to my delighted surprise Bombé moved out of the *mbanjo* and in with her.

One afternoon a ten-minute staccato burst of popping leaves rose from the nearby forest. The Bayaka told me that Ejengi was on his way back to his "village" in the forest. Was his village nearby, I asked? The Bayaka laughed — no, no, it was very far away. For a few afternoons the leaves popped and Ejengi's thoughts were proclaimed, but Ejengi himself never appeared. Then one afternoon I realized that I hadn't heard the leaves for days, and when I asked, the Bayaka told me Ejengi had gone.

ONE MORNING I set out with Adamo for Amopolo on a *mbingo* run. Along the way we encountered a group on their way to the forest camp. A child had died at Amopolo during the night, one of Dimba's sons. I asked a few questions. The boy hadn't been sick, they replied. He had merely gotten a headache and died. Adamo and I proceeded on our way with grim speed.

Amopolo was a mess, or perhaps I'd never seen it quite so clearly before. I was shocked by the transition from forest to road, as if I were emerging from the calm depths of the soul into a state of burning delirium. Flies buzzed everywhere. The rancid odor of human excrement hung over the settlement like a miasma. I could smell it fifty yards away. Amopolo seemed to shimmer in the sun, as though I were looking at an overexposed photograph taken at the beach. The only shade that afforded my eyes a refuge from the brightness was the thin strips and tiny patches along the sides of the huts. Most of the Bayaka were inside. The few who remained outdoors were squeezed into the bits of shade, looking dazed and listless.

As was usual for the death of a child, the *élélo* was a subdued family affair. I found quite a number of people suffering from malaria and spent an hour trying to push back the tide of illness by administering medicine. Afterward I sat in the remains of the *mbanjo,* which had pretty much disintegrated during Ejengi. Ngbali appeared at last, and when she glanced in my direction something seemed to strike her. She walked over to Etubu's hut, passing close by the *mbanjo,* and I could see her looking at me out of the corner of her eye. After a few words to Etubu's wife, Kukpa, she returned to Mowooma's hut, now looking at me out of the corner of her other eye. Suddenly I realized: it was my beard! I hadn't shaved in two weeks.

I made my purchases in the village and left a share of them at Amopolo. Then with Adamo I set off. We reached our forest camp at sunset, to the cheers of those who were counting on us to return by nightfall.

I CONTINUED TO WRITE, and the book gradually became my reason for being. It seemed, too, that the book provided me with a genuine function among the Bayaka. It was all very well for me to go hunting with them, but I would have been kidding myself had I believed that I was being productive. Now I had a genuine role: I had become a sort of village scribe.

Sometimes in the mornings before I set out with my notebook, the Bayaka would warn me not to stray too far in a certain direction, because elephants had moved into the area to eat *payu,* or gorillas had been smelled on the trail the day before. The elephant warnings I was bound to heed, but as for the gorillas, I always replied that unlike the Bayaka I was not afraid of them. If any gorillas came along and decided to charge me, I would sit quietly and mind my own business. The Bayaka were astonished by my attitude. Of course, once I was alone in the forest, the prospect of an actual gorilla charge seemed suddenly much more threatening. Would I really sit still? I had the feeling I would even panic if confronted by a chimpanzee.

Every day more Bayaka arrived from Amopolo, tipping the population balance now in favor of the forest camp. Some of the arrivals were almost like statements of support: Dimba, who came out only days after his young son's death; and Zabu, whose arrival, considering the rumors still flying around about Mindumi's death, was positively an act of courage. I made more *mbingo* runs to monitor conditions at Amopolo. Without fail I found malaria cases needing treatment.

Yet despite the steady state of apprehension that lay beneath the whole spectrum of my moods like a kind of background radiation, I felt optimistic regarding my future with Ngbali. Hope is resilient, and in the absence of evidence to the contrary, it is almost bound to rise unchecked. But also, I was beginning to sense, with a faculty even less amenable to rational explanation than intuition, that things were happening "behind the scenes." At first there was nothing concrete to support my feeling. During my *mbingo* runs the glances I caught of Ngbali were not particularly reassuring — but they were not overtly discouraging either. A glance from her became an event of utmost significance, given that she was so careful not to impart them too freely; the few she did grant were almost certainly calculated. And so each of my *mbingo* runs doubled as a quest for one of her glances. Sometimes I did not see her at all, but when I did I would not be satisfied until she threw a glance my way.

One *mbingo* run stands out in my memory above the others. I set out early that morning with Adamo, my usual *mbingo* companion, and two or three boys. We traveled by a different route this time, crossing the Mombongo some fifty yards farther downstream than usual. Thereafter the walk was of an entirely different character. Often the trail seemed to disappear under our feet, and fallen trees forced us into many arduous detours. We emerged on the road a couple miles south of the bridge.

When we reached Amopolo an *élélo* was in progress. The mother of a man named Bokia had died during the night after several days of fever. I remembered having treated her during my last run. I was feeling increasingly frustrated by the ineffectiveness of my medicines against some strains of malaria coming from the swamp. I found several other people I had treated still suffering, so for the first time I resorted to injections. I hated the thought of giving injections, but the Bayaka, who had been clamoring for the needle all along, welcomed them. The confidence and even enthusiasm with which patients presented their buttocks would have been comical were it not a measure of how desperate the Bayaka had become.

My anxiety over Ngbali's health was assuaged even before I reached Amopolo by a view of her bathing at the bridge. She gave me one look of surprise, then submerged out of sight. I wasn't exactly pleased to see her bathing by the road, but at least I knew she was all right. Later I caught sight of her several times as I made the medical rounds, and our eyes met frequently. I concluded that she was watching me. By the time Adamo and I set off for the forest, I was floating on air.

We were returning the way we had come, and I realized the new route was a permanent one; its purpose was to bypass the earlier camp where Banda had died. As we walked along the road I bubbled with talk. The settlement at Amopolo was too close to Bomandjombo, I said. When we finally left our forest camp, we should make a new village on the far side of the bridge. There was an ideal spot just at the top of the hill. It was only a few hundred yards farther from Bomandjombo, but having to cross the bridge (always profoundly dark at night) and ascend the hill would, I argued, discourage many villagers. Adamo agreed enthusiastically. Yes, when we came out of the forest we would found a new village. Those who wanted to remain at the old one could do so, I added. It would serve as a decoy for the new village. I, however, intended to leave Amopolo forever. I would live at Amopolo II. "Amopolo II!" Adamo cried in ardent endorsement.

Up to this point the road was bordered on either side by plots of manioc and the occasional patch of degenerate forest. I had forgotten the precise spot where we had come out of the forest, and now, as we passed the final overgrown garden, beyond which the forest closed in over the road, Adamo indicated that we had reached the turnoff. He clambered over the immense trunk of a felled tree and vanished in the tall weeds on the other side. I turned to follow and was suddenly overcome by a surge of euphoria so irresistible that for a moment I felt I was experiencing an emotional revelation.

The detail that triggered it was simple enough: several flowering vines curled and snaked over the tree trunk and up several of its branches, forming an arch at precisely the point where Adamo had climbed over — an arch of radiant white and yellow flowers. It was entirely natural, an enchanting though accidental configuration that would probably change beyond recognition in a month's time, but at that moment it struck me as deeply significant. I almost laughed out loud at the preposterously blatant meaning it presented: the entrance into a new world, a new life. The vision before me was infused with promise, as if shouting: here I am, here I am. I had the glorious feeling that by simply passing under that arch my life would undergo some mysterious change. Could this forest camp signal the beginning of a new life? Though I misinterpreted some of the details, my vision turned out to be startlingly prescient.

I must have stood there for several minutes, because Adamo suddenly shouted at me to get a move on — only a couple hours of daylight remained. I scrambled hastily over the tree and under the arch.

The walk was strenuous at any pace, and we were speeding along in a race against the sinking sun. Yet I was scarcely aware of my feet. Each twist in the trail revealed a different facet of the forest's changeless beauty. At one moment I was marveling at the serpentine coils of a liana, only to be distracted by the way the moss spread over only one side of the trees, like an iridescent green shadow cast by an invisible source of light. On we rushed without a word, the hush of the forest enveloping us, the rays of the sun slanting through the canopy and splashing here and there across the understory. All of nature seemed to be drawing a quiet breath before whispering some deep secret. I trembled as though in the grip of fever or ecstasy. Did the others not feel it too?

One of the boys broke the silence suddenly. He began to sing a little ditty, more a rhythmic repetition of a phrase than a song with a tune. Yet his voice did not shatter the spell the forest had cast on me but only heightened its effect, for in the context of my thoughts the words had a direct relevance.

"*Ya tay! Ya tay, Sombolo! Ya tay!*" (Come here! Come here, Sombolo! Come here!)

The other boys took it up, and soon Adamo himself laughed and began to sing too. Immediately my vague and unfounded feeling of optimism became grounded in a concrete hope. What else could they be referring to but Sombolo's imminent arrival at the forest camp? For weeks I had not believed that Ngbali and her family would join us. On this day, however, I had left Amopolo with the distinct feeling that Ngbali would join us soon. And now, with their ditty, Adamo and the boys seemed to confirm it. There had been a subtle but definite change in everyone's mood, a manifestation of the communal intimacy I had detected several times before. Usually Bayaka life was chaotic, a conglomeration of independent, anarchic elements that cooperated only enough to guarantee survival. Now and again, however, the individual elements would align themselves into a collective whole and a profound sense of communal purpose would emerge. Often the change was triggered by an *eboka*, which seemed to rally everyone into a single identity that persisted days or even weeks after the dance was over. One could feel it in the air, and every gesture, every smile, every spoken word, was a part of it.

Through chinks in the canopy we saw flashes of bright sky, but here below twilight had already fallen. Details of the terrain were gradually absorbed by deep shadow rising like a mist. Several times I stumbled over tree roots. Our last stream crossing was behind us, and we had reached the final stretch. My mind raced on, searching to understand that collective identity. Again I found myself considering the idea of telepathy. I had retreated from my belief in direct thought transfer despite my experience with Ejengi. Now I had in mind a less focused type of telepathy, one that operated somewhere in the realm of the subconscious. At times its influence was palpable.

Adamo and the boys were still singing the *ya tay* ditty as we came within earshot of the camp. That night, and over the next few days, the *ya tay* ditty was on everybody's lips. Children sang it in chorus, girls said it while clapping and then laughed. Even Bombé repeated it a few times.

ONE MORNING I wandered off, notebook in hand, eager to start my day of writing. The work had been progressing well lately, and today I hoped to finish the first installment. On the spur of the moment I passed by my regular writing spots and eventually turned off the trail into dark and unfamiliar forest. Soon I was in the throes of creation, and I wrote straight into the afternoon. When I finished, not thinking of where I was, I headed back toward the trail as if I'd been at my familiar afternoon spot. After a few minutes, failing to find the trail, I realized my mistake and backtracked toward the tree I'd been sitting under. Small juxtapositions of detail — a sapling here, a termite mound there — led me on with the false appearance of vague familiarity. I retraced my steps again, then tried to retrace what I'd retraced. Finally I stopped dead still: I was lost!

For a moment I was intensely disappointed in myself. Here I was beginning to think of myself as Mr. Rainforest and now I'd gotten lost within a hundred feet of a well-trodden footpath! I made a last attempt to locate the trail by walking in what I hoped was an outward spiral, but after half an hour I gave up. Several times I caught the barely audible sound of women's voices. The snatches were so brief I had trouble determining their direction. I began to shout, my voice startlingly loud and resonant. But there was no response. Finally I took a deep breath and howled out a long booming yodel that might have been the death cry of a brontosaurus. There is something about a yodel — the voice's transition from head to chest — that enables it to travel far in the forest. As the reverberation from my desperate whoop died down, I heard an answering cry full of surprise. I let out another monster yodel, another cry answered, and so I stomped my way through trackless undergrowth and finally emerged into camp on the opposite side from where I had left it. When the women and children saw the source of the bizarre cries and realized that I'd been lost, they shrieked with merciless laughter.

AROUND THIS TIME chigoes began to bother our camp. For more than a month there had been no sign of them, and I had enjoyed spending the evenings barefoot. But the larvae had arrived in the feet of the children, and now as they hatched in the hundreds and even thousands, I found myself digging them out of my own toes, too. We decided to move camp a hundred yards up the hill, and over the next few days men and women set about clearing the chosen site of underbrush.

In the meantime there was another major migration from Amopolo. Mitumbi and his group came, and set up camp at the new location. Many people at Amopolo were sick, he told me, and from his description I knew that malaria was rampant. Unfortunately the forest seemed but a poor refuge from it. Although the mosquitoes were few, many people suffered from outbreaks or lingering forms of the malady. I began each day treating patients. Wadimo had been sick for days and scarcely left his hut, and Bokumbi's wife, Ngbali, had a fever that reached the critical stage, abating only after two injections of quinine. Alarmed as I was by these developments, I still preferred to have everyone with me in the forest. The number of parasites in the blood, I reasoned, was bound to lessen once the Bayaka had been away from the mosquitoes for a while.

One day Sombolo and his family arrived. They passed through our camp without a word and continued up the hill to the new site. I was so happy to see them that I did not even mind that Ngbali hadn't even glanced my way as she passed through. That evening her cousin Mango delivered a gift of manioc flour from Ngbali, and I knew our relationship was on an upswing.

Two days later we all moved to the new location. My hut, along with many others, had already been built. Mbina, Bosso, and Simbu's wife, Mandubu, all had a hand in its construction. Ngbali had not lifted a finger to help. Still, I was glad to move out of the *mbanjo* and into my own space.

I now spent the days copying out what I'd written in a large, neat script to send off. It was tedious work, but it didn't require any special concentration, so I worked in camp. Biléma and Engulé even constructed a makeshift table and chair out of sticks for me. When the weather allowed (rain was becoming more frequent), everyone left camp early for the hunt. The evenings were filled with feasting on meat and honey, and the nights often enlivened by *eboka*.

One evening I had a meal in Bakpima's hut. I had watched his wife, Ajama, construct the hut, but I had not been inside it before. Easily the largest hut in camp, it was in fact the largest beehive I had ever seen. It was actually several beehives merged together, looking like a bundle of saddles and humps from the outside. The entrance I used (there were two) was a short tunnel so low it practically forced me onto my hands and knees. Once inside, however,

I could only marvel. Huts always look bigger from the inside, but this one was a leaf mansion. I could stand erect near its center. A young tree had been incorporated into the design, its trunk like a column rising up through the ceiling. As I ate I kept looking around, discovering ever more nooks and crannies with beds and smoking racks. In amazement I shined my flashlight at one unexpected room or alcove after another. The hut was a masterpiece. "A big hut is *good*," Bakpima said, and laughed at my continued astonishment.

I saw little of Ngbali during this period, though we lived within a hundred feet of each other, but I was content just knowing she was around. So far Sombolo and his family were the only members of his group to come out. Akunga, I was told, would be joining us any day now, and Mowooma planned to move into the forest as soon as his bamboo hut was completed. He'd been working on it for nearly a year now. Often Sombolo visited me at my hut; less frequently I visited him. If Ngbali was around, she ignored me. Yet whenever I saw her in the distance, she seemed to send me a different message. Once, through a break in the foliage, I caught sight of someone swinging Tarzan-like on a dangling liana. I could see only the arms and hands, but was intrigued that someone was engaging in such jungle fantasy behavior. Then the liana swung into view and I saw that it was Ngbali. She noticed my look of candid interest before I could mask it, leaped from the liana, and performed a brief but wild jig for my benefit before running up the forest path after her parents for a day of gathering. My heart was racing.

On other occasions I would be bent over my table copying out my book while a group of women sat in front of a nearby hut and chatted. Suddenly Ngbali's voice would join in. Instinctively I would look up, and for that one instant our eyes would meet. Thereafter, however, she went back to ignoring me.

One morning word arrived from Amopolo that Akunga's wife, Awoka, was seriously ill, as well as their little daughter Gonjé. Before I knew what was happening, Yéyé and Ngbali had packed their carrying baskets and were heading out of camp.

"Where are they going?" I asked Sombolo with some concern.

"They're going back to Amopolo to take care of Awoka," he replied. Shocked that no one had thought to tell me, I grabbed my bag of medicines and hastened after them. Balonyona and the teen-age Mobila followed. I heard Esoosi call out to them to keep an eye on me.

The heat at Amopolo was more oppressive than ever. I wondered aloud how the few families remaining could bear to continue living there.

"We're guarding the village," Joboko and Simbu explained.

"What's there to guard here," I retorted, "besides the chigoes in the sand?" They laughed, but it was the laughter of condemned men, and I regretted my remark.

Both Awoka and her daughter were burning with fever and re-quired injections. I was beginning to find it perverse to be on terms of such intimacy with the buttocks of so many Bayaka.

I assumed that Ngbali would be spending the night, so I an-nounced that I would stay too. Under no circumstances was I going to leave her behind at Amopolo. I was dreading the onset of night and the prospect of staying several days at Amopolo. And what if Ngbali decided to stay for good? Just then Balonyona stuck his head into my hut to tell me that Ngbali was all ready to go back to the forest camp. She was waiting for me.

ONE DAY MOWOOMA'S SON Mbunda arrived with a note for me. It was from Roland, a villager acquaintance of mine. Roland had had some vague connection with the now defunct village infirmary, but he seemed to spend all his time sitting under mango trees and drinking palm wine. He had taken a cursory official interest in our progress with the latrines and initially had been impressed by the number of holes we were digging.

"You must return to Amopolo at once!" his note declared. "Al-ready five latrines are finished at Mosapola. So far Amopolo has none. All you care about is the hunt. You must return and finish the latrines! Your friend, Roland — officer responsible for village hygiene. P.S. When you return, please think of me for a modest morsel of meat."

Ordinarily I ignored such demands, orders, and entreaties by vil-lagers to return to Amopolo — a feature of every one of my forest stays — but this time I felt compelled to reply.

"The problem with Amopolo," I wrote with a genuine sense of outrage, "is not simply one of latrines. Already three people have died from malaria, and many more are sick. I have used up almost all of my quinine, and even had to inject myself during a serious illness. There are so many mosquitoes at Amopolo that sleep is impossible. Amopolo is dangerous, and I fear more deaths if we return. So for the moment we are not moving from the forest. Your friend, Louis. P.S. Very little hunting lately because of the rain."

The detail about injecting myself I had thrown in to give an appropriately alarmist edge to my letter. I believed such a tone was justified, but it turned out to be prophetic.

A few more days passed without event. I was nearing the completion of my copying work, and I was feeling optimistic about my marriage, even though there were no concrete developments. Word came that Awoka and her daughter were better and that Akunga would soon arrive at our camp. I was still administering to a fair number of sick people, but I believed that the situation was under control.

My complacency was thoroughly shattered by the commotion that ripped into my sleep in the early hours one morning. I knew immediately that someone was dying. The moment had a frightening familiarity, as though Banda's death were being reenacted, as though I could hear in the helpless passion of the voices the foregone conclusion of another death. Who was it this time?

One of the men called over, "Mobila's head is really hurting!" It was a ridiculous understatement. Mobila was in a coma, oblivious to our frantic efforts to revive him. When we poured some water down his throat he coughed, his eyes opened a slit, and his hands pushed away the cup in an automatic reflex. I injected quinine, but I had not the slightest glimmer of hope. Then we sat around the motionless teenager and waited, and I listened to the men's account of events leading up to this nightmare.

Mobila had gone walking in the forest, they said, meaning that he had set off in the morning with a spear and a machete to see what he could find. Toward afternoon he had met Mobo on the trail and complained of a headache. Mobo, renowned for his knowledge of medicines, treated him from his portable kit, making little nicks in Mobila's temples and rubbing in his special "family recipe" medicinal paste. Mobila had returned to camp at dusk, his headache worse, and gone straight to bed.

At first light Mobila began to groan, long, deep, excruciating groans that seemed to rise from the very wellspring of agony. One would expect such groans to be accompanied by powerful writhings, but Mobila lay as motionless as a corpse. All the women of the camp gathered in front of his mother's hut, huddling together quietly in the cold morning air as the forest dripped with condensation, sounding like a light rain.

The men were far from silent. Mobila's older brother, Dembé, on the verge of tears, began to rage at Yongo. What was he saying, I asked Adamo. Dembé was accusing Yongo of murdering Mobila, he replied. I was frankly stunned.

"Why would Yongo want to murder Mobila?" I asked.

"I don't know," Adamo replied.

Yongo vehemently denied responsibility. He kept shouting, "Give me *mbanda* — I'll drink!" Finally Bakpima went off into the forest and returned thirty minutes later with some strips of bark. They were brewed up in water, and Yongo gulped down the potion without hesitation. Before he had even finished, Bombé began a rapid, rhythmic chant, each incantation ending with the word *ngaké*. "Ngaké!" echoed the rest of the men. On and on Bombé chanted, with scarcely enough pause between phrases for a single thought, and each time the men answered, in one voice, "Ngaké!" Once I might have cherished a recording of such a ritual, but now I found myself an unwilling witness, and I cringed as though I were glimpsing the raw nerve of a people's despair.

Yongo wandered slowly back and forth, a strange detached smile on his lips. Every now and then he clicked his tongue and shook his head in frustration. Bombé held a fistful of twigs, and at each *ngaké* he broke off a piece and tossed it away. When he reached the last piece of the last twig, Yongo had still failed to come up with any sort of vision, and the men seemed to snap out of their spell. Mobila, still groaning, was hoisted onto Dembé's back, and his family set off immediately down the forest path for Amopolo.

I fully expected a mass migration back to Amopolo, as had happened after Banda's death, so I was grateful when Mobo told me that everyone was remaining in the forest. The next moment I saw Ngbali and her family preparing to leave. They had packed everything. When I asked why — they had no connection to Mobila's family — I learned that during the business with the truth potion and the chanting, a messenger had arrived to inform Yéyé that her sister Awoka had had a relapse and was desperately ill. As they filed out of camp, I grabbed a few things and followed, calling back to Mobo and the others that I would return in a day or two. In my heart of hearts, however, I knew I had seen the last of that forest camp.

Mobila died on the trail. In his honor, and to acknowledge his status as a man, the following night the men who were at Amopolo wandered around the settlement singing *so*.

The next morning, though I was low on cash, I went into town straightaway and at Ngunja's shop bought a mosquito net for Ngbali. My mosquito net was the envy of the entire camp, and the one I purchased for Ngbali was of an even finer mesh. That afternoon I presented it to her and insisted that since she wouldn't share my net with me, she must at least sleep under her own. I should have realized that a mosquito net was too grand a possession for someone as young as Ngbali to be allowed to keep; a couple of days later I discovered that she had given it to one of her aunts upon request. Thereafter, every evening, I brought Ngbali a mosquito coil, which, when lit, burned slowly through the night with a smoke that repelled mosquitoes. The coils had the advantage of extending protection to everyone in the hut, and any decision to give one away would have to be approved by Yéyé and Sombolo. Ngbali readily accepted the coils. Still, few Bayaka shared my belief that the recent spate of deaths had anything to do with mosquitoes, and I got the impression that Ngbali was humoring me to some extent.

Within a week members of the forest camp began to drift back to Amopolo, until scarcely anyone was left but Yongo and Mobo and their families. I felt guilty about leaving them out there, as though I had abandoned them. One day I prepared a package of village goodies — cigarettes, coffee, sugar, marijuana, soap — to

send out to them, when suddenly they appeared with all their be-
longings, the last to leave the forest. The following morning Yongo
approached me to complain that he had never gotten a sheet in the
days when I gave them away. I promised him one as soon as I had
sufficient funds, but he seemed dissatisfied as he walked away. No
wonder: the next day, fearful of revenge for Mobila's death, he fled,
and I never saw him again.

THE WEEKS THAT FOLLOWED were the most disturbing of my
life. So sustained was the sense of catastrophe, of outright doom,
that without even thinking I abandoned my practice of jotting down
daily events, as though they were too obscene to record. Most terrifying was the gradual accumulation of paranoia that affected the
Bayaka, and, by a kind of osmosis, myself.

Amopolo had something of the desperate air of a refugee camp.
Hunger was widespread, and everywhere I turned there was sickness. Awoka was suffering from both malaria and pneumonia, and
no sooner had I gotten her on the road to recovery than Bokumbi
called me over to examine his wife, Ngbali. I had last seen her a few
weeks before, in the forest. She had recovered from her malaria by
then but suffered from some lingering malady that I thought might
be flu. She had called me over to her hut and given me a baked
yoko. We sat and chatted for a while. The mother of three healthy
young boys, she was a very strong and beautiful woman. Now at
Amopolo I was shocked by her condition. I hardly recognized her,
she was so emaciated. What could have made her waste away so
quickly? She complained of pain in her chest, so I started her on a
course of penicillin, hoping it might be nothing more mysterious
than pneumonia, but as I walked away I cursed the stars for what
was happening.

Then "the hammer" struck again. I was aroused in the middle of
the night and called over to Joboko's. His young teenage son — I
never learned his name — was in a coma after suffering from a
headache earlier in the evening. Even as I stood over the dying boy,
paralyzed by my own helplessness, his family began the death lament. He died at dawn. It was a recurring nightmare.

In the morning, as the *élélo* was reaching a crescendo, and Joboko
sat outside his hut screaming out and asking why it had happened,

pounding the earth with his hand, Akunga came over and quietly asked me to take a look at his boy. I found his son in a fever. Did he have a headache? I asked in alarm. No, Akunga and his wife explained, it was his neck that hurt. I had no idea what to make of it. I was so confused by this onslaught of sickness and disease, so exhausted by my impotence in the face of it, that I almost began to hate the Bayaka for being so vulnerable to death.

That night as I lay under my net I listened with a mixture of abhorrence and fascination to the ceaseless, ubiquitous hum of the mosquitoes. The air was thick with them. In the distance I could hear a couple of hunting dogs the Bayaka kept at camp, crying and running crazily back and forth, back and forth. I seethed with rage at the thought of the Bayaka, and Ngbali in particular, being fed upon like dumb brutes, night after night. I knew I could not rest until we all left Amopolo for good.

It took a genuine effort of will to get out of bed in the morning. The *élélo* in Joboko's hut, after subsiding into an eerie sob for most of the night, was gathering force once more as preparations were made to bury the boy. I could hear the sounds of Sango from villagers who had already arrived to collect on debts; their voices were quite distinct from those of the Bayaka, less rich in overtones. The early morning sun was beating down on the settlement, sending shadows into retreat and exposing the ugliness of Amopolo in a merciless glare. The loud, tense babble of voices coming from Akunga's hut was anything but reassuring. I wanted to keep my eyes closed, but in the end I braced myself for the worst and went to check on Akunga's son.

The boy showed no improvement, and I was more baffled than ever by his symptoms, a cross between spinal meningitis and tetanus or perhaps both at the same time. I was not equipped to deal with the case, and I decided to appeal to Andrea Turkalo for help.

Both Andrea and her husband, Mike Fay, the new director of the Dzanga-Sangha Project, were of vital importance to me during this period. Like me, Mike was a native of New Jersey, and we had been amused to discover that we two, living by chance in the same small area of the Central African Republic, had younger brothers who worked for the same company in New York. Andrea and Mike helped me in many ways, lending me money and, more important, providing moral support and companionship. Andrea was working on health and sanitation problems at Mosapola, and I found a much-needed emotional release in discussing the terrible situation at Amopolo with them. In one of our talks the subject of moving the Bayaka settlement came up. They agreed that it was necessary, but we all knew that the authorities in Bomandjombo and the villagers themselves would be adamantly opposed to the move. That conversation was a watershed for me, giving me more confidence in my own private, heretical thoughts about the situation.

Andrea had made many emergency visits to Amopolo over the months, and sometimes she was able to help. Once, when Sosolo's wife's arm suddenly swelled like an inflated sausage, Andrea's treatment probably saved her life. On this occasion, however, when she examined Akunga's son, she was as much at a loss as I.

In the afternoon a group of tourists — still a rare sight — arrived and strolled around Amopolo taking photos. One remarked on the "strange sounds" of the *élélo* coming from Joboko's. When I told them that today was not a good day for a dance because a boy was dying, another tourist, moved by curiosity (which she might have mistaken for compassion), went into Akunga's hut for a look. I gritted my teeth at the abominable indignity of the situation.

The next day I awoke to a loud and emotional *élélo* coming from the direction of Akunga's hut. Had his son died? I asked fatalistically. No, Mokoko grimly replied, it was Zabu's baby son, Mindumi, who had died. The tragedy of that little death was simply too much to bear, and my eyes filled with tears.

Akunga's son died the following morning. Now three *élélos* were going at the same time. And to think that I had once been eager to record *élélo*! At the first sighs my heart went frantic, and as it mounted in intensity I found the sounds emotionally overwhelming.

Every day seemed to add a new horror. Baku's wife, Bwangi, confined to her bed by the cauliflower tumor blossoming below her knee, was a frightening sight. Sometimes as I passed by her hut she would call out to me like a living corpse for a hundred francs to buy salt or peanuts. I always gave her the money, and each time I wondered how much longer she could live. One day her leg below the tumor fell off. In an attempt to sterilize the stump, Baku rubbed salt on the wound. No corner of the settlement was out of range of her screams. A group of men huddled together in my hut, shaking their heads dismally.

We made several attempts to transport Bokumbi's wife to the hospital at Belemboké. Circumstances, however, seemed deliberately contrived to thwart us. Both WWF vehicles were out of operation; there was a nationwide shortage of fuel, so that even the local bush taxi had suspended its daily runs; and the road was in atrocious condition, so that even if a vehicle were available, Bokumbi's Ngbali might not survive the trip. Every day I had to report my failure to Bokumbi and Ngbali. She knew that she was dying and that her only hope lay in getting to Belemboké. Sometimes she looked at me and pleaded, "Looyay, isn't there a car?" "No, Ngbali, not today," was all I ever managed to reply. How could I explain the whole damned world to her, with its machinations, its godforsaken economics, and its crackpot circumstances that could lead to the unavailability of a car? How could I explain that fate was bent on this cruel mockery, that luck was perverted?

Later both Ngbali and Bokumbi became possessed by a strange calm. Emotionally this was easier for me, though deeply unsettling. I would visit and ask how Ngbali felt. "She's sitting," Bokumbi invariably replied, and in the even, placid tone of his voice there was resignation and acceptance. I had seen it before, in Akunga as his son lay dying, and by now I knew what it meant, though I had been unwilling to admit it. It was the belief in *gundu* — sorcery.

In the course of my readings about Pygmies, I had come across a statement that Pygmies attribute certain deaths to sorcery, but I was unprepared for the sudden pervasiveness of this belief at Amopolo. The Bayaka now seemed to believe that sorcery was at the root of every death — of death itself. There was no such thing as natural death. Disease, accident, even death from old age, all had their origins in *gundu*. Despite their excitability, the Bayaka had always struck me as realists, and my new realization of the widespread belief in *gundu* came as a shock, as if I hadn't even begun to understand their inner lives.

Much later I tried to find out how *gundu* supposedly worked. At best the Bayaka were vague, as though unwilling to discuss it. It had something to do with creeping about at night. As Mobo cautiously put it, "Perhaps someone sneaks into your hut at night while you're sleeping, and carries you outside and leaves you in the forest."

"If someone tried to carry me when I was asleep," I replied, "I would wake up."

"Perhaps you don't wake up," Mobo suggested. "Perhaps he has a power that keeps you asleep."

"Then when I wake up in the morning, am I in the forest?"

"Perhaps you think you are still in your hut," was his cryptic reply. "Have you ever seen anyone using *gundu?*" I asked.

"Never," Mobo admitted.

"Then how do you know it's real?"

"Perhaps it is," was all he would say.

At the time, however, I only knew that *gundu* meant sorcery. Talk of *gundu* was rampant, and the Bayaka were in a frantic state of mind. Accusations flew back and forth, arguments erupted and threatened to turn violent. When two more teenagers died suddenly, probably from cerebral malaria, the effect on the Bayaka was harrowing to watch. I had never tried to influence their customs before, but now I found myself trying to persuade them that *gundu* had nothing to do with the deaths. I might as well have tried to stop the incoming tide with a teaspoon. "Louis doesn't really know us Bayaka well enough," Joboko remarked to the others after one of my tirades against *gundu.* "If he did, he'd know how much we use *gundu.*"

My own hysteria regarding the mosquitoes easily matched their fear of *gundu.* The fact that so many of the victims had been teenagers now made me especially fearful for Ngbali. I still brought her a mosquito coil every evening, but word of their effectiveness had spread, and I was bombarded by requests from others. I doubt they believed that burning the coils protected them against death, but they certainly welcomed the relief from mosquitoes. If I refused a request, I worried, Ngbali might give hers away, so I distributed more and more coils, which became a major expense.

I continued to press Ngbali to make up her mind about our marriage. I even appealed to her aunts for help. After a couple of weeks my persistence seemed to pay off: one afternoon her aunts arranged a meeting between us, in which they acted as go-betweens. Speaking to her aunts, though she was sitting next to me, Ngbali listed her objections: her father, Sombolo, always boasting in Bomand-jombo that his daughter was sleeping with a white man, had filled her with shame; if she moved in with me, he would never leave us in peace but constantly harass us for drinking money; and once we slept together I would probably lose interest in her and start looking for another woman.

I did my best to allay her fears: she shouldn't be ashamed to be my wife — I myself was proud that she was and wanted the whole world to know it; I would warn her father in no uncertain terms that he was not to bother either of us for drinking money; and finally, I would never have eyes for any woman but her. Ngbali spoke rapidly to her aunts again, and when they explained what she said I could hardly believe my ears: Ngbali would sleep with me that very night!

That evening, full of excitement, I went to her hut for our rendezvous. Ngbali, however, looked sullen and explained that she had a headache. Immediately I was filled with alarm. A headache meant only one thing: cerebral malaria! I ran to fetch my medicines. By the time I returned, bearing half a dozen different medicines and a syringe, I realized that I had probably misinterpreted her meaning. She wasn't ill — she had merely resorted to the oldest excuse in the book. For several minutes I pleaded with her: if she didn't want to sleep with me she had merely to say so, I wouldn't force her. But please, please don't claim to have a headache if it wasn't true. She had told me that her head hurt a lot, but now she relented slightly. "My head hurts a little." I gave her an aspirin and returned to my hut alone.

THEN, AS MYSTERIOUSLY as it had begun, the season of deaths came to an end. The mosquitoes were as multitudinous as ever and malaria was still widespread, but death itself seemed to withdraw its shroud. Who could ever know why? Gradually there came an almost imperceptible lightening of mood, a relaxation of tension, as if instinctively we all knew that the worst was over. Death had not left us entirely, however. Bokumbi's Ngbali and Baku's wife lingered on, but it was understood that they would die soon.

The teenagers, the group worst hit by the crisis, were the first to recover. *Elanda* became a nightly event even as individual families continued to mourn their dead. I was not a fan of *elanda*, but the first few times I heard it again I felt as though I were listening to a benediction. Sometimes I went so far as to record a session. Ngbali was nearly always present and thoroughly enjoying herself. I marveled at her resilience.

As life returned to its normal, post-Ejengi footing, I became increasingly disquieted by a thought that had occurred to me late one night. *Elanda* often took place in the large clearing near my hut and would go on long after the adults, including me, went to bed. One night as I lay listening to a session, my ears alert for Ngbali's voice, I noticed that almost every time I heard her high-spirited laughter, she was shouting out Kukpata's name. Kukpata was Amopolo's favorite teenage drummer. My ears put out antennae. What was going on? The *elanda* continued until very late, and though the ranks gradually thinned, Ngbali and Kukpata remained until the end.

In the morning my suspicions seemed absurd, a phantom of darkness and doubt that dissipated in the first rays of the tropical sun. True, my so-called marriage was enough to drive anyone over the deep end. I was never sure whether to lose myself in all-out admiration of Ngbali because she was mine or to maintain a critical eye because she was not. In the space of that uncertainty and doubt, jealousy crouched like a hungry panther. I must, I told myself in the light of day, guard against it. But that night, as another *elanda* began, uneasiness came creeping back. Both Ngbali and Kukpata took part, and several times she cried out his name.

Over the next few days my suspicions found support: Kukpata was definitely smitten by Ngbali. He began to spend much of his time sitting on a log that gave him a full view of her neighborhood. Once when I passed near him I actually heard him sighing. Did Ngbali reciprocate those feelings? I had no doubt that she was aware of Kukpata's infatuation and that she encouraged it, for she was a merciless flirt. Once, during an *elanda*, I watched as she picked Kukpata twice in a row to dance his solo after hers. But was her flirting serious?

Now I often saw Ngbali wearing a pink T-shirt. One of the most charming habits of couples "going steady" was to exchange items of clothing back and forth. Most popular of all were T-shirts. I vaguely remembered having given Kukpata a pink T-shirt, but I could not recall if the shirt I had given Ngbali was pink. It hardly mattered; there were at least a dozen pink T-shirts floating around, and Ngbali could easily have gotten one through trade. How I agonized! Was it coincidence that whenever Ngbali wore the pink shirt, Kukpata went without? And that when Kukpata wore the pink shirt, Ngbali went without?

Sometimes I would persuade myself Ngbali had no interest in Kukpata, that she wanted only me. I was, by Bayaka standards, a multi-billionaire, a strong inducement in any culture. I was interested in marriage, not an affair. I was willing to meet Ngbali's conditions and prepared to renounce both family and country for her sake alone. Her parents and relatives were in favor of the marriage — the whole village would benefit from the union. An hour later I would reverse my opinion: Ngbali was such a traditionalist, it would be logical for her to prefer the settlement's favorite drummer to the wealthy white man, who couldn't even gather honey! And so I debated and counterdebated, and it all seemed to hinge on that pink T-shirt.

AROUND THIS TIME Bokumbi's Ngbali died. I had believed the Bayaka would take her death in stride, but I was wrong. The *élélo* reached an emotional intensity that was distressing to hear. Bokumbi sat in his hut, which was crammed with mourning women. Now and then the lament subsided into a lull. Then Bokumbi's deep voice, overflowing anew with inconsolable grief, would roar out hoarsely, and the sighs and wails of the women would start up once more, mounting until the very hut seemed to rock and quake with that spooky polyphony. After a while I could not stand it anymore and retreated to my hut.

Late that night the women roamed the settlement, performing their ritual *lingokoo*. It was beautiful beyond description, filled with deep, warbly undercurrents, a moving farewell to one of their own.

As the days became weeks, my uneasiness about Kukpata grew. At night he was often in my hut, standing in the shadows cast by my lamp, watching me as I wrote. Others did the same, but there was something eerie in Kukpata's silent presence, looking at me steadily hour after hour, and thinking — what? Whenever Sombolo dropped by and started to talk about Ngbali, Kukpata always happened to be nearby, listening.

And then, strangest of all, I began to hear Kukpata's name spoken in whispers all over the settlement. One day as I was sitting with a group of men, Sombolo emotionally blurted out that if Kukpata ever murdered Ngbali, he would personally kill him with a knife. "*What?*" I blurted back. But the men pretended there was nothing to explain.

Kukpata himself became more and more like one of the shadows he seemed to lurk in. Late at night I would be at my table, scratching out my words by lamplight, when the faintest stir of air, the briefest flutter of darkness, would prompt me to turn around as if someone had entered my hut. At first, blinded by the brightness of the lamp, I could make out nothing. But as my eyes adjusted to the dark I would see Kukpata floating in the farthest, blackest corner of my hut. When I asked if he had anything on his mind, he replied simply, "No."

A few days later all the apprehension that had been brewing just beneath the surface broke out into the open: Kukpata had fled, though why I still could not tell.

The next night I was sitting with Adamo and a few others when a violent scuffle broke out behind me. I turned to see Kukpata's father, Wadimo, dragging his son out of his hut by a rope wound around his neck. Kukpata, his hands clasping the rope at his throat to prevent it from tightening, resisted. Akunga, Joboko, Singali, and many others shoved and pulled him along. Once Wadimo boxed him on the head, shouting, "People are dying! People are dying!"

I felt somehow responsible for Kukpata's plight, and now all signs indicated that the Bayaka were going to murder him.

"What's going on?" I asked, my voice weak and shaky from a repugnant sense of guilt.

"I don't know!" Adamo exclaimed, though it was obvious that he did. Kukpata was still struggling as his father and the others dragged him up a jungle path.

Shaken, I went over to visit Mobo, who had not been part of the foregoing scene. He was calmly loading coals into the bowl of his bamboo pipe.

"Why have they dragged Kukpata off?" I asked.

"He's been killing people," Mobo replied matter of factly. "Kukpata's *gundu* is incredibly powerful."

Coming from Mobo, renowned for his power to turn invisible, it was quite an endorsement. But I argued that this was not possible, and that Kukpata of all people had no reason to kill anyone. Even as I spoke, however, I was aware that at some deep, inaccessible level I was unmoved by my own arguments; in fact I was relieved that the cause of my anxiety had been removed.

During the night I brooded relentlessly over the ugly turn of events, my thoughts following me in and out of sleep. I detected something beyond coincidence in the fact that my uneasiness about Kukpata had paralleled so perfectly the growing suspicions of the community. There must have been some telepathy between us. The Bayaka's belief in *gundu* was so deeply rooted that I began to wonder, even fear, if there was not something to it. Perhaps *gundu* was the Bayaka's way of explaining a genuine phenomenon. I still believed in a kind of subconscious telepathy, and this experience put the matter beyond doubt. I had picked up on the community's thoughts and feelings and translated them into an irrational jealousy against Kukpata. But no — it was the other way around. My jealousy had been based on something real, if innocent — it was the Bayaka's fears that were groundless, for poor Kukpata had certainly not murdered anyone. My unguarded ill feelings had contaminated the community, had gone floating out along the telepathic network wreaking havoc. Yes, I thought in that hyperlogical limbo between full consciousness and sleep, it was simple, really: evil thoughts — envy, jealousy, hate — could kill, without so much as the lifting of a finger.

FOR SEVERAL DAYS I saw no more of Kukpata, and Amopolo's crisis seemed to pass. I relaxed. The mystery of the pink T-shirt dissolved into irrelevance. One day I mustered the courage to ask Sombolo if "the problem of Kukpata" had been resolved. His cheerful expression transformed for a moment into deep melancholy, and he nodded his head sadly. I was sure then that Kukpata had been banished to restore harmony to the community.

Although nothing in my experience with the Bayaka had suggested that they would resort to such a drastic measure, I had been truly shaken by their belief in *gundu* and the genuine terror it inspired in them. I felt I no longer knew them and thought they might be capable of anything.

But then, lo and behold, Kukpata reappeared, and there was no sign in his demeanor to suggest what he had been through. It was as though nothing had ever happened. Remarkably, my own former suspicions vanished without a trace. Soon he resumed his routine of nocturnal visits to watch me write, but now his persistent lingering in the shadows had nothing ominous about it; it was only a habit that sprang from endearing, childlike shyness. Instead of menace, my heart was filled with warm affection toward him.

As Amopolo emerged from its collective hysteria, the day-to-day misery of the community was thrown into stark relief. The Bayaka had slid deeply into debt, and Amopolo had become a kind of *mbo* factory. Every afternoon the men, with hardly an exception, returned from the raffia swamps with bundles of palm leaves balanced on their heads. Every evening villagers came to collect them, bargaining down the purported value of each bundle, so that in the end a day's work was scarcely worth a quarter. Villagers typically made a four hundred percent profit when they resold the finished thatching. Bomandjombo had fallen on hard times, and the villagers were acting out of desperation. But Amopolo had sunk to the very bottom of the economic barrel and looked likely to remain there. Yet when I once meekly suggested that we move back into the forest, the Bayaka's reaction was strongly negative. I thought it extraordinary that Joboko, whose son had gotten sick and died at Amopolo, should remark that the forest was dangerous, that too many people died there.

Real starvation, not just acute hunger, was cropping up here and there. Baku's four-year-old son, Baja, was dying. He no longer associated with other children. He never even walked anymore. Every day he sat behind his hut, calm and still and seemingly aware of the imminence of death, his colossal head balanced on the skinny pole of his neck. He looked old and wise. Each time I passed he called

out my name, softly and distinctly, and when I turned to acknowledge his greeting and say his name in return, he merely gave a brief
nod in response. It became a strangely powerful reproach, that sage
little nod of his, and on occasion I went a different way to avoid
him.

In the stultifying heat of early afternoon, the stench of human
ordure hovered over Amopolo. The Bayaka complained about it, but
no one made an attempt to improve the situation. Children crapped
directly behind the huts, and days might pass before someone removed the pile. When the men were not in the raffia swamps collecting leaves, and the women were not laboring in the villagers'
manioc fields, the Bayaka just sat among the chigoes, the filth, and
the refuse, nibbling on palm nuts or eating pieces of boiled manioc
tuber, which smelled like vomit. One day I realized with a start that
they were living in their own cemetery.

I hung on, I suppose, only because I was still in love with Ngbali,
even though it seemed hopeless. But I began to remember that I
had the possibility of a life apart from these doomed souls. I felt a
pang of wild regret when I thought of Ngbali as one of them, but
by an effort of will I projected myself into the world beyond, where
Ngbali would be only a memory, and I started to believe that I *could*
go back. Perhaps it wasn't too late. My mounting anger against
Ngbali might provide the jump-start I needed. I decided to nurture
that anger, until it grew into an irrevocable fury that could launch
me out of Amopolo.

I was in the habit of passing the sweltering afternoons sprawled
out on my bed in a daze. One afternoon a group of children between three and five years old, led by Singali's indomitable son
Elimbo, crept slowly into my hut chanting, "Looyay, Looyay, Looyay!" When I opened a bleary eye at them, they fled giggling, but
soon they were back. Thereafter they came every day, so my attempts to nap became a mere pretense, while I waited for them to
begin their game. I began to think about those children, most of
whom were too young to remember a time when I was not there.
I adored their sweet, pure laughter, their unreserved affection for
me, their faith in the permanence of my presence. Knowing what
was probably in store for them at Amopolo, how could I abandon
them? And so I rationalized staying just a little bit longer.

ELEVEN

Yondumbé

I HAD OFTEN SPOKEN about founding a second settlement at the
top of the hill beyond the bridge. The higher altitude, I believed,
would make a significant improvement. If we moved farther away
we would surely run into opposition from the village authorities.
But in the midst of their suffering and paranoia, the Bayaka had
hardly listened to me. I was therefore surprised when one day Singali came into my hut and told me, with some emotion, that he was
tired of playing chief for the *bilo*, and that the time had come to
move farther from Bomandjombo, to Amopolo II. He and the men
had already found the ideal location.

The next day I went with Mabuti and Singali to check it out. We
crossed the bridge, climbed the hill, and continued walking. Soon
we were well beyond the site I had had in mind. Though I was
personally happier the farther we went, I worried that the authorities would block such a move. Mabuti and Singali argued the whole
way over whether the site was two or three kilometers away. After
a mile or so we came to a halt. "Here it is," they said.

We stood before the very last overgrown plantation, beyond
which pure forest took over. I recognized the spot at once: there in
front of me was the flowered arch that had once inspired my vision!

It was no longer in flower, and the arch itself was concealed under festoons of greenery. But I knew it right away, and now the true meaning of that vision became gloriously lucid. *Here* was our new life. I knew we faced a struggle; living for a few months in the forest was one thing, but starting up a new village was a major change, and likely to run into legal problems. I also knew the Bayaka were correct to reject any halfway measures, such as the site I had proposed. I would fight for this place, the site of my vision, even if it meant that in the end I was forced to leave.

In the morning I returned with a work force, including Sombolo, and we began the awesome task of clearing the site. By noon a villager had spotted us and informed the authorities. The next day the mayor called me to his office and told me to stop this nonsense. I couldn't just move a village like that — I needed official permission, *his* permission, and he wasn't going to give it. He had his reasons, I knew. Frequently his guards swept through Amopolo in the early morning hours to drag men off for a day's unpaid labor in the village. Since my arrival the Bayaka had taken to resisting this form of slavery by fleeing into the forest, with the result that the guards often returned empty-handed. Already the mayor had cause to regret my presence. Now I was trying to take his whole labor pool away.

But I persisted. I submitted a written proposal to move the Bayaka settlement for reasons of health and sanitation. The mayor countered by ordering an official police investigation into my activities, with specific instructions to the police chief to find a reason to get rid of me. For two days I was interrogated. I presented my case to Chief Biléma of the Sangha-sangha, and he gave me his unqualified support. Villagers, many of whom were dependent on the Bayaka's *mbo* work to make ends meet, came to me to complain about the move. I always took the time to explain to them why the Bayaka had to leave Amopolo. Ultimately, albeit reluctantly, most of them agreed with me.

I was not at all certain I would succeed, and was even afraid I would be forced into exile. But I had found at last a meaning to coming here. As soon as I set foot in Amopolo, I felt that I had been drawn here for a purpose. The urgency with which I had embarked on my first visit, with my one-way ticket and five hundred dollars, had a fateful quality.

I now understood my reaction to the *mokoondi*, which had puzzled me. Although I had always known that they were the men, I had believed that they were also something more. Their discordant cries on the recordings from my first visit had filled me with agitation each time I heard them and had called me back a second time. Now I thought I knew why: they had been crying out for their own survival. Even as the men sank deeper into destitution and degeneration, the *mokoondi* had raised their voices in a siren song to lure and capture the heart of someone who would be the agent of their deliverance. I even understood the destruction Ejengi had wrought. He had accelerated the process of degeneration to make it evident, bringing all the latent contradictions of Amopolo to a head so that they could no longer be ignored.

Seeing the whole picture for the first time, I admired how the Bayaka had prepared me for this moment, drawing me into the heart of their world, slowly conditioning me to accept the idea of remaining with them, of forgetting I even had a choice. They had invested me with an illusory authority over them, however unwilling I was to accept it, so that without even thinking about it I was now leading them to a promised land. The program seemed far too subtle, complex, and long-range to have been conscious, the details of daily events too random and chaotic to reveal any overall trend. But the trend was undeniably there, as if the Bayaka had been guided by a wisdom or instinct greater than the sum of its individual parts.

I wondered if Ngbali was aware of my confrontation with the mayor, the struggle I was going through, and the risks I was running. Nothing in her outward manner suggested it. Her sole concession was to make herself neutrally available to my gaze. Paradoxically, my fear that I had lost her made me more daring in my daily encounters with the authorities as they conducted their investigation. I became recklessly audacious — after all, what more could I lose? — and made wild predictions about the rewards of moving to the new site.

In a written statement I boldly prophesied that before the end of the following year, the Bayaka would perform their music in America. Bomandjombo would shine in glory, and money would come rolling in. (In fact, the Bayaka did perform in Paris, and they returned as heroes, with lots of money.) The police chief recommended my proposal to the mayor. The mayor, hinting that he would like to visit America too, gave it his official sanction. We were free to move.

But THE BAYAKA were far from ready. For one thing, Amopolo had debts to Bomandjombo amounting to more than a hundred dollars. Now the Bayaka wanted to pay them all off, which they calculated would entail another month or two of labor in the raffia swamps. If I promised to supply them with their minimal daily requirement of tobacco and marijuana (*mbaku* I refused), as well as the occasional bar of soap, pair of batteries, bag of salt, and fistful of peanuts, they promised to work diligently to pay back every last debt and to not incur any new ones. They were as good as their word.

To keep alive our claim to the new site, as well as to fulfill the first of my many forecasts to the village authorities, I organized a work force of six teenage boys under Andrea's command. Their task was to construct ten latrines at the new site. Andrea had been remarkably successful in keeping the Mosapola Bayaka on the job, and she proved equally successful with the Amopolo crew. Every morning she showed up at seven in her pickup. The crew never missed a chance to ride to the site, and in the afternoons they returned in the back of the pickup, singing. The sound of their voices as they approached Amopolo brought a smile to everybody's lips and bolstered us with a feeling of confidence.

Life continued much as before, but with the promise of renewal at Amopolo II, things did not seem nearly so depressing. Mokoko's wife, Sao, gave birth to her first child. Unlike most, hers was a difficult labor, lasting two days. On the second night she lay in her hut, crying out in pain, a crowd of concerned women around her, a group of anxious men sitting on the ground outside. Mowooma began to address her, speaking in a loud voice in the direction of her hut: she was an important woman, the wife of the chief's oldest son, so why was she giving us all such a fright? Just have the baby and get it over with, so that we could all sleep in peace that night! At that instant Sao gave birth to a girl.

There were the usual ups and downs with Ngbali. Days might pass without so much as a glimpse of her; then her mother and grandmother would visit my hut, and finally I would be invited over for a meal, served by Ngbali herself. But when I paid more visits or brought small gifts, Ngbali withdrew into indifference or shyness. Discouraged, I would give up and wait for her mother's visits to start again. Once, over a period of a few days, a number of the women busied themselves with acquiring new tattoos. Talking to them one afternoon, I mentioned that I found *matelé* very attractive. The next day Ngbali emerged with one of the most heavily tattooed faces at Amopolo. Was it in response to what I'd said, I wondered, or would she have gotten the tattoos anyway?

Perhaps inspired by my optimism about the future, I wrote more than ever. I often wondered if any book had ever been written under the scrutiny of so many onlookers. One night Ndoko and Bokia stood at opposite ends of my table while I struggled with the fourth chapter. They took turns praising me to each other, as if I weren't present, each trying to outdo the other in extolling my virtues, the accolades mounting until I was being compared to Jesus Christ. Having properly established my munificence, they went on to describe the very special gifts they expected I would give them. Bokia wanted a "little radio," Ndoko nothing more extravagant than a flashlight. Would the white man give them these things? they speculated in a momentary flicker of doubt. But faith triumphed: of course he would! They were starting up with their testimonies again when I chucked them out.

Sometimes the Bayaka seemed to visit me for no other reason than to perform little theater pieces. Once Dabusu and Musako entered my hut, both dressed up in their finest and looking exactly like two villagers. Musako even wore a pair of sunglasses. For nearly an hour they held a mock argument in Sango, seemingly for my benefit, which I did not understand a word of. Then, without so much as asking for a cigarette, they departed. Other visits were eminently practical and did not concern me at all, such as when Engulé, Biléma, and Lalié showed up to remove a splinter by the light of my lamp. For fifteen minutes I listened to Engulé's gasps of pain as Lalié dug into his finger with a safety pin, while Biléma offered a nonstop stream of advice. One time an old man named Momboli, tipsy on palm wine, came into my hut to insist that when I wrote about him in my "paper," I was not to call him Momboli. There were too many Mombolis; no one would know which one I meant. There was a Momboli at Mosapola, there was a Momboli at Emona, there was even a Momboli at the Mokala River in the Congo! No, I was to call him *Contre-boeuf*. That way there could be no mistake.

Late at night, very late, when it seemed that everyone was asleep, Balonyona would slip silently into my hut, tiptoe up behind me, and whisper in my ear, "Chocolate." I had once, with an air of secrecy, given him a sip of my hot chocolate, and he had concluded that chocolate must be a very powerful drink, a kind of supercoffee, to be consumed clandestinely, away from the eyes of others, especially children. He would stand in my hut solemnly sipping his cocoa, averring that never, ever would he allow a child so much as a single whiff of chocolate. It could be dangerous! Already he, an adult, could feel the chocolate "grabbing his eyes," and he still had half a cup to drink! There was no way he would ever get to sleep now, the chocolate was too strong tonight. And so he would go on until the very last drop. Then, with a final vow never to tell the children about chocolate, he would slip back out into the night.

ONE DAY I WAS TOLD that the latrines were finished. I announced the news that evening, and I thought everyone would start moving to the new site in the morning. But the next morning the Bayaka started the day like any other. No one was packing. Since their debts to the villagers were about paid off, I asked them why they delayed. They weren't delaying, they replied, but first the women had to go and clear the site and build the huts. Okay, I said, then do it.

For a week a group of women led by Esoosi worked at clearing space for the first huts. Mine and two others were completed, and then work stopped again. Days became weeks, and still no one made a move. I began to hear rumors of discontent, and many Bayaka complained behind my back to Mike and Andrea that the new site was too far from Bomandjombo. I noticed men resuming work on their bamboo huts at Amopolo. Mowooma had only recently finished his, a genuine palace, and it suddenly occurred to me that he might be understandably reluctant to abandon it. About the only one still eager to move was Baku's wife. She had so wasted away that she scarcely made a crease in the sheet she lay under day and night. Every day now she called me over and asked if we were moving yet. And every day I told her perhaps tomorrow. Eventually I realized that I would have to make the first move, but I also knew that I was afraid to leave Ngbali behind. I wanted some guarantee that she and her family would follow me. None of the women in her extended family had even visited the new site yet.

A month passed. Once when I went to look at the site, I became alarmed at the extent to which the jungle had reclaimed it. Then one day, only an hour after asking me if we were moving, Baku's wife died. As the *élélo* began I felt a wild, thrashing despair. But ten minutes later the *élélo* suddenly stopped, and Mokoko came and told me that Baku's wife had returned to life. God didn't want her yet, he explained, and had sent her back.

One afternoon I was called over to Mowooma's hut. Big deal, I thought cynically as I made my way over, Ngbali's going to serve me another meal. But I was wrong. Mowooma had a large piece of meat he wanted to sell me. Since I had no money, he would give it to me on credit. My wife, Ngbali, would prepare it for me, he said. She would cook it that evening, and I would eat it first thing in the morning. Ngbali was present the whole time, lying with seductive indolence on a reed mat, her head in her aunt's lap, looking at me long and unabashedly.

At last a message with no ambiguity, endorsed evidently by Ngbali herself: she *was* my wife after all! I left Mowooma's hut considerably happier than when I'd entered it. But the next morning when I returned to Mowooma's for my meal, there was no sign of Ngbali. Her mother served me instead. When I casually asked where Ngbali was, they told me she had gone to sleep in the forest with Sosolo's group, which had already been out there for a month. She would be gone for two weeks.

I spent a good hour brooding in my hut. Then I saw that with Ngbali gone, there was nothing to keep me in Amopolo. I could move to the new site. The next day I went into town and bought a supply of sardines and bread. Back at Amopolo I packed my bags and waited for my ride. The Bayaka gathered around me.

"Are you really moving today?" they asked.

"I'm really moving," I told them. "I'll eat sardines and bread and enjoy the peace and quiet. You can all stay here — you make too much noise, anyway. I'm leaving Amopolo forever forever."

In the afternoon Anna Kretsinger picked me up in the truck. She had been the first Peace Corps volunteer ever posted to Bomand-jombo and now, two years later, she had returned to work for the Dzanga-Sangha project. As we were about to drive away there was a shout. Simbu and his wife, Mandubu, hopped into the back with a hastily packed carrying basket. Anna drove us the mile and a half to the new site and dropped us off. She would check up on me in a few days, she promised, and bring me some sardines.

And then the three of us were alone.

SIMBU, MANDUBU, AND I had Yondumbé (named after the Ndumbé, a nearby stream and the source of our drinking water) to ourselves for three days and nights. That pressing but vague feeling of mission, the illusion of destiny that had grown stronger over the years, creating its own kind of tension, suddenly left me now, as if I had been riding the crest of an ocean swell that had finally deposited me on this distant shore. From now on my existence would have no more sense of urgency than a beachcomber's.

I loved the motion and activity in the sky above us, as the sun sank behind the forest, and our pioneer camp grew cool in deepening shadow. Clouds sailed by with stately speed, and beneath them a pageant of airborne life unfolded. Gray parrots winged past on their way to roost, filling the air with their richly toned whistles. Black hornbills soared overhead with an occasional squawk, perching briefly on the tops of trees before launching on their way again. Smaller black and white hornbills gave impressive aerial displays as they nosedived across the open space and vanished over the forest. Bats swooped and wheeled everywhere, their piercing squeaks just within range of the human ear. Crested blue touracos congregated in the trees in fours and fives, and for several minutes their loud gobbling cries rose into the clear evening light even as dusk overtook the forest.

At night the forest rang with the long, self-renewing wails of the tree hyraxes. Owls called back and forth — always a series of deep hoots from one direction, followed by a soprano *wooo!* that sounded disconcertingly human. One morning Simbu and I were discussing what a good place Yondumbé was because of all the wildlife. Monkeys and tree hyraxes were a blessing as far as Simbu was concerned, but when I started to imitate the *wooo* of the owl, he interrupted me hurriedly to say, "Don't worry — those will go away when more people arrive."

Within a few days Bayaka from Amopolo began to visit. They came to see how we were faring, to ask for cigarettes, but above all to check out their new home. They were all unusually happy, as if doing their best to keep a wild joy under control, and they looked around with obvious approval. Those who remained late enough to see the air show could not suppress a gasp of delight.

Biléma and Bosso were the first to join us. They told me that the day after I left, Balonyona's rickety hut had suddenly collapsed, and now he and his family were living in mine. Engulé and Mbina moved out next, followed by Mobo and his family. Thereafter a steady migration began, and when Sombolo arrived with Yéyé to stake out and clear an area, I could not have been happier. By the end of the second week, only Joboko and Wadimo and their groups remained at Amopolo. Even Mowooma had forsaken his grand hut to the elements without apparent regret.

One of the earliest to move to Yondumbé was Baku, who carried his wife out and installed her in a hut built by Mandubu. Then he went back and brought little Baja out. I remember that afternoon sitting with Baku and some other men on an old termite mound a few yards into the forest. Suddenly Baja appeared down the trail, picking his way with infinite care, stopping to clear away twigs and leaves from each spot where he intended to place a foot. It took him thirty minutes to reach us. Then, as he came to a towering, smooth tree, he placed his hands against the trunk to steady himself, drew back his head, and stared up at that tree, all the way up to the leafy kingdom of its crown spread out against the sky. He stood that way for ten minutes, now and then gently patting the tree.

That night his mother died, but for once death did not bring hysteria and accusations of *gundu*. Only immediate family took part in the *élélo*, and in the morning she was quietly buried. I carried Baja out to his tree every day for a week and gave him a tin of sardines to eat, which he consumed, bit by tiny bit, over the course of an hour. At first I had no hope that he would live, but like the rest of us he had been through the worst. He, too, was a survivor.

One tradition our move put a definitive and welcome end to was *mbo* work. Many months would pass before any men descended into those raffia swamps again, and when they did, it was to gather leaves for the thatching of their own bamboo homes. The men were free to go hunting again, which they did every day, as though they had only just discovered the pleasures of their ancient way of life.

One night the owl with the human cry perched in a tree behind Baku's hut. Every thirty seconds or so it cried *wooo*. Baku was soon moved to respond, "Aw! Leave me alone!" *Wooo!* the owl cried. "Go away!" Baku continued. "Go find someone else! I have nothing. I've buried my wife in the earth. I just want to sleep tonight." *Wooo!* "Okay, what have I ever done to you? Why are you bothering me? There are lots of people at Yondumbé. Go away!" *Wooo!* "Okay, that's it! I'm not sleeping tonight. I'm just going to lie here with my eyes open until dawn. So you might as well stop wasting your time with me and go somewhere else." *Wooo!*

I could not help laughing to myself, but finally I took pity on Baku and called out that it was only a bird.

"Yes, that's right — only a bird!" half the population of Yondumbé called back nervously at once, and I knew then that everyone had been listening anxiously to the exchange between Baku and the owl.

I FELT QUITE HAPPY at Yondumbé. I even felt I had a reason to be proud. I had yearned to find *real* Bayaka, with a forest culture uncontaminated by the outside world. Yet what, I now wondered, could I have brought such a culture but corruption, jealousy, and rivalry, with my cigarettes and my gifts? What could I have been to them but a kind of Pandora's box, unleashing hungers that could never be satiated? At least with the Bayaka of Amopolo I could say that my coming had brought some benefits.

But I was a long way from congratulating myself. What would Ngbali think when she saw Yondumbé? Sometimes I convinced myself that she had wanted just such a deed as proof of my intentions. But then I argued just as persuasively that she was too young to have had such a desire.

The afternoon she returned, I sat with her and her family and listened to her stories of forest adventure. Now and then she paused to look around, and I could tell she was pleased. In the evening I was called back for a meal, and when Ngbali served me I knew that we were on another upswing. This time, I decided, I would not destroy it by probing too much. Perhaps Ngbali was as wise as I sometimes imagined, despite her youth. I realized what she had probably known all along: that she could never have abandoned her people to live with me in America, and I could never have spent the rest of my life at Amopolo, watching the Bayaka degenerate and be exploited.

Shortly after Ngbali's return, Joboko and Wadimo arrived with their families. They had stayed behind to bury Joboko's younger sister, who had died after a sudden and violent illness. It was Amopolo's final tragedy. I took a walk there a few days later and felt a deep satisfaction looking at the derelict huts, the piles of refuse, the sun beating down silently and furiously upon the filthy sand. What a wreck, I thought. We had escaped in the nick of time.

One night the men wandered around our new village performing their *so* music. I wandered with them, making my first recording in months. It was an event of great healing power, as if by their dance the men were restoring balance to the whole cosmos.

The following evening Ngbali and several girls began to roam around Yondumbé singing *lingokoo* songs. The singing was lovely, but I knew that what would come later in the night, when the men retired and the women conjured up their *mokoondi*, would far surpass it. I sat outside my hut and listened to the girls, and my body began to tingle with a pleasure I had not felt for decades, as though

I were a child again, sleepless with excitement on the long night before Christmas morning. I had thought such pleasure forever obliterated by age and experience. Yet here I was savoring it again, a joy inspired by my anticipation of the night to come and the time when Ngbali would finally be mine. Even though I myself might drift in and out of sleep, the women would sing into the dawn, their voices filling the night with benediction.

As the men began to withdraw into their huts, and I prepared to enter mine, old Esoosi came up to ask, with some concern, if I planned to record the women's *lingokoo*. "Not a chance," I replied. "I'm a man, aren't I? I'm going to listen from my bed like the others." Esoosi laughed and went to join the choir.

That night I heard the most beautiful singing on earth.

APPENDIX 1

The Dzanga-Sangha
Dense Forest Reserve

THE EVENTS IN this book take place in the southwestern corner of the Central African Republic, in territory that is now the Dzanga-Sangha Dense Forest Reserve. Two newly created national parks abut on the reserve: Dzanga Park in the eastern sector and Ndoki Park in the extreme south. The reserve and both parks are sponsored by the American branch of the World Wildlife Fund, in collaboration with the government of the Central African Republic.

All forms of hunting, development, and exploitation are forbidden in the two parks. The reserve, on the other hand, has several thousand human inhabitants, whose needs have been accommodated in the reserve's charter. Regulated rural development and hunting by traditional methods are permitted. A zone is open for the hunting of big game, primarily bongo (the largest of the forest antelopes). These safari hunts are carefully controlled and bring in much needed revenue to the local economy.

Sadly, the reserve's charter also allows for logging, and recently several logging companies have expressed interest in resuming operations at the Bomandjombo sawmill. Although the rain forest can recover from selective logging to a certain extent, other adverse effects of logging are more insidious. Logging roads open large areas of the forest to poachers. And in the long run logging is not economically sound; the first company to operate in the reserve went bankrupt, and an attempt to revive the sawmill in 1989 ended in failure.

For the Bayaka, renewed logging will be an unmitigated disaster. Attracted by the salary, however small, many Bayaka will abandon their traditional pursuits to work for the sawmill. For what amounts to a few pennies a tree, they will help to cut down their forest. The money they earn can never compensate for their loss. Alcoholism will definitely rise, social order in the community will break down, and the incidence of violence (fights, wife beating) will certainly increase, together with hunger and malnutrition. Several of the social and economic factors leading to such a scenario are beyond the Bayaka's control.

The Dzanga-Sangha Reserve and its charter offer many exciting possibilities for the Bayaka, some of which are already being realized, but for them logging is a dead end. I, for one, would like to see logging excluded once and for all from the reserve. The only way this can be accomplished is to raise the funds to buy or rent the forestry concessions in the reserve.

Conservation of the rain forest, and protection of the culture of its indigenous inhabitants, is not the responsibility only of those nations where rain forests exist. On the contrary, the primary responsibility lies with the industrialized nations, which have the means to provide alternative economic incentives to nations striving for economic development.

To help make the Dzanga-Sangha Reserve a success, contributions earmarked for Project Dzanga-Sangha may be sent to the following address:

The World Wildlife Fund
1250 24th Street NW
Washington, D.C. 20037

APPENDIX 2

Discography of
Pygmy Music

MANY ANTHOLOGIES of traditional African music include one or two Pygmy songs. The following discography, listed in alphabetical order by recordist, includes records devoted mostly or exclusively to the Pygmies. It was compiled by Fred Gales of the University of Amsterdam. I have added some comments.

Arom, Simha. *Music of the Ba-Benzelé Pygmies*. Barenreiter Musicaphon Bm 30 L2303. 1965. The fifteen selections give an excellent introduction to the Ba-Benjelé. Some of the Bayaka recorded here, including Adamo's father-in-law, now live at Monasao. The five sung fables are especially good.

———. *Anthologie des Pygmées Aka*. Ocora 558526/7/8 (3 LPs). 1978. Also on CD. Superb-quality recordings of the Aka near the village of Mongoumba, some seventy miles south of Bangui. Lovely recording of *mobandi*, music on the eve of gathering honey.

———. *Aka Pygmy Music*. Philips 6586016. 1973. More recordings from the same region.

———. *Baka Pygmy Music*. EMI/Odeon 3C 064-18265. 1977. Also on CD. The only available album of the Baka in southern

Cameroon. Includes some beautiful water-drumming music, in which young girls sing and beat the water of a forest stream for percussion.

Arrigoni, Georges. *Cérémonie du Bobé chez les Pygmées du Nord Congo.* Ocora C 560010. 1991. CD only. I don't know this recording. Three different Pygmy groups take part: BaNgombé (Baka), Ba-Benjellé (Bayaka), and Mikaya. Recorded near Ouesso in northern Congo.

Bonnaud, Fredy. *Pygmées.* Playasound PS 33509. 1970s. Recorded among the Aka.

Demolin, Didier. *Pygmées du Haut-Zaire, Kango-Efe-Asua.* Fonti Musicali FMD 190. 1991. CD only. Excellent overview of music from the Ituri forest.

————. *Polyphonies des Pygmées Efe.* Fonti Musicali FMD 185. 1990. CD only. I don't know this recording, but it is certain to be good. The Efe are unique in that they hunt almost exclusively with bow and arrow.

Guillaume, H. *Chasseurs Pygmées.* ORSTAM.SELAF Ceto 795. 1982. More music from the Aka, giving a good impression of the acoustics of the forest. Includes the only recordings of the *mbiti*, a musical bow made only by the women from a sapling, a large leaf, and raffia string.

Huchin, C. *Chants et Danses Pygmées.* Chant du Monde LDY 4176. 1957. Recorded in northern Congo. I am not familiar with it.

Quersin, Benoit. *Polyphonies Mongo: Batwa, Ekonda.* Ocora OCR 53. 1971. The Batwa Pygmies seem to have lost their original style of music and now excel at imitating the music of their non-Pygmy neighbors. The Twa recorded here live in conjunction with the Ekonda, who are not Pygmies. The music of the Ekonda is very interesting and also polyphonic, showing some Pygmy influence in the past. Side A is the music of the Batwa; side B, music of the Ekonda. Recorded in central Zaire near Lake Tumba. A fascinating record.

Sallee, Pierre. *Musique des Pygmées Bibayak.* Ocora 558504. 1975. Also on CD. Recordings of the Baka in northern Gabon from 1966 and 1973. Includes an excerpt from an Ejengi dance, here called *Ishiagbi*

Tracey, Hugh. *Mbuti Pygmy*. International Library of African Music, *The Sound of Africa* series TR-125. 1952. Many short selections from the Ituri forest.

Turnbull, Colin. *The Pygmies of the Ituri Forest*. Folkways Ethnic Series FE 4457. 1958. Recording technologies have improved since Turnbull made these, but they are still among the best.

————. *Music of the Rain Forest Pygmies of North-east Congo*. Lyrichord LLST 7157. 1967. More recordings from the Ituri. Excellent.

Unknown. *Polyphony of Deep Rain-Forest: The Music of Pygmy in Ituri*. Victor VDP 1100 CD/Ethnic Sound. 1983. Not as interesting as the Demolin or Turnbull recordings from the Ituri. Notes in Japanese.

Some of my recordings are available on cassette:

Boyobi. Available from Sound Photosynthesis, P.O. Box 2111, Mill Valley, CA 94942-2111. Excerpts from a single ceremony in which the Bayaka call the *mokoondi* to prepare for an important hunt. Recorded at Amopolo in 1989.

Voices of the Forest. Available from Henry W. Targowski, 16 Langridge, Rhyl Street, London NW5 4LY, England. Anthology of Bayaka music and sounds from the forest. Very evocative. Includes the only available recording of an earth bow. Recorded at Amopolo, Mombongo, Sao-sao, and Yondumbé, 1986–1992.

Bayaka Harp Songs. Available from Sound Reporters, P.O. Box 10214, 1001 EE Amsterdam, Netherlands. An anthology of *geedal* music, featuring three players: Balonyona, Mamadu, and Akété. Most pieces have chorus and percussion accompaniment. Recorded at Amopolo in 1987.

ACKNOWLEDGMENTS

No one should be under the illusion that this is a work of anthropology. Although I have lived among the Bayaka for years, I am the first to admit my vast ignorance regarding many aspects of their life. Some passages in this book may outrage many anthropologists. I can only stress that my experiences among the Bayaka are highly personal in nature, and I could not ignore their subjective content. My attitude of acceptance of the forest spirits played a large role in shaping my subsequent experiences. Unlike Alice in *Through the Looking-Glass*, I find that I *can* believe impossible things.

I can never repay my debt to Colin Turnbull, author of the classic anthropological study *The Forest People*, whose kind replies to my letters groping for encouragement started me on my journey. Walter Slosse of VPRO radio in the Netherlands, the first person to broadcast my recordings of Bayaka music, also helped me acquire a solar battery recharger, designed by Renewable Energy Systems, which I still use. His early support was crucial. The Pitt Rivers Museum at Oxford University has steadfastly and generously supported my musical research through the Swan Fund. Illuminating discussions with Walter Maioli, probably the world's foremost authority on prehistoric musical instruments, helped shape my philosophy of recording. Dr. Fred Gales, who researched the discography of Pygmy music, along with Scott Rollins and Stefan Lanshoff encouraged me at a time when my plan to make recordings among the Pygmies was little more than a pipe dream.

Jim Jarmusch and Sara Driver were often my only contact with the outside world. I owe them my sanity. Their friendship inspired me to complete the book despite formidable obstacles. I am obliged to Luc Sante for timely counsel when I was in desperate need of it.

I have often had to rely on the hospitality of friends, and they have never failed me: Henry Targowski, Roslyn Martin, and Freya Alice Breitenbach; Phil Kline; David Katz and Alexis Adler. And family: my brothers Robert and Steven; and my dear grandmother.

In Africa help was never far off, whether a loan of cash, medicine, a meal, a stamp for a letter, advice, or simply a sympathetic ear. I value the friends I have made there: Richard and Rita Carroll, Mike Fay and Andrea Turkalo; Anna Kretsinger, who earned my undying gratitude for helping me keep in contact with Ngbali when circumstances forced me away; Rebecca Hardin; Arthur Green.

Among the many Central Africans I am indebted to, my thanks must go to Gustav Doungoubé, who presided over the Dzangha-Sangha Dense Forest Reserve during its formation. His keen interest in the welfare of the Bayaka led to many enlightening talks on ways they might benefit from the reserve. The reserve itself owes much of its unique character to his broad and generous spirit of humanity.

My gratitude extends also to the Boganda Museum in Bangui, under whose auspices I made my original forays to Amopolo; I especially thank Maurice Licky. In the Ministry of Communication, Arts, and Culture I wish to thank Marie-Hubert Djamani and the minister, Tony da Silva.

Throughout my years in the Central African Republic I have met nothing but kindness and hospitality that would do credit to any nation on earth. Above all I want to thank François Djebrinne and Jean-Pierre Bale'pou and their families in Bangui and Bernard Koy in Bomandjombo. My gratitude also extends to Alain Ambroise Kpata; Bavone; Serge London; André Bunduwuri and his wife, Jeanne; and Eugène Mbea.

A special word of thanks must go to Ngunja, owner of the finest shop in Bomandjombo. Time and again he extended me credit when my funds were exhausted and helped me through long stretches of destitution. I shall never forget his generosity.

Every author depends for the success of his venture on the tolerance of his editor, but rarely has the concept been stretched so far as in this case. Elizabeth Lerner was simply wonderful in persuading my publisher to cater to some very unorthodox needs. And Peg Anderson's contribution to the text was invaluable.

Finally, I owe special gratitude to my agent, Eric Ashworth, without whose assistance this book could never have been written. From the beginning his encouragement and advice were instrumental in shaping the concept of the book, and his unflagging enthusiasm helped me through some pretty dismal periods. Rarely has an author owed so much to his agent, and I happily acknowledge my debt.